T0399693

"This book is timeous, thoughtful, pragmatic and visionary. It is based on voices from the field: researchers, practitioners, teachers, policy makers and civil society organisations working at the coalface of education when one of the most extraordinary educational events in modern day history occurred. The book distils deep insights into the complexities of education during a global pandemic, yet it is fiercely future-focused... A most worthy read and an extraordinary resource for anyone working in education."

–**Professor Irma Eloff**, Chair of Global Network of Deans of Education and University of Pretoria, South Africa

"This book is a good reference book for policy makers and practitioners when planning and adapting policies to continue education services during and after pandemics and other crises and calls on policy makers to consider a holistic approach to ensuring ongoing educational development of the most marginalised children."

–**Purna Kumar Shrestha**, Education Lead, VSO (Voluntary Service Overseas)

"This book provides advice in futures thinking for school leaders so that they can plan to provide continuity of high quality teaching and learning for all during normal times as well as during times of crisis. This book endeavours to aid decision-making to prevent marginalisation of learners when schooling is disrupted."

–**Carl Smith**, secondary headteacher, UK

"This book documents teachers' experiences during an unprecedented time in education... This book is invaluable in supporting staff to continue to develop provision, not only in preparation for another whole-school lockdown, but for those individual pupils who, for a number of reasons, are unable to access day-to-day schooling."

–**Rachel Peckover**, primary deputy headteacher, UK

Education for All
in Times of Crisis

This book is a response to the loss of learning experienced by children and young people during the Covid-19 crisis. It examines the measures which were taken to fix the disruption of education and their limitations particularly in reaching marginalised groups.

Drawing on data and experiences from around the world, the book examines education systems as ecosystems with interdependencies between many different components which need to be considered when change is contemplated. Chapters explore the challenges involved ensuring continuity of education for all learners in times of crisis and disruption and set out practical solutions that are relevant when preparing for natural disasters and disasters caused by humans as well as for climate change challenges and future pandemics. The focus throughout is on building the sustainability of learners' education into education systems to ensure educational continuity for all learners in times of disruption and crisis.

Including tools for planning, prompts for reflection, and future possibilities to consider, *Education for All in Times of Crisis* will be valuable reading for school leaders, educators and policy makers.

Marilyn Leask is Professor at De Montfort University, UK. She has held roles in central and local government, universities, schools and research institutes and through her role as co-chair of the MESHGuides initiative (www.MESHGuides. org) is committed to supporting international collaboration between teachers and educational researchers for the benefit of learners everywhere.

Sarah Younie is Professor of Education Innovation and previously Director of the Institute for Education Futures at De Montfort University. She is a member of the ICET (International Council on Education for Teaching) Board and is the UK BERA (British Education Research Association) Convenor for the Educational Research and Policy Making Special Interest Group. She is the current Editor-in-Chief for the international *Journal of Technology, Pedagogy and Education* and also co-chair of the *Mapping Educational Specialist knowHow initiative* (www.MESHGuides.org).

Education for All in Times of Crisis

Lessons from Covid-19

Marilyn Leask and Sarah Younie

Routledge
Taylor & Francis Group

LONDON AND NEW YORK

First edition published 2022
by Routledge
2 Park Square, Milton Park, Abingdon, Oxon, OX14 4RN

and by Routledge
605 Third Avenue, New York, NY 10158

Routledge is an imprint of the Taylor & Francis Group, an informa business

British Library Cataloguing-in-Publication Data
A catalogue record for this book is available from the British Library

Library of Congress Cataloging-in-Publication Data
Names: Leask, Marilyn, 1950– author. | Younie, Sarah, 1967– author.
Title: Education for all in times of crisis : lessons from Covid-19 / Marilyn Leask and Sarah Younie.
Description: Abingdon, Oxon ; New York, NY : Routledge, 2022. | Includes bibliographical references and index.
Identifiers: LCCN 2021009671 (print) | LCCN 2021009672 (ebook) | ISBN 9780367726201 (hardback) | ISBN 9780367726232 (paperback) | ISBN 9781003155591 (ebook)
Subjects: LCSH: Educational equalization—United States. | COVID-19 (Disease)—United States.
Classification: LCC LC213.2 .L45 2021 (print) | LCC LC213.2 (ebook) | DDC 379.2/60973—dc23
LC record available at https://lccn.loc.gov/2021009671
LC ebook record available at https://lccn.loc.gov/2021009672

ISBN: 978-0-367-72620-1 (hbk)
ISBN: 978-0-367-72623-2 (pbk)
ISBN: 978-1-003-15559-1 (ebk)

DOI: 10.4324/9781003155591

Typeset in Optima
by Apex CoVantage, LLC

Our books are dedicated to all teachers, with particular recognition of long-serving teachers and head teachers around the world, who work within challenging political contexts, but who manage to put the learning and wellbeing of their students first.

We particularly dedicate our books to all those training to be teachers now and we welcome them to this rewarding profession.

We also dedicate this book to those policy makers who are able to step aside from party politics and consult with communities, businesses, parents/carers and learners to create the best education system possible providing pathways to self-realisation, lifelong personal fulfilment and community wellbeing.

Teachers and learners need politicians who have a humanitarian world vision, who, understanding the power of the internet will step forward to help UNESCO to realise the vision (outlined in the last chapter) of harnessing digital tools to provide freely available educational resources to teachers and learners everywhere.

The UN's sustainable development goal 4 – providing the best education possible for children everywhere by 2030 – is perfectly attainable but political will and vision is needed. In recent times, some national leaders of economically strong countries have not displayed any understanding of the leadership role that they could play in bringing governments together through existing organisations such as the United Nations. We hope that those who come after them have a stronger sense of what is possible and the will and vision to realise this.

Contents

SECTION 4
Moving forward   169

10 Reopening schools   171

Figures and tables

Figures

Tables

Acknowledgements

Thanks are given to the MESHGuides International Council members whose contributions to the coronavirus weekly meetings enabled us to draw up these guidelines for planning continuity for education in emergencies; specifically: Dr Bc Akin-Alabi (Nigeria); Dr Linda Devlin (Wolverhampton University, UK); Professor Irma Eloff (Pretoria University, South Africa); Dr Temechegin Engida (UNESCO-IICBA, Ethiopia); Carol Hordatt Gentles (International Council on the Education of Teachers and University of the West Indies, Jamaica); Stephen Hurley, (VoicEd, Canada); Professor N.B. Jumani (International Islamic University, Pakistan); Khalid Khan (Ministry of Education, Pakistan); Mohamed Mukhtar (Development Line, Somalia); Professor Ruksana Osman (UNESCO Chair, Witwatersrand University, South Africa); Purna Kumar Shrestha (Voluntary Services Overseas International, NGO member UNESCO Teacher Task Force); Dr Ling Siew Eng (Universiti Teknologi MARA, Malaysia); Professor Tracey Tokuhama-Espinosa (Ecuador and Harvard University, USA).

Thanks also to the MESHGuides Executive Board members: Jon Audain (chair of Technology, Pedagogy and Education Association, University of Winchester, UK); Mike Blamires (RIPPLE, UK); Jonathan Doherty (Leeds Trinity University); Stephen Hall (Staffordshire University); Dr Richard Procter (De Montfort University); Dr Chris Shelton (Chichester University), who met under the direction of the MESHGuides co-chairs Prof Marilyn Leask and Prof Sarah Younie (both of Education Futures Collaboration Charity and De Montfort University).

We also acknowledge and thank colleagues from the International Council on Education for Teaching (www.icet4u.org), particularly Dr Carol Hordatt Gentles from the University of Jamaica and Dr Deb Eldridge from Western Governors University in the USA, for their organisation of the data collection from colleagues around the world on their experiences of Covid-19 and the following international ICET/MESH-Guides Symposia during October 2020.

We thank senior leader and teacher Chris Harris for his insights into 'rick task' pedagogy.

Lastly, we acknowledge the contribution of the Emergency Advisory Group for Learning and Education (EAGLE) Group of teachers, teacher educators and researchers led by Professors Helen Gunter, University of Manchester; Pam Jarvis, Leeds Trinity University; Liz Todd, University of Newcastle; Terry Wrigley, Northumbria University.

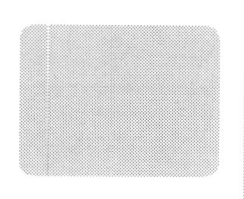

Author biographies

Marilyn Leask has held roles in central and local government, universities, schools and research institutes. She is visiting Professor at De Montfort and Winchester Universities, UK, and is committed to supporting international collaboration between teachers and educational researchers for the benefit of learners everywhere. In 1992, she initiated the Learning to Teach in the secondary school series of textbooks which she co-edits. She is co-chair of the Education Futures Collaboration Charity which oversees the MESHGuides initiative (www.MESHGuides.org) addressing the UN's SDG 4, and with Professor Younie and Ulf Lundin from Sweden, initiated the European SchoolNet in 1995 (www.eun.org). She is an elected board member of the Council for Subject Associations and the Technology Pedagogy and Education Association. She has previously held elected roles on the British Educational Research Association national council and the national council for the Universities Council for the Education of Teachers. With a network of educators in 1994, she initiated TeacherNetUK which became the Department for Education's TeacherNet website. As a public servant at the government agency, the Training and Development Agency for Schools, 2000–2007, she led an initiative to put the knowledge base underpinning teacher education online – developing the Teacher Training Resource Bank and was a member of a cross-government agency working party developing the use of the internet to support teachers' professional development.

Sarah Younie is Professor of Education Innovation and previous Director of the Institute for Education Futures at De Montfort University. She is an elected member of ICET (International Council on Education for Teaching) and is the UK BERA (British Education Research Association) Convenor for Educational Research and Policy Making SIG (Special Interest Group). She is a trustee and founder member of the Education Futures Collaboration (EFC) charity and MESHGuides (Mapping Education Specialist knowHow) project, which provides research evidence to inform teachers' professional practice, and represents MESHGuides on the UNESCO supported International Teacher Task Force (ITTF) panel; MESHGuides contribute to UN SDG4. She has been involved in international research on technologies in education for UNESCO, EU, UK government agencies, local authorities and educational charities. As the UK Chair of the National Subject Association of IT in Teacher Education (ITTE) she has submitted evidence to several Parliamentary Select Committees on Education. Professor Younie is currently the Editor-in-Chief for the international *Journal of Technology, Pedagogy and Education*.

Contributors

As part of the research undertaken in collecting data to write the book, the authors acknowledge the contributions from the following colleagues, who gave of their time in undertaking focus groups and phone interviews to provide case studies, practitioner expertise and extended consultations on multiple and complex matters that arose as we collaborated to record the significant challenges of managing the Covid-19 pandemic from March 2020 to September 2020.

Jon Audain is Senior Lecturer at the Institute of Education, University of Winchester. He has worked as a primary teacher, Head of Year, Senior Teacher, Learning Platform/VLE Consultant and peripatetic music teacher. In 2006, he was appointed as a county-based Advanced Skills Teacher (AST) specialising in Primary ICT. He has advised and worked with schools, teachers as well as award-winning children's author Judy Waite and companies, such as BrainPOP, 2Simple, Promethean, Rising Stars, Scholastic, MirandaNet and MESHGuides. Jon is the author and collaborator of over 20 books, chapters, peer-reviewed journal articles and papers.

Jon is an Apple Distinguished Educator (ADE) and a member of the Promethean Advisory Council/ActivAdvocate. He is Chair of the Technology, Pedagogy in Education Association (TPEA), an Executive Board member for the Education Futures Collaboration (www.MESHGuides.org) and Fellow of the Chartered College of Teaching, the College of Teachers and the Royal Society of Arts.

Carol Hordatt Gentles Senior Lecturer in Education, Teacher Education and Development, University of the West Indies, Mona. Jamaica. She is Chairperson of the Joint Board of Teacher Education, Western Caribbean, and Chair of the International Council on Education for Teaching (ICET). Research interests include Critical Pedagogy in Teacher Education and Education for Sustainable Development, Teacher

Educator Development and the scholarship of teaching and learning of qualitative research methodology.

Hugh Greenway is CEO of the Elliot Foundation and sits on the education advisory board to the British Council. His interests include behavioural change and organisational design.

Stephen Hall is Senior Lecturer in Education at Staffordshire University. Previously he was a primary school headteacher, and he has been closely involved in the British Council's e-twinning programme. Stephen teaches on initial teacher training and continuing professional development programmes and works with schools' networks on a range of professional initiatives. He is a member of the executive board of the Education Futures Collaboration charity (www.MESHGuides.org).

Brian Matthews taught science in London schools, then trained science teachers on the PGCE at Goldsmiths, and now at King's College. He has researched ways of developing emotional literacy and equity in science classrooms and has published *Engaging Education*.

Jwalin Patel is a Cambridge International scholar and final year PhD candidate at University of Cambridge. He also works in the developmental/social action sector and runs a grassroots level organisation called Together In Development and Education Foundation in India.

Rachel Peckover is Deputy Headteacher at Burbage Junior School and Doctoral Researcher at De Montfort University. Her research interests are Primary School Leadership and Initial Teacher Education.

Purna Kumar Shrestha is an expert in education and international development with 30 years of experience in classroom teaching, education leadership, teacher training, project management of grassroots-development works, research and advocacy works and participatory facilitation skills. He started his teaching career as a pre-primary teacher in rural Nepal in 1990. He holds a Master of Education (M.Ed) from Tribhuvan University and MPhil (Education and Development) from Kathmandu University. He is currently based in the UK and works for VSO International as Education Lead technical advisor. He led an innovative home-based early childhood education programme for Rohingya children in Jamtoli camp, Cox's Bazar and developed a mobile application, VSO School app, to empower ECE teachers and caregivers with young children. He contributed to the development of MESHGUIDES on Early Childhood Care and Education in Emergencies, a collection of evidence-based open-source resources for ECE teachers available in different languages.

Purna is a member of the steering committee of the International Task Force on Teacher for Education 2030 and a member of United Nations Girls' Education Initiative International Advisory Committee. Purna, father of two young children, founded the Early Years Education Society – UK (www.eyes-uk.org) in the UK in 2017.

John Sibbald Specialist leader in education: John has over 30 years of experience working in Manchester schools. He is passionate about how we should harness technology to improve learning, teacher effectiveness and student outcomes including the development of digital literacy, work, life and specialist skills.

Carl Smith is Principal of Casterton College Rutland, shortlisted for Secondary School of the Year in 2019 and one of the highest performing comprehensive schools in the East Midlands. He is the East Midlands representative on the National Council of the Association of School and College Leaders (ASCL) sitting on the teaching and learning committee and has written widely on educational topics, including making regular humorous contributions to the popular Last Word column in the ASCL magazine *Leader*. He has appeared on Radio 4 and in national debates on issues, such as reforming independent schools, and he has written books on supporting teacher trainees in schools, KS3 history, Departmental CPD and Walter's Voice – a secondary resource based on oral accounts of the First World War. In 1997, he was made Britain's first Advanced Skills Teacher of history. Carl is currently working on a pilot projects on mass saliva testing in schools with the National Institute for Health Research and on managing teacher morale and improving recruitment and retention with University College London Institute of Education.

Caroline Whalley CBE is founder of The Elliot Foundation and has held executive positions in public, private and charity sectors. She researches connections across knowledge boundaries to enrich understanding of how and why to educate.

Rowan Williams grew up in South Wales and studied theology at Cambridge. After research in Oxford on Russian religious philosophy, he taught in Yorkshire, then returned to Cambridge, where he continued with teaching and pastoral work until 1986 when he moved to a Chair at Oxford. In 1992, he became Bishop of Monmouth in Wales and from 2002 to 2012 was Archbishop of Canterbury. He retired from the Mastership of Magdalene College in 2020 and now lives in Cardiff. He is the author of numerous books, most recently *Justice and Love: A Philosophical Dialogue* with Mary Zournazi.

Foreword

The Covid-19 pandemic of 2020 brought to light a very wide range of inequalities and disadvantages that seem never to have been noticed, in our own society nor worldwide. Not the least of these have been the deeply damaging injustices around access to education. In the UK, we have seen how school students whose parents have easy access to internet connections and digital resources gain immense educational advantage unrelated to their comparative capacities. Parents with limited resources and children at different stages of school life have had to choose which child to support. Working parents and single parents in these circumstances have had to juggle their own personal and professional needs alongside those of their children. It has been estimated that a gap of about a year in educational attainment will have opened up between children who enjoy this kind of access and support and their less well-placed peers.

Project this inequality on to the global scene and its seriousness becomes even more obvious. In many countries it is a challenge to persuade students, especially female students, to stay in full-time education rather than going immediately into the world of work and family – a particularly important choice as far as women's opportunities are concerned. But for male and female students alike, an early end to school education means a huge loss for their communities as well as for them as individuals: it means a lost generation of potential teachers, doctors, engineers, entrepreneurs and the like.

At the moment we have no exact way of measuring these losses, but we know that in one way or another they will shape the lives of young people from low, middle and high income countries. But there is nothing automatic about this. Technologies exist that can carry educational provision to remote or under-resourced environments. Many teachers are actively willing to explore new cultures of teaching. Some of the contributions to this book describe successful ventures in reshaping patterns of pedagogy and supporting the creativity of teachers; others look at examples of innovative technology in Kenya and Australia and elsewhere.

What seems to be lacking is the political will to turn this situation around. It should be obvious that challenges to educational justice and effectiveness cannot be dealt with by hastily improvised strategies, switching tracks without warning or training in ways that are damaging to teachers and students alike (not to mention families who have to stretch their resources to the limit). And once again, we have to remember the challenge for societies where educational freedom and opportunity are hard-won and fragile matters.

This timely book sets out the urgency of the situation and offers practical and achievable ways forward. As with many other areas of our social life, it is essential that what we have learned in the period of the pandemic about problems that have largely gone unnoticed should be a driver of prompt and creative action by governments and professional bodies. Too much has been lost already; but we can still transform the hopes of children worldwide if we act now.

Dr Rowan Williams
Sometime Master of Magdalene College,
Cambridge and Archbishop of Canterbury 2002–2012

Introduction and context

Aim of the book

This book, written during the Covid-19 pandemic in 2020, sets out solutions and challenges for ensuring continuity of education for all learners in times of crisis and disruption. The solutions are relevant for preparing for natural disasters, manmade disasters as well as for climate change challenges and future pandemics. The book focuses on how sustainability of learners' education can be built into education systems to mitigate the risks to the stability and development of nations if young people miss out schooling because schools are closed for extended periods.

Who the book is for

The book is aimed at those responsible for developing and implementing policy changes in the education sector, school leaders and teachers, whom we hope will find much in this book to guide their thinking and planning.

We support the World Health Organisation (WHO 2009) and European Commission (EC 2009a, b) advice that being prepared for crises is essentially about ensuring school business continuity is built into day-to-day plans, so that a transition to operating in times of disruption is smooth.

WHO/EC advice is to build systems (structures and processes) which work well in non-crisis times and are flexible enough to support continuity of learning and assessment in times of crises. The years 2019 and 2020 saw across the world, many extreme natural disasters – floods (East Africa, UK, Italy, France), fires (USA, Australia), droughts (India) as well as human disasters of terrorism, war and genocide (West Africa, Middle East, Myanmar/Bangladesh). So, whether disruption of schooling is

DOI: 10.4324/9781003155591-1

caused by natural or human disasters or pandemics, disrupted schooling is an ongoing reality for many children in many countries.

The 'futurecasting' scenarios in the book provide options which support or conversely work against the continuity of education during crises. It provides sobering reading for all who wish to see their country's education sector moving forward rather than retreating into breakdown and failure to provide learning.

How to use the book

The structure of the book allows you to dip into the sections relevant to your work. To support stand alone use of chapters, some powerful examples are repeated in different chapters.

The book examines education systems as ecosystems with interdependencies between many different components which need to be considered when change is contemplated. Each chapter considers an element of an education system and provides factual input, comparisons between systems in different countries, analysis of unintended consequences of policies together with possible future scenarios. The authors draw on their international networks and their extensive experience in education systems in a number of countries, including low-, middle- and high-income countries (LIC, MIC, HIC). Data about the impact of Covid-19 were gathered through international focus groups undertaken by educators in over 30 countries and a series of webinars: detail is provided subsequently.

The book is divided into four sections:

Section 1: Planning – for continuity of learning and assessment during disruption of schooling. The section addresses planning and futurecasting processes.

Section 2: Leadership and management – lessons learned during Covid-19. The section addresses leadership challenges at national, regional and local levels.

Section 3: Teaching – during Covid-19. The section addresses the challenges for curriculum, assessment, pedagogies and educational technology.

Section 4: Managing uncertainty – continuity of learning and assessment during crises. This section looks to the future and poses a challenge to national and international bodies to act together, using existing resources more effectively, to protect the education of young people.

Where relevant, the chapter structure includes:

* an introduction giving the context,
* a discussion of the overall and specific challenges faced in the particular area,

* a lessons learned section, followed by a
* planning toolkit,
* then a 'futurecasting' section where 'What if . . . thinking' is encouraged to identify possible scenarios for your context which you may wish to plan for.

The Annexes provide real examples of schools' planning documents which demonstrate the complexity of planning required to support continuity of learning and assessment during crises.

Lessons learned

A number of significant lessons have been learned since the Covid-19 international lockdown and closure of schools, initially in Wuhan in China in January 2020 and then worldwide from March 2020. Each chapter provides examples of specific lessons learned in relation to the foci of the chapter, for example, which types of pedagogy are best placed to facilitate remote learning, how can digital technologies be best deployed to support learning at home and so on.

Worldwide, where governments opted to support online remote learning, they exacerbated existing digital divides: in high- and low-income countries, significant numbers of learners had no internet access or devices (West 2015). Several pre-Covid initiatives are worthy of note in bringing internet-connected learning to remote communities. The World Bank[1] identifies mobile internet buses as a solution for remote communities and these are used in many countries for example, in Texas, USA, communities with no electricity were supported with this solution: 100 school buses converted to provide digital connections to learners (Click2Houston April 2020). In the Philippines, the innovative portable digital classroom 'School in a Bag' solution is carried in backpacks over tracks to 'Last Mile' schools to provide remote communities with online connection.[2] In Kenya, stratospheric balloons bring internet connection.[3] In Australia, low orbiting satellites bring connection to remote communities, and in Canada, the Telephone school in Manitoba provides yet another solution for reaching out to remote communities. Other countries focused on radio and TV. Further information about these initiatives is provided in the book.

Another major lesson learned during the Covid-19 pandemic period was that when students were no longer in front of teachers, it was harder to assess when children were becoming disengaged; to this end we argue that all learners are potentially 'at risk' of becoming marginalised with remote learning. Therefore 'education emergency plans' must include pedagogies relevant to maintaining student motivation at times of remote teaching. Such careful planning will ensure engagement and progression for all learners as much as is possible in challenging circumstances.

Planning toolkits

Where relevant, *planning toolkits* are included at the end of a chapter. The planning toolkit provides key questions, to be considered at the national, regional and local levels as appropriate, to aid your strategic planning. They identify areas that need thinking about in relation to your own context: from the learner and teacher experience to the infrastructure necessary to support learners for remote schooling, to pedagogical approaches which ensure continuity of learning. The questions are linked with the challenges, problems and solutions identified in each chapter. The goal is that such plans ensure continuity of learning and assessment and are immediately available to activate for whatever type of crisis may emerge, whether pandemics, natural disasters, or indeed, during the expected cycle of reopening and re-closing of schools that is set to continue due to Covid-19 through 2020 to 2021 and possibly beyond.

We reviewed policy documents from governments and global organisations outlining planning for pandemics, and interestingly, whilst these provided general advice, they omitted specific information for education and extraordinarily little, if any, detail was provided on how to assure continuity of learning and assessment (WHO 2009; EC 2009a, b; see also the references in MESHGuides 2020; Inter-Agency Standing Committee-UNICEF, WHO and IFRC March 2020; International Labour Organisation 2020). The planning toolkits support you in addressing this gap between general advice and what has to be put in place in schools and classrooms.

Futurecasting

As the Covid-19 crisis intensified globally, in low-, medium- and high-income countries, governments found it difficult to ensure quality learning continuity in their education sectors. This failure of existing education sector pandemic plans highlights the need for detailed 'futurecasting' of scenarios for continuity – focused at the individual community and individual learner level – to ensure learners are not marginalised.

Annexes

The annexes contain advice for senior school leaders from the union ASCL (Association of School and College Leaders, www.ascl.org.uk 2020) and worked examples of school plans and risk assessments covering the primary age range 4–11 years and secondary school, 11–18 years.

Research base of the book

Global webinars: gathering research data

The research underpinning the book is based on a series of global webinars, organised and hosted by ICET (International Council on Education for Teaching www.icet4u.org), MESHGuides (Mapping Educational Specialist knowHow (www.MESHGuides.org) and VSO (Voluntary Service Overseas, www.vso.org) that were undertaken from May–October 2020. These were planned and arranged by Leask and Younie from MESHGuides, Shrestha from VSO and Hordatt Gentles and Eldridge from ICET at the start of the coronavirus outbreak and ran through the period of the first wave of the global crisis and the return of the second wave.

An international webinar with video technology experts, IRIS Connect, on 2nd July addressed the challenges of continuing initial teacher training when schools were closed and beginning teachers could no longer complete their qualification program.

Similarly, further international research was undertaken with a two-day E-Conference hosted by Professor Muhammed Anwer, a MESHGuides International Council colleague in Pakistan, on 26–27th August with over 100 educators attending. This was followed by a series of global webinars in October 2020 which extended the dataset.

International focus groups: 30-plus countries

This book was commissioned following the first international webinar that was held on 15th May 2020 which brought together 90 educators from 30 countries to share their frontline knowledge of practices and what was happening with schools' provision for learners and especially marginalised learners. Their contributions are integrated into this book.

In collaboration with the members of the International Council on Education for Teaching and MESHGuides network members, focus group interviews were held with teachers in more than 30 countries from August to December (ICET/MESHGuides 2021). This enabled extended data collection and the use of Teacher Voice to inform the discussion and analysis offered in this book.

Desk research, individual interviews and peer review

In addition to desk-based research, the authors also undertook interviews with teachers and senior school leaders from different countries. Some gave written contributions and case studies, and then provided extended consultations on multiple and complex matters that arose as we collaborated to record the significant challenges of managing the Covid-19 pandemic, from March 2020 to December 2020.

 ## Conclusion

This book is important as education systems provide the foundations for the future well-being of every society. In addition, teaching is the one profession that makes all other professions possible. The book explores the impact on learners, teachers and senior school leaders and extrapolates lessons learned. The book builds on and complements the text: *Education System Design: foundations, policy options and consequences*, Hudson et al. (2021).

It is hoped that the research and the analysis of findings reported in this book provide a benchmark for preparedness for providing educational continuity in times of disruption and crises.

Sarah Younie and Marilyn Leask
July 2021

 ## Notes

1 Mobile Internet buses https://blogs.worldbank.org/edutech/mobile-internet-buses-vans-and-classrooms
2 Philippines School in a bag https://smart.com.ph/About/learnsmart/programmes-projects/school-in-a-bag
3 Loon 4G balloons https://guce.techcrunch.com/copyConsent?sessionId=3_cc-session_9a1c3e9b-682c-4143-8e12-5d21982101ebandlang=en-GB

Section 1

Planning – for continuity of learning and assessment

Planning for continuity during periods of disruption

Introduction and context

Unfortunately, as always in education, the consequence of a failure to act decisively will be borne by others long after the main decision makers have deserted the political stage. National and international leaders have the opportunity in their hands to minimise marginalisation of learners. Will they grasp it?

Carl Smith Headteacher, August 2020

In early 2020, the Covid-19 global pandemic erupted. While some countries had existing detailed pandemic plans, built on WHO guidance (2009) which advised that national pandemic plans should ensure 'school business continuity', many countries did not.

Even where national pandemic plans existed, we found that they mentioned that school closure would only be undertaken as an extreme measure. No mention was made of how to ensure learning continued for all learners in this extreme case. The damage caused by this international failure is incalculable.

By March 2020, around the world, schools, colleges and universities (along with all businesses except for essential services) were closed for weeks initially and then months, as countries went into 'lockdown', with some closing their borders, to limit transmission of the coronavirus through the population. Lockdowns eased during May/June but by July/August, (when schools were reopening after the summer break in some countries), the spread of the virus was surging and local area lockdowns were imposed by governments along with many travel restrictions and countries imposing typically two-weeks quarantine on travellers returning from hot spots. Schools were reopened then closed again then reopened then closed again as outbreaks occurred

DOI: 10.4324/9781003155591-3

(EAGLE Report 2020). By November at the time of writing, the spread of Covid-19 virus was accelerating across Europe with schools in some countries being closed for weeks at a time again. Closing of schools had different consequences for different stakeholders – parents, teachers, pupils – and brought into sharp relief inequalities in societies. Children who had personal internet-connected devices were able to continue their education at home if their teachers moved swiftly to teaching online. Other children from poorer families or with special needs simply missed out (UNESCO 2020a) and were disadvantaged through inequalities in provision.

The Covid-19 crisis laid bare the challenge of ensuring continuity of education at times of disruption. In low-, medium- and high-income countries, governments found it virtually impossible to enable continuity of learning when schools were shut down at short notice. Many thought online learning was the solution only to find the digital divide across all countries marginalised large numbers of learners, denying them education, while for the children of the wealthy (in low-, medium- and high-income countries), their education continued for the most part (ICET/MESHGuides 2020).

Increasing marginalisation of learners during the Covid-19 pandemic

Originally, we had intended to focus in this book on marginalised learners, but as the research data were analysed, we found that all learners were at risk of becoming marginalised when they were no longer in front of teachers. With remote teaching, teachers found it difficult to assess when children were becoming disengaged. So the lessons in this book are not just about continuing education for existing specific groups of marginalised learners but also for the many learners who are 'at risk' of becoming marginalised at times of crises as their contact with their teachers and friends contracts, their hopes and plans for the future are put into question and their family lives disrupted. To this end, we seek a greater understanding of what happened to all learners during the Covid-19 pandemic and outline a range of solutions that address the needs of all learners in the future. We found that particular groups of marginalised learners are at risk of being forgotten and in need of additional support such as SEND and EAL learners and those living in disadvantaged households, in remote rural areas, islands or coastal regions. We are also aware that many of the needs of these particular groups are best served by the local schools that have the in-depth understanding and appreciation of their individual circumstances.

We found that as schools and support systems were 'locked-down', learners without reliable internet and personal devices rapidly joined the already extensive group of marginalised learners across low-, medium- and high-income countries. The disruption and possible loss of learning for the upcoming generation of young people has the potential to impact seriously on every country's talent pool, the chance of rapid recovery from a pandemic and the long-term knowledge base of the society (United Nations Development Programme 2020). Young people may end up not possessing the essential knowledge necessary to develop solutions required to address challenges of the future and, even, to maintain the status quo.

Looking to the future

A significant amount of the disruption learners experienced was avoidable because:

* pandemic planning advice existed but was ignored
* open (free) online resources to support schooling, developed by governments in the late 90s and early 2000's in the emergent internet era in education, developed in the spirit of knowledge being shared for the common good, had been closed, put behind firewalls or privatised (Blamires 2015; White and Parker 2017; World Bank 2017)
* technologies are available to connect remote and marginalised communities to the internet via low orbiting satellites or high altitude balloons as well as to locally generate electricity.

It did not have to be like this, and continuity of learning and assessment can be better in future crises through:

* 'futurecasting' techniques and exercises to build preparedness
* pandemic plans being integrated into existing operations to support smoother transition to remote learning in times of crises
* harnessing national and international resources through existing international bodies to co-ordinate access to extensive curriculum resources: schools can only do a certain amount alone. See UNESCO (2020b) for the potential of the Global Education Coalition to do this.

Building on the lessons from Covid-19, this chapter provides an overarching framework for what should be considered in national, regional and school pandemic/crisis plans which strengthen existing practices at national, regional and local levels. Subsequent chapters address specific aspects of the operation of the education sector in turn.

To note: The research data underpinning this chapter were gathered through desk-based research, focus groups in more than 30 countries and through a series of global webinars and interviews from May to October 2020 (as outlined in the Introduction).

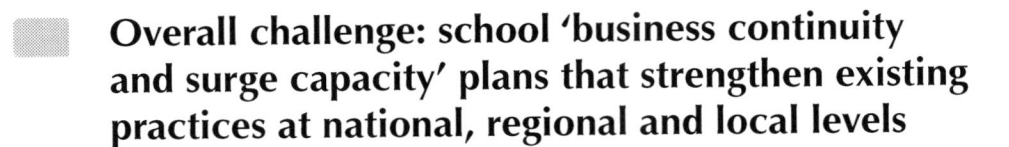

Overall challenge: school 'business continuity and surge capacity' plans that strengthen existing practices at national, regional and local levels

While the Covid-19 pandemic and the subsequent national lockdowns and closures of schools may have come as a surprise in early 2020 to many, a simple internet search shows that governments, regional authorities and some schools have had pandemic management plans ready for decades (Uscher-Pines et al. 2018; MESHGuides 2020a; NZ 2011, 2020). However, few plans provided advice on how teachers and schools could ensure continuity of learning and equity of access to education provision during pandemics.

Pandemic planning advice from the World Health Organisation (WHO 2005, 2009) and European Commission (EC 2009a, b) for managing and assessing readiness for pandemics updated earlier advice. These documents outlined steps which those who have experienced national lockdowns in 2020 will recognise. School closures feature as one of the containment measures:

> Influenza spread will be accelerated in schools and other closed communities leading to a potential need to close schools.
>
> (European Centre for Disease Prevention
> and Control 2006, p. 45)

Advice for English schools from the ministry (DCSF 2008) was that every school should have a pandemic plan linked with regional and national plans. However, this online advice was removed by the 2010 incoming government and has not been updated or replaced since (World Bank 2017). The USA, Canadian and New Zealand government advice was similar, and schools, regional and national bodies have made their plans freely available on the internet (see MESHGuides 2020a for a list of examples).

However, the dilemma at any time of crisis is when to act and what to do. School closures are one of the last actions to be considered, because of the disruption to the learning and well-being of children alongside the impact on the economy and the functioning of society without teachers providing, as a minimum, mass childcare. Experience of other pandemics/epidemics led the European Commission (EC 2009a, b) to suggest school closures as a last resort:

> During pandemics with lesser severe disease and of fewer falling sick, such as those seen in 1957 and 1968, some possible community measures (proactive school closures, home working, etc.), though probably reducing transmission, can be more costly and disruptive than the effects of the pandemic itself. Hence such measures may only have a net benefit if implemented during a severe

pandemic, for example one that results in high hospitalisation rates or has a case fatality rate comparable to that of the 1918/19 'Spanish flu'.[1]

(EC 2009a, p. 1)

The risk in keeping schools open is that teachers and schools provide a meeting point linking nearly all community members so the potential for cross-infection and the risks for staff, children and communities can be expected to be higher than for most employment sectors apart from some areas of health, hospitality and public transport. Outbreaks among learners and teachers as schools and universities reopened late in 2020 after six months of lockdowns illustrate the risk.

National pandemic planning is one of the responsibilities of governments and guidance from WHO (2005, 2009), the European Commission and others (ECDC 2006; EC 2009a, b; NZ 2011, 2020) outlines good practice. Planning for the continuance of education is recommended as one element of national plans with consideration of interdependencies between sectors being essential.

The European Commission's (EC 2009a, b) advice provides a generic framework for developing national pandemic plans which strengthen current systems. Planning for *business continuity and surge capacity* (overwhelming demands on a service) are highlighted. See Table 1.1.

Table 1.1 European Commission advice on pandemic planning

Pandemic preparedness is most effective if it is built on general principles that guide preparedness planning for any acute threat to public health. This includes the following:	
1	Pandemic preparedness, response and evaluation should be built on generic preparedness platforms, structures, mechanisms and plans for crisis and emergency management.
2	To the extent possible, pandemic preparedness should aim to strengthen existing systems rather than developing new ones, in particular components of national seasonal influenza prevention and control programmes.
3	New systems that will be implemented during a pandemic should be tested during the inter-pandemic period.
4	Adequate resources must be allocated for all aspects of pandemic preparedness and response.
5	The planning process, implementing what is planned, testing and revising the plan in order for key stakeholders to familiarise themselves with the issues at hand, may be even more important than the pandemic plan itself.
6	Pandemic response requires that *business continuity plans and surge capacity plans* (authors' emphasis) be developed for the health sector and all other sectors that could be affected by a pandemic to ensure sustained capacity during a pandemic.
7	The response to a pandemic must be evidence-based where this is available and commensurate with the threat, in accordance with the IHR. Planning should be based on pandemics of differing severity while the response is based on the actual situation determined by national and global risk assessments.

Source: European Commission EC (2009a, p. 1)

This book focuses on actions to ensure *business continuity and surge capacity* (i.e. how to assure continuity of learning and assessment), how to minimise spread of disease in educational settings and how to ensure that sufficient teachers are available as the disease affects teachers and as teachers leave their posts through fear of catching the disease.

The book is divided into four sections:

> Section 1: Planning – for continuity of learning and assessment during disruption from pandemics, disasters and crises
> Section 2: Leadership and management – lessons learned during Covid-19
> Section 3: Teaching – during Covid-19
> Section 4: Managing uncertainty – continuity of learning and assessment.

Each section focuses on specific elements of practices in education which together provide a framework for emergency planning for the education sector. In Table 1.2, we identify a list of these elements. The contents list shows where these are addressed in this book.

In considering each element we suggest you consider:

* Who needs to be engaged in this provision?
* How can you use existing infrastructures?
* How will you refresh your plans?
* How will you communicate your plans?
* What children are not catered for in your plans?
* What unintended consequences may there be?

The following section on futurecasting provides a process for future scenario planning and what if thinking.

Futurecasting for education: 'being forewarned is forearmed'

It is clear that pandemic planning based on evidence should have already been in place for nation states to be able to respond to crises as and when they occur. The European Commission, advised:

> Response to a pandemic must be evidence-based where this is available and commensurate with the threat, in accordance with [human resources], planning should be based on pandemics of differing severity while the response is based on the actual situation determined by national and global risk assessments.
>
> (EC 2009a, p. 1)

Table 1.2 Core elements of education pandemic/disaster plans – national, regional, local and where they are discussed in this book

* Your underpinning philosophy and goals which provide the foundation for your policy and plans; decisions about how to allocate resources, for risk management and what losses are acceptable; whether you make provision for *all* learners
* Resources: human and material including equipment provision
* Infrastructure
* Health and safety
* Special cases
* Maximising learner experiences
* Teacher workload
* Teacher training: continuing and initial
* Communications
* Risk assessment and risk management
* Mental health and well-being of teachers and other school staff, students, families
* Ensuring continuity and synergy between national strategy and local plans
* Parental/carer involvement strategy
* Home worker strategy
* Community/NGO/Charity roles and resources
* Community engagement: mapping educators' specialist expertise and networks; linking local and national level plans
* Curriculum resources: online/TV/radio content
* Assessment
* Teaching and learning pedagogy, including remote pedagogies
* School closures
* Exit from lockdown: reopening plans
* Each of the areas identified in the preceding Pandemic/disaster recovery readiness checklist, including strategies to exit from school closure

Intelligent planning can be done through the process of futures thinking: forecasting, hypothesising based on scenarios, drawing on scientific knowledge – 'futurecasting'. Because the future cannot be known, national contingency planning has to accommodate uncertainty.

At a 12th February 2002 news briefing, USA Secretary of Defense Donald Rumsfeld explained the uncertainties and thus limitations of intelligence reports:

> There are known knowns. There are things we know we know. We also know there are known unknowns. That is to say, we know there are some things we do not know. But there are also unknown unknowns, the ones we don't know we don't know.
>
> (Shermer 2005)

Shermer goes onto to argue that 'Rumsfeld's logic may be tongue-twisting, but his epistemology was sound enough . . . Rumsfeld's wisdom was first invoked by University of California at Los Angeles paleobiologist William Schopf, who, in a commentary on a lecture on the origins of life, asked: "What do we know? What are the unsolved problems? What have we failed to consider?"' Shermer (2005).[2]

In brief, in planning for the future, consider:

We know what we know
We know what we don't know
We don't know what we don't know

This leads us onto consider the area of futurecasting for the education sector. To help plan for crises and manage ongoing waves of the coronavirus pandemic, we draw on futurecasting as a way of preparing for emergencies and disruption to provision.

Futurecasting is a process of building scenarios for the future through exploring options and extensive contingency planning. Worldwide, all countries will continue to face the challenge this book addresses: how to maintain continuity of learning for an upcoming generation at times of crises and concomitant disruption. If high-quality education for all cannot be maintained at such times, then the long-term outcomes for the country of loss of potential of young people to drive the country forward may be catastrophic.

The chapters which follow make a unique contribution to the field of education through futurecasting by focusing on the practices, techniques, methods, exercises and toolkits necessary to future-proof education systems against disruption from unforeseen events. The additional international context for the book is provided by the ongoing preoccupation of governments with improving their education systems and the setbacks to these plans caused by Covid-19.

So as the crisis hit, in low-, medium- and high-income countries, governments found it difficult to ensure learning continuity in their education sectors. This failure of existing education sector pandemic plans highlights the need for detailed future-casting of scenarios for continuity, focused on the individual learner level, to ensure learners are not marginalised.

Introducing futurecasting for education

What follows is an introduction to the process of futurecasting. The future can-not be known so planning for possible future scenarios or futurecasting provides a tool for developing contingency plans. This means knowing 'your knowns' and seeking 'unknowns' – planning for contingencies and working through unintended consequences

Futurecasting at the school level is useful in identifying for your context (your school and your learners) your known knowns, known unknowns and having in place processes for managing unknown unknowns once they become known.

Known knowns: Perhaps the most important need is the rapid retrieval by leaders of their known knowns or what others know: those solutions already discovered that work for particular issues.

So, what is known in your context? What were the lessons learned from the Covid-19 pandemic and other crises your school/community/nation has experienced? What worked well, what were the challenges, risks and losses? What flexibility and responsiveness can you build into your system so that existing structures support teachers and learners in times of crisis. Can collaboration with other countries/schools provide a foundation supporting positive outcomes for learners. We argue that knowledge management (KM) tools (Leask et al. 2020; Younie et al. 2021c) will help you do this. They enable you to identify tacit and explicit knowledge already in your system so you can make this knowledge available to those who need it and identify gaps.

Known unknowns: Hypotheses are created by using known knowledge with known tools – leadership teams analyse the hypotheses against agreed headings and formulate broad actions needed to mitigate. Choose perspectives that will give you the most information and be most useful to analyse your unknowns, considering the following contexts:

* **P**olitical
* **E**conomic
* **S**ocial
* **T**echnological
* **E**thical
* **E**ducational
* **E**cological
* **E**nvironmental
* **L**egislative

Well-known tools use the following acronyms:

* STEP or PEST – social – technological – educational – political
* STEEP – social – technological – educational – economic – political

This method elicits the areas that may need contingency planning, for crises. Although we may not know when or if these will occur, plans can be put in place which can be immediately actioned and which ensure continuity of learning and assessment for all. Plans that work for marginalised learners will work for all learners.

Unknown unknowns: By learning from known unknowns, most unknowns can be managed. In other words, we will have strategies in place and be in a better position to cope with unanticipated challenges (unknown unknowns) when they arise.

Regional and local education emergency committees, that have agreed structures and are given delegated power, can enact processes for organising and communicating both local and regional emergency planning based on 'what has worked' (i.e. known knowledge).

The futurecasting process

Here we outline the process of 'futurecasting' which is used in business as a tool for planning 'forward'.

> Futurecasting as a theory, and knowledge driven predictive practice, can be used across private, public and third sectors. It enables strategic planning for an organisation's as yet unforeseen future. The process evaluates underlying business dynamics, then employs predictive analysis to decide on possible futures and finally decides on a variety of strategies to help develop a manageable vision of the future.[3]

In summary, there are 3 main steps:

* Identify and understand key trends.
* Create multiple 'what if' scenarios of plausible futures you may face.
* Decide on the most relevant scenarios and develop strategies to act on them.[4]

Futurecasting builds upon traditional forecasting practices to look beyond the face value of a number of issues and to understand more fully *how* and *why* a particular outcome occurred or may occur. It helps to understand the factors that are driving possibilities. This informed view of the future enables intelligent planning and informed decision-making.

Futurecasting presumes that the future is uncertain, in a world that is rapidly changing. Making strategic decisions would be so much easier if the future were known!

> Life can only be understood backwards, but it must be lived forwards.
>
> – Soren Kierkegaard

The global Covid-19 pandemic has sharply drawn this to our attention, while organisations predicted the catastrophic impact of a pandemic leading to international lockdowns followed rapidly by country-wide school closures, few governments and schools seemed to be prepared with plans.

Futurecasting is used to imagine 'future scenarios' and 'what if ' events, such as schools closing. Had governments used this methodology then their plans would have accounted for scenarios, including the need for learners to have alternative schooling provision and with remote learning predicated on well-planned models of distance delivery inclusive of all learners.

Whilst futurecasting cannot predict specific crises or disasters, or for that matter future innovations, what could have been imagined for schooling was the need to ensure 'continuity of learning and assessment' to be ready to be operationalised for *all* learners when required.

We argue it is possible to have prepared the education sector for the likeliest scenarios and to regularly update plans to make sense of broader trends and changes taking place globally and locally so as to have contingency planning in place to act fast when, and if, required.

Futurecasting encourages us to change our position from reactive to proactive. The aim of this book is to help ministries and schools become proactive in planning for the future to ensure 'continuity of learning and assessment'. Such planning would protect against the marginalisation of learners (from poor families, remote areas or with special needs and disabilities) when a change suddenly stops learning in school classrooms, as was the case in the Covid-19 pandemic, and children were required to stay home and be homeschooled.

Policymakers trained and able to use futurecasting methodology would be more effective in choosing efficient solutions – fewer U-turns would be needed with the accompanying wastage of resources and potential ensuing loss of public trust and confidence (ICET/MESHGuides 2020).

Specific challenges: for national pandemic planning for education

Schools cannot solve the challenge of disruption to learning at times of crises, alone. National planning provides the backbone supporting local responses.

The following specific challenges relating to national planning are covered in this chapter:

* The framework for school-based education sector planning
* Operationalising the policy elements: allocating roles and responsibilities
* Resources for learning: human, financial, material, technological
* Health and safety: risk assessments
* Continuing and initial teacher training
* Special cases and marginalised learners.

Specific challenge 1.1 A framework for education sector planning

Contingency plans need to consider in detail how a number of interdependent elements can continue to function together during a crisis. Each element listed in Table 1.2 forms a specific challenge with accompanying problems and solutions.[5] What is possible depends on your particular context, the relationship between government and the schools and the resources – financial, human, material and technological – that are available. Table 1.3 shows the planning tool suggested by the European Centre for Disease Control (ECDC 2006).

Specific challenge 1.2 Operationalising the business continuity plans: allocating roles and responsibilities

The EU advice (EC 2009a, b) to build on existing structures seems worth bearing in mind at all points. Our research shows that the way that roles and responsibilities are shared and managed between the national, regional and local levels can be grouped into three different modes.

Mode 1: Top-down mode: national leaders determine what happens at the local level and devise and manage a national education 'business continuity plan' for the school sector.

Mode 2: Bottom-up mode: This mode, for central and regional government, is the do-nothing mode – in a crisis leave the education of learners to individual teachers, schools, commercial bodies, NGOs.

Mode 3: Hybrid collaboration mode: This mode works when there are shared values and trust between governments and education organisations, notably teachers and teacher professional organisations, teachers' curriculum subject associations, education unions, other education networks and teacher training institutions. For example, in New Zealand, the ministry of education worked with educational researchers, teachers and teacher educators to launch two new educational TV channels within three weeks – this shows what can be done with collaboration.[6]

Table 1.3 Example: Assessment planning tool for checking pandemic or natural disaster preparedness from ECDC (2006)

Goal	Key indicator	Current status	Instructions in italics
1			Comments and notes by those filling in

Specific challenge 1.3 Resources for learning: human, financial, material, technological

Each country, region and school will have different resources at their disposal. Supplementary to equipment that schools might offer their pupils, there may be a need to provide, at short notice, certain equipment and resources to ensure continuity of educational provision both for pupils at home and those attending a setting that is different to their normal experience – but imagine if such provision were available to each learner in non-crises?

Examples of how countries built on existing media provision of learning resources come from, for example, Mexico and Portugal for television and Mexico and Somalia for radio. Collaboration between governments, educators and the media ensured that there were programmes supporting ongoing learning at times to fit with parents' and learners' lives.

Specific challenge 1.4 Health and safety and risk assessments

We found that in public debates about re-opening schools to all pupils, while the risks of transmission between young people and the potential impact of the virus on their health were discussed, the potential impact on teachers hardly featured. Advice on the provision and use of PPE for teachers (Nuki 2020; CDC 2020; DHS 2020) varied from the clear advice of USA's CDC (2020), which acknowledged that there would be resistance from some quarters to the recommended mask-wearing, to the UK's DHS advice (2020) which in August 2020 provided advice for a wide range of workplaces (transport workers, for example, were specifically mentioned) but neglected the school sector. Mask-wearing was a well-established norm in East Asian countries particularly but was highly politicised in the USA where mask-wearing became to be seen as an infringement of liberties, particularly by supporters of then-president Trump. As time went by in 2020 mask-wearing in public settings was either mandated or strongly encouraged. In November 2020, mask-wearing by secondary school students in Scotland was mandated in areas where viral spread was at a high level.[7]

During Covid-19, misinformation, misconceptions and myths, including conspiracy theories, circulated. These were potentially dangerous, and head teachers reported that community members turned to them for trusted advice although they were not medically trained (ICET/MESHGuides 2020).

Specific challenge 1.5 Continuing and initial teacher training

Ensuring supply of teachers is a national government responsibility. Some national governments amended teaching certificates to take account of the different experience of trainee teachers during Covid (e.g. accrediting their online teaching experience), others did nothing. There is clearly a need for the training of teachers, now and in the future, to include relevant and appropriate skills, knowledge and understanding in order to be prepared for teaching within a world that is subject to the sudden disruption to 'formal' education due to emergencies such as pandemics, epidemics and natural disasters. Teachers need to be able to mix online/remote learning with both face-to-face teaching and intergenerational learning at home. During the Covid-19 period some schools were reluctant to allow trainee teachers onto the school premises. Others treated the student as a member of staff and tutoring and observations have been undertaken using remote video technology such as IRISConnect so that external tutors and assessors did not attend the school site. In one country, teacher training qualifications were amended to recognise they had been trained to teach online.

These new scenarios require a different approach to evaluation, assessment and validation of achievement which takes account of online/distance learning environments and informal settings as well as more traditional formal learning environments.

Specific challenge 1.6 Special cases and marginalised learners

Each community faces unique challenges for supporting continuity of learning for marginalised learners in the best of times. In planning for times of crises particular types of learners may need special attention (e.g. children in care, children with special needs, children from poor families and other emotionally and physically vulnerable children).

Every education system leader and teacher should be able to answer the question: 'what steps are being taken to ensure there is continuity of learning *for all*?'

Lessons learned: planning for continuity during periods of disruption

1.1 Planning for business continuity and surge capacity: Virologists predict that epidemics and pandemics will continue to occur periodically as new viruses emerge (recent examples being Ebola, SARS, MERS, swine flu, measles and HIV) so it is clear that plans for ensuring continuity of learning and assessment need to be already in place and ready to be implemented within hours. There is no guarantee that another pandemic/crisis will not occur in months or within a few years so regularly updating contingency plans is essential. This will also help mitigate the effects of other crises which may suddenly erupt and cause disruption to schooling.

In the context of the education sector, 'business continuity planning' means plans must be specific enough to ensure continuing education and public assessment processes. Careful planning, as recommended by the WHO (2009) and the European Commission (EC 2009a, b), could have avoided a situation where teachers and pupils, particularly pupils preparing for final exams of their school careers, were placed under considerable stress. Teacher shortages have to be expected and planned for. In October 2020, with schools resuming full-time teaching and at a time where groups were supposed to be small, grouped in 'bubbles', in one high-income country, teachers reported class sizes of 90 as so many teachers were off 'self-isolating'.

1.2: A framework for school continuity planning: Without prior education contingency plans, schools will be suddenly subjected to reacting to crises, which puts undue stress on staff and material resources. Giving prior thought and attention to the elements of the framework outlined in Table 1.1 may help schools prepare for crises and enable schools to be proactive in providing continuity of learning for all, including marginalised learners, from the outset of any disruption.

1.3 Updating plans: Whatever mode is used to develop and operationalise them, plans will need updating regularly to avoid what happened in England, where school pandemic planning advice (DFES 2006; DCSF 2008) had not been updated for nearly 15 years and, in the meantime, the lines of accountability mentioned in the plans, from central government to the local schools via local education authorities, had been dismantled. The European Centre for Disease Prevention and Control (ECDC 2006) proposes that plans are checked regularly and updated. The ECDC provides an assessment tool which would need adaption for education specific plans. Table 1.2 shows the headings they suggest for such a plan.

1.4: Continuity planning for learning resources: Continuity planning if education is to be continued for as many learners as possible includes harnessing the power of radio and TV – not just the internet. In countries with rapidly developing technology which relies heavily on sustained connectivity to the internet, politicians thought that internet programmes were the answer only to find that many learners had no access. In England much was made of marginalised learners being supplied with internet-connected devices, but further examination showed that laptop devices took many months to arrive, somebody had to configure them, provide the internet connection and train the young people and that not enough were supplied.[8] Also, in low-, medium- and high-income countries, rural locations in particular may have no internet coverage or electricity and the costs of data rule out access in any case. World Bank data on access to electricity gives an approximate indication of access to electricity round the world.[9] However, USA colleagues told us the 100% figure in the World Bank for rural access in the USA to electricity is inaccurate.

1.5 Risk Assessments – teachers' and learners' lives: Who carries the risk if a teacher or child dies of Covid-19 from school? One of the most challenging problems for school leaders is how to keep teachers and young people and their families safe. The issue of teacher safety has to be balanced with the priority of getting parents back to work and economies restarted. Risks to mental health of staff and pupils also have to be considered.

1.6 Teacher training: Teacher training programmes need to include a study of assessment and pedagogical approaches that are suitable for online/distance learning, formal and informal learning, and intergenerational learning to an equal level and standard as their specialist subject knowledge. Teacher training needs to equip teachers with the ability to draw on learners' own interests and motivations as well as the part that parents, siblings and other family members can play in teaching and learning and the specialist knowledge and support that schools and outside professional agencies can provide as and when necessary.

1.7 Special Cases and marginalised learners: The identification of marginalised and potentially marginalised learners and the mitigation of risks to the continuity of their schooling should be addressed as part of the planning process.

1.8: Futurecasting – national pandemic plans: Prepare emergency plans for a rapid implementation based on robust existing processes and structures and update such plans regularly.

Ensuring the provision of continued learning for all children is a national concern; no country's education system should be unprepared for a national crisis, ever. Risk management requires us to plan for worst-case scenarios. So, if the country wants an education service preparing all children and young people for the future, each country's government needs to develop a strategy for making education happen during times of crisis.

In short, strategies for crisis management for schooling need to include risk assessment, whether for global pandemics, national epidemics or natural disaster/s, and to include provision of online resources or viable alternatives (radio or printed packs) that could be immediately called upon to support learners across all ages and phases.

Recognising that the situation is different in different countries, we stress the need for governments to understand that teaching is a profession with recognised experts, whose work is quality assured through recognition by professional subject associations, which have, as a core purpose, identifying and promoting excellent teaching of their subjects.

Planning toolkit: planning for the unknown

Table 1.4 provides key questions to aid your strategic planning relating to the overall and specific challenges outlined previously. You will need to adapt and add to these to suit your circumstances and context.

Table 1.4 Planning toolkit: strategic planning for disruption of schooling

Decision 1.1 Ensuring business continuity, allocating roles and responsibilities

Questions to resolve	*Examples:* Infrastructure – is the infrastructure there and sufficiently robust to carry your plans out? What provision is there for maintaining communication and accessing online-learning materials and support – for all learners? Are you providing equity of access to pedagogically appropriate resources? Can teachers access materials needed to teach their curriculum? Are your plans realistic? Are there links between national and local plans? This ensures that there is coherence between a national strategy and links to operational plans at a local level. Does your plan include how you will access experts and networks of educators who can support online/distance/home learning? Being able to provide access locally and nationally to expert and credible knowledge may foster calm and help teachers and parents educating children at home to draw on 'trusted' knowledge with confidence. This can help to challenge fake news and myths and misconceptions. Commercialisation opportunities: commercial offers may often have hidden costs. For example, in the coronavirus crises, a search engine revealed over 1000 'free materials' which were offered by a variety of companies that turned out to be – free trials for a week, free for the period of crisis and which were linked to paid-for materials. Out of 1047 'free' resources, only 28 were genuinely 'free for all time' to the user (date of search 20 April 2020).
Solutions	*Examples:* Solutions are context dependent – they depend on national values and deployment of resources.

Decision 1.2 Resources

Questions to resolve	*Examples:* We found no patterns to the allocation of extra resources. Some governments provided funding for additional teachers so as to reduce class sizes and acted quickly to provide extra toilets and wash stations; others left school leaders to sort out problems with no additional resources. We also were told of schools in rural areas being left with no teachers, because the teachers returned to their own villages.
Solutions	*Examples:* The most effective solutions we have come across are where central and local government worked with representatives of teachers and community leaders to agree on solutions, including the allocation of new resources which gave flexibility to adapt at the local level. The least effective solutions were those where government tried to blame professionals for failures. Authoritarian approaches caused chaos at the local level.

(Continued)

Table 1.4 (Cont).

Decision 1.3 Health and Safety	
Questions to resolve	*Examples:* What personal protective equipment (PPE) is to be made available to teachers, other staff and pupils? Where will this be kept? Are instructions and resources available to make PPE? What standards are there for the facilities' health and hygiene protocols? What has to happen to enable these standards to be met in all settings? How do your plans mitigate misinformation, misconceptions and myths, including conspiracy theories? How do your plans ensure accurate knowledge that is evidence-informed is available? Does your plan acknowledge mental health issues arising from the impact of a crisis on those involved in providing education provision/homeschooling as well as coping with family and community challenges?
Solutions	*Examples:* During the coronavirus, schools have used design and technology equipment to make protective visors, community groups have made masks and indeed gowns for medical staff; goggles used for science lessons have been used for protection against virus transfer. In some countries, there are building standards about the ratio of pupils' hygiene facilities which may give reassurance to parents and school leaders in decisions about safety. Have you strategies to ease stress? Networking teachers to share solutions may ease pressures. Creating easy access to tools and resources supporting teaching as well as individual well-being is another. (There are specific charities providing expertise for mental health with resources available through their websites). Do you need to act to ensure key workers can access food and medicines so that they are able to continue to work. In terms of Maslow's hierarchy of needs, those needs at the bottom of the triangle need to be met first (McLeod 2007).

Decision 1.4 Continuing and Initial Teacher training	
Questions to resolve	*Examples:* Are processes in place to ensure all teachers and support staff are upskilled in the pedagogies which most effectively support remote learning including digital technologies? Is this training also available to trainee teachers and teacher educators to help plan for any such future events, too? Have you strategies for ensuring that teacher training continues?
Solutions	*Examples:* Solutions are context dependent – they depend on national partnerships. Remote video observations where possible minimise visits of tutors to schools – otherwise they may be visiting a number of schools.

Decision 1.5 Special cases and marginalised learners	
Questions to resolve	*Examples:* Do you have systems that allow you to identify learners who are marginalised or likely to become marginalised if schools close? Do you have plans to support them in keeping up with their peers? How will learners catch up after a crisis? What will inform your recovery curriculum for when schools reopen?

(Continued)

Table 1.4 (Cont).

Solutions	*Examples:*
	Local solutions during Covid-19 included:

* Printed packs: For those without internet, teachers produced printed packs, posted or delivered to pupils or pickup points. Would your plan cater for this, and are funds and resources to print packs available? Respondents in the research for this book reported that some teachers paid for such materials from their own pockets (ICET/MESHGuides 2020). What distribution plans are in place that do not require pupils or their parents/guardians to travel personally to collect such learning materials and resources? (see DCSF advice 2008).
* Teachers delivered food or food vouchers to homes and also checked on learners' well-being through telephone contact.
* Schools remained open for marginalised learners and children of key workers.
* Recovery curriculum was planned, with particular attention on marginalised learners.
* Catch-up plans put into place, including formative assessment on return and individual interventions by teachers or tutors.

Futurecasting: for education continuity planning for crises

This chapter encourages education stakeholders to plan for crises that disrupt schooling and require continuity of learning to be re-imagined and delivered in new and alternative ways.

The World Health Organisation (WHO 2009) advises governments and ministries of education to have a national strategy for remote schooling during a time of emergency, whether a pandemic or natural disaster, and to regularly update this. Virologists (WHO 2009) say that epidemics and pandemics are to be planned for as a factor of life. The seriousness of the coronavirus contagion rates were identified in January 2020 in the Lancet (Wang et al. 2020), but in some countries, leaders were slow to react. That not all governments implemented the WHO (2009) advice became apparent during the 2020 worldwide coronavirus pandemic when, within a couple of weeks of rising political concern of a global health crisis, schools were closed but plans to provide continuity of education were not in place

While it is not possible to future-proof education fully for times of crisis nor to know what form a crisis will take, it is possible to plan for known challenges and what we can anticipate will cause challenges. With respect to Covid-19, what was a relief for those who remember polio and smallpox epidemics is that children and young people were considerably less affected than older members of the population so that the risks of attending school were not as great as during polio and smallpox epidemics. However, this did not mitigate against the risks to adults and the teachers who continued to deliver education. The debate about risks to children with coronavirus cited the 'lesser' effects of the disease, but the teachers remained subject to contagion and were at risk from contracting, from the children, a disease which would affect them with greater severity than the children.

Continuity and contingency planning are vital for a robust education system design for every region and country. As European Commission (ECDC 2006; EC 2009a, b) documentation recommends, there should be national strategies in place for education for times of crisis. Governments may have previous examples of guidance (e.g. in England DfES 2006; DCSF 2008), but these must be refreshed and not, as happened in England, ideologically rejected due to a change in political party following an election; education and children's lives are worth more than that.

We propose that, from now on, educators look to their governments to provide a well-planned national strategy for education that is able to be operationalised at the local level for schools during times of crisis.

Acknowledgements

Parts of this chapter are adapted from Sarah Younie, Marilyn Leask and Stephen Hall in Hudson et al. (eds) (2021) *Education system design: foundations, policy options and consequences*. Abingdon, UK: RoutledgeTaylorFrancis.

Thanks are given to the MESHGuides International Council members whose contributions to the coronavirus weekly meetings enabled us to draw up these guidelines for planning continuity for education in emergencies; see full list of contributors in the acknowledgements.

Notes

1 This virus originated in the USA and was carried to Europe through troop deployments in World War I.
2 Rumsfeld and Schopf (ibid) are applying Meno's Paradox to their respective areas. The **learning paradox** – also an application of Meno's paradox – refers to a set of arguments that, in the 1980s, questioned the received way of conceptualising **learning**. The core of the argument was that novel knowledge cannot be derived completely from old knowledge, or it would not be new.
3 Definitions www.hospitalitytech.com/future-forecasting-futurecasting
4 Definitions https://www.remembertoplay.co/files/17.11.14_Futurecasting-rtp.pdf
5 The information in this chapter is derived from the analysis of existing strategy documents and planning advice from different international and national bodies (MESHGuides 2020) and the MESHGuides International Council weekly meetings held during the coronavirus crisis. Council members collaborated across UN regions to

analyse practices occurring during the lockdown period of school closures. (See list of Acknowledgements for contributors).

6 NZ government move to TV https://nzareblog.wordpress.com/2020/10/15/television-changed-our-day-jobs-part-i/.

7 Mask-wearing mandatory for 15–18 year olds in areas of Scotland www.independent.co.uk/news/education/education-news/coronavirus-school-face-mask-rule-restrictions-pupils-covid-teachers-b1447546.html

8 Provision falls short: https://schoolsweek.co.uk/coronavirus-85m-free-laptops-scheme-falls-short/

9 World Bank data https://data.worldbank.org/indicator/EG.ELC.ACCS.RU.ZS

National vision and values

The foundation for contingency planning

Introduction and context

The values of a society are reflected in national priorities and can lead to different opportunities for a society's children as these quotations show:

> *The crisis we have experienced this year poses serious challenges to policy makers and professionals. It exposes fault lines in society and reveals problems which had previously only been noticed by a minority. It can also highlight the distance between policy makers and practitioners and the gap between their understandings of how schools work.*
>
> *At the same time, such a crisis presents opportunities to address serious problems and make lives better. This requires more than short-term technical fixes, it requires vision.*
>
> (EAGLE Report July 2020 p. 24)[1]

> *'Oran a azu nwa': it takes a community or village to raise a child: Nigerian Igbo cultural proverb. The Igbo's also name their children 'Nwa ora' which means child of the community.*
>
> (van der Rheede 2010)

> *There is no such thing as society.*
>
> (Thatcher 1987)

These quotations from different cultures, illustrate two quite different philosophies which influence the functioning of countries and their ability to respond to emergencies. One talks about collective responsibility, the other decries collective responsibility and leaves the effective operation of society to individual efforts.

DOI: 10.4324/9781003155591-4

The values of national leaders and, within local communities, shared values and history of collective effort, influence the development of contingency plans and then what can be achieved in times of crises.

If you are undertaking contingency planning whether at national, regional or local levels, what you do and how you use resources reflect your vision and values.

Overall challenge: developing a shared vision for the operation of the education sector during crises

The Covid-19 pandemic exposed the issue that politicians and their advisors may not necessarily have the depth of specialist knowledge to understand how their policies and planning for and during pandemics will be operationalised and what the unintended consequences will be. In the ICET/MESHGuide member surveys, teacher support was positive for government-initiated educational pandemic strategies where ministers of education and senior staff had educational backgrounds (ICET/MESHGuides 2020).

In countries where education is centrally organised, the education service may be organised around the political vision and values of the party in power. In other countries, consensus at regional and local levels sets the vision and values underpinning decisions.

In analysing the responses of different governments to the Covid crisis, we identified four modes of national leadership, each with different values influencing their philosophical approach:

* Mode 1: devolved responsibility – to individual regions, communities, schools
* Mode 2: collaborative – working with teacher unions, NGOs, professional associations
* Mode 3: authoritarian – central diktats and mandatory instructions
* Mode 4: ad hoc – centralised and partly localised (chaotic and fragmented).

These approaches informed their expectations of and communications with schools during the pandemic. For example, in England, education seemed to be a 'political football' with Mode 3 leadership in place. As one headteacher said in our survey, 'What the Prime Minister decides on a Friday night, headteachers are implementing on Saturday' (27th August[2]). The chaos this caused during the pandemic, as decisions were centralised where more regional and local decision-making would have been more sensitive to local conditions, created a strong argument that education should be decoupled from politics or managed through a cross-party system. (The present arrangement in England allows for total change with the education system every time there is a change of government.)

School leaders at local level also have sets of values which guide the organisation of their school – these may be different to those of the incumbent government in a country, depending on the degree of freedom headteachers are given.

These national and school values have direct impact on the actions taken to protect continuity of learning and assessment for the marginalised.

Our research during 2020 indicated that many teachers and community volunteers felt a moral and professional imperative to provide continuing support for learners during the crisis. This work ethic seems similar to the work ethic of medical staff who put their lives and those of their families on the line in treating infectious patients. There were numerous reports of schools (ibid.) and their teachers providing food to poor families, teachers paying for learning materials from their own pockets and delivering these to students as well as schools donating and making PPE (Personal Protective Equipment) to health workers (e.g. science departments donating their safety goggles and making 'scrubs' (protective clothing) or face shields). The commitment of teachers driven by a moral imperative is notable.

The coronavirus crisis highlighted the need for effective knowledge mobilisation strategies. Those countries which had developed nationwide, knowledge management platforms for education were at an advantage when the Covid-19 crisis struck. For example, South Korea (KERIS – Korea Education and Research Information Service), Scotland (GlowConnect) and the Netherlands (KennisNet) have national digital platforms to house content and pedagogical knowledge to support teachers and learners during normal times and times of crisis. These platforms were already developed and in use, and could then be further mobilised during the crisis to provide ongoing 'Covid-19 updates' for parents, governors, teachers and learners as well as giving immediate further provision to ensure continuity of learning.

Specific challenges: developing a realistic national vision for education

The following specific challenges are covered in this chapter:

* The national vision and values for education
* National values and the curtailing of the curriculum during crises.

Specific challenge 2.1 The national vision and values for education

Vision statements make public the values of an organisation. So what national vision statement might underpin contingency planning in your setting?

Is your country's vision to ensure as much as possible, continuity of learning and assessment for all, or is your country content with an elite system where resources are cornered by the already privileged? The answer to that question affects relationships and the functioning of your society and contingency planning. At the heart of education is access to knowledge, with many countries having a defined curriculum and assessment structure. The educational vision for a country influences how this knowledge is viewed and managed: whether knowledge is valued as a public good and therefore freely available for all to access (perhaps online or on radio or tv), or whether the knowledge is viewed as a private commodity and monetised.

Open access to knowledge and equity

Knowledge and access to it must be carefully considered in education contingency plans as inadvertently, many learners may be excluded (e.g. subscription services can exclude the teachers and schools who would benefit the most). Some countries (India, Australia) use low flying satellites, others use balloons to provide internet access to previously remote areas, others do nothing.

At a time of crisis where contingency planning is not in place, decisions may need to be made about what is included in any emergency curricula and what is excluded. Such a decision may impact on learners and their societies for the rest of their lives. We found some examples where learners have not had to face a restricted curricula during the Covid-19 period. For example, Table 2.1 provides an example of a school service for learners in remote areas that puts the vision of inclusion of all learners at the heart of its operations. The vision and values and mission statement of the Alice Springs (virtual) School of the Air shows a commitment to the education of all children. The school catchment area covers 1.3 million square kilometres including the desert areas of most of the Northern Territory, the northern area of South Australia and eastern area of Western Australia. This example demonstrates how a vision of how to provide equity of access to education can be implemented in the most difficult of environments. Low flying satellites are used to support remote teaching in areas with no internet and with home-generated electricity.

Table 2.1 Values and mission statement for remote schooling of the Alice Springs (virtual) School of the Air[3]

> **Delivering excellence in education to remote Australia since 1951**
>
> The Alice Springs School of the Air provides a virtual school experience, offering a wide range of educational services and activities to isolated school children, from Preschool to Year 9, in the southern half of the Northern Territory and the extreme north of South Australia. The School operates for 40 weeks of the year and follows the same school calendar as other Government schools

in the Northern Territory, sharing the same term and holiday schedule. The Principal states, many of our students live on cattle stations but they also come from Indigenous communities, camel farms, national parks, mining camps, roadhouses, remote police stations and tourist ventures. Some students stay with the school from the start of their primary education all the way through until the end of Year 9 when they either continue in distance education via the Northern Territory School of Distance Education, or move into a regional centre or interstate to attend boarding school.

Our Vision

Inspiring isolated students to recognise and realise their potential.

Our Mission

We educate isolated and diverse students to recognise and realise their potential through world-leading educational approaches:

* interactive technologies
* engaging teaching practices
* fostering independent learners
* strong partnerships with families.

Our Values

We recognise and respect everyone's rights, knowledge, aspirations and experiences.

We value diversity and the benefits that different perspectives and experiences bring to our work.

We encourage reflective and open dialogue that is timely and constructive.

We collaborate to promote innovation and solutions-focussed thinking.

We continually evaluate our impact to improve student outcomes.

We learn and improve through practice and persistence, by risk taking, mistake making and through embracing challenge.

The inclusive values of the (virtual) School of the Air are worth noting. In other countries, children living in similar circumstances may be among the most marginalised. In developing an education sector contingency plan for crisis management, decisions are influenced by the values, culture/s and resources specific to country, context and school.

> Values are principles and fundamental convictions which act as general guides to behaviour; enduring beliefs about what is worthwhile; ideals for which one strives; broad standards by which particular beliefs and actions are judged to be good, right, desirable or worthy of respect.
>
> (Halstead and Taylor 2000, p. 3)

Values shape actions, and in a pandemic or crisis in education, these values shape responses and new actions. What each country and each school does in response to a pandemic depends on the values espoused at different levels of the system and these values include whether the *rights of all learners* to the best possible education are recognised and respected.

Areas influenced by values based decision-making when contingency planning include: equity, access, curriculum/assessment, teacher empowerment, infrastructure, communications, community/volunteer engagement, evaluation strategy, and leadership. See the planning toolkit for suggestions of questions to be addressed when contingency planning in these areas.

Specific challenge 2.2 National values and the curtailing of the curriculum during crises

National values affected the choices made to restrict curriculum and assessment strategies experienced by students during the time of Covid-19.

In any curtailing of the curriculum envisaged in contingency plans, the following information from the OECD is worth considering. Matthews (2021) cites international studies which stress the need for children and young people to develop what are called the 4Cs – Collaboration, Communication, Critical thinking and Creativity (European Commission EC 2016; Jayaram 2012; O'Sullivan 1999; Pellegrino and Hilton 2012; Voogt and Roblin 2013), which are a set of global competencies for contemporary living and working.

These could form the basis for stimulating and engaging educational experiences, both during crisis and non-crisis schooling. Normally tradition and the consequent demands of national examinations and set curricula may prevent the development of these, but times of crisis when there is disruption and re-evaluation of priorities may provide an opportunity to fully engage with these core skills. For example, in England the *Confederation of Business* (CBI) argues that the curriculum is too narrow, that attitudes are important and that elements such as teamwork, self-management

Table 2.2 21st-century skills

21st-century skills include:

* Critical thinking, problem solving, reasoning, analysis, interpretation, synthesising information
* Creativity, artistry, curiosity, imagination, innovation, personal expression
* Perseverance, self-direction, planning, self-discipline, adaptability, initiative
* Leadership, teamwork, collaboration, cooperation, facility in using virtual workspaces
* Information and communication technology (ICT) literacy, media and internet literacy, data interpretation and analysis, computer programming
* Civic, ethical, and social-justice literacy
* Economic and financial literacy, entrepreneurialism
* Global awareness, multicultural literacy, humanitarianism
* Scientific literacy and reasoning, the scientific method
* Environmental and conservation literacy, ecosystems understanding
* Health and wellness literacy, including nutrition, diet, exercise, and public health and safety.

Source: Great Schools Partnership (2018)

and problem solving should be taught in schools (CBI 2010a, b, 2012). Arguably, during a crisis, if examinations are cancelled, schools could use the time to focus on developing more 21st-century skills, see Table 2.2.

Importantly, the development of these skills are seen to help with well-being and mental health central to young people's ability to cope during a crisis as well as for the future – to be employed and function in a changing society.

We argue that education should include global competences, which are about more than employment and offer a holistic approach to educating children that is beneficial to society and individuals' well-being which is a priority at a time of uncertainty and disruption which affects children's mental health.

> Global Competence includes the acquisition of in-depth knowledge and understanding of global and intercultural issues; the ability to learn from and live with people from diverse backgrounds; and the attitudes and values necessary to interact respectfully with others . . . cross-cultural engagement should balance clear communication with sensitivity to multiple perspectives and . . . equip young people not just to understand but to act. The greatest of these is the need

to find a new concept of growth. This . . . [is] a multidimensional concept that includes care for the environment and social harmony, as well as acceptable levels of security, health, and education.

(Ramos and Schleicher 2016, p. 3)

These are also beneficial skills for managing crises when they occur and at whatever level, whether it is local, regional, national or a pandemic across multiple countries.

Matthews (2021) draws our attention to the inclusion of practical and physical skills, which are often undervalued. Figures 2.1 and 2.2 illustrate the importance of the 21st century values to education, as the world becomes more internationalised, partly because of technology. Pupils, in order to gain global competency, need to develop such attributes as tolerance, resilience, being able to handle uncertainty, self- and critical-reflection as well as empathy. Learning from mistakes and being able to deal with uncertainty and confusion is a crucial part of learning.

Figure 2.2 is useful in that it indicates common international issues. (There are 34 countries in the OECD. Albeit that these are high income countries, the concerns of middle and low-income countries are also relevant, particularly as these may look to high-income countries for knowledge transfer and system developments, including education).

The values that emerge in this discussion, listed in Table 2.3, cover many aspects of the 21st-century skills mentioned earlier.

In particular. Matthews (2021) suggests that it is worth unpicking the meaning of a focus on collaboration, the first on the list. This is understood to include cooperation and being communal, even developing a sense of community, which would stand in stark contrast to the stress on individualism in education in some countries. Notedly, during Covid-19, the public health advice across countries was reliant on cooperation and compliance from people in relation to social distancing and wearing of face masks, which required a collaborative, communal effort to tackle the spread of the virus. Such compliance was found to dip when politicians were seen to flout the rules, as research from UCL found in England when the prime minister's senior government adviser broke lockdown, refused to apologise and was supported by the Prime Minister Boris Johnson and his close associate Michael Gove. (In the video referenced here, you can see shocking evidence that Gove doesn't believe what he is saying himself[4] thus potentially furthering public distrust.) Later in the pandemic, when the Prime Minister wanted teachers to look after children so parents could work and the economy to restart he had the temerity to say it was teachers 'moral duty' to open schools regardless of the risks.[5] In other cases, in different countries, senior people resigned their posts when they were found to have broken the rules.

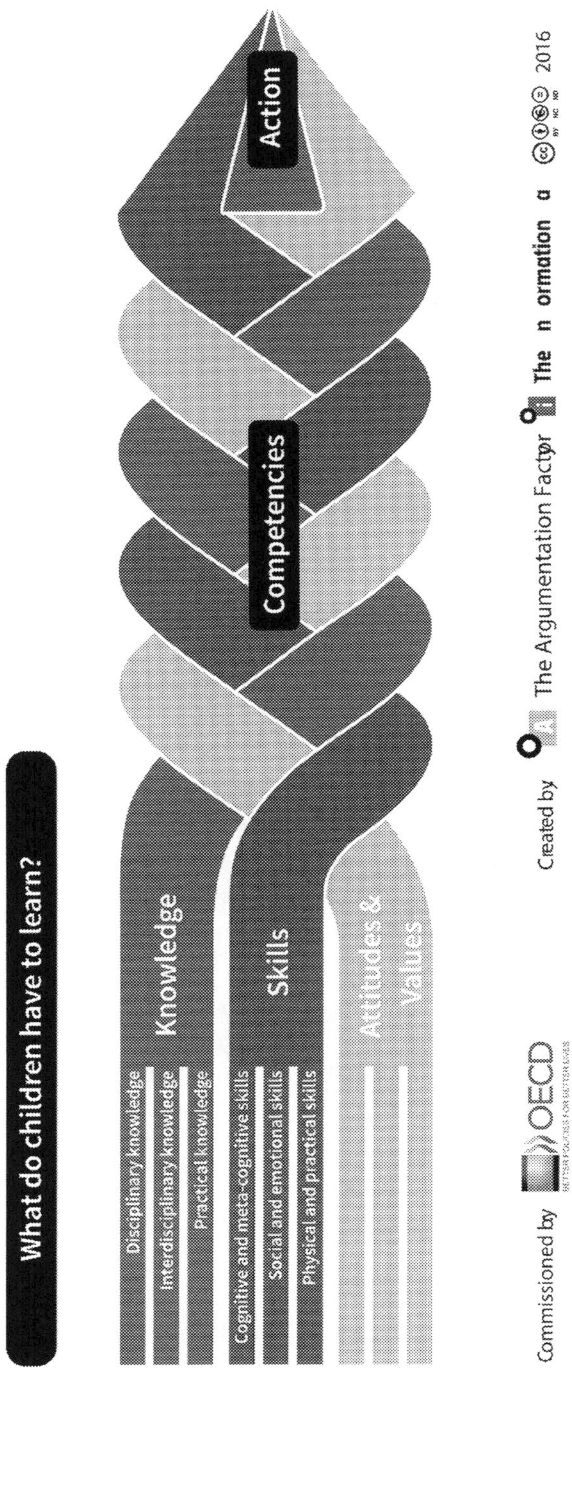

Figure 2.1 Strands of provision in an education service, including values

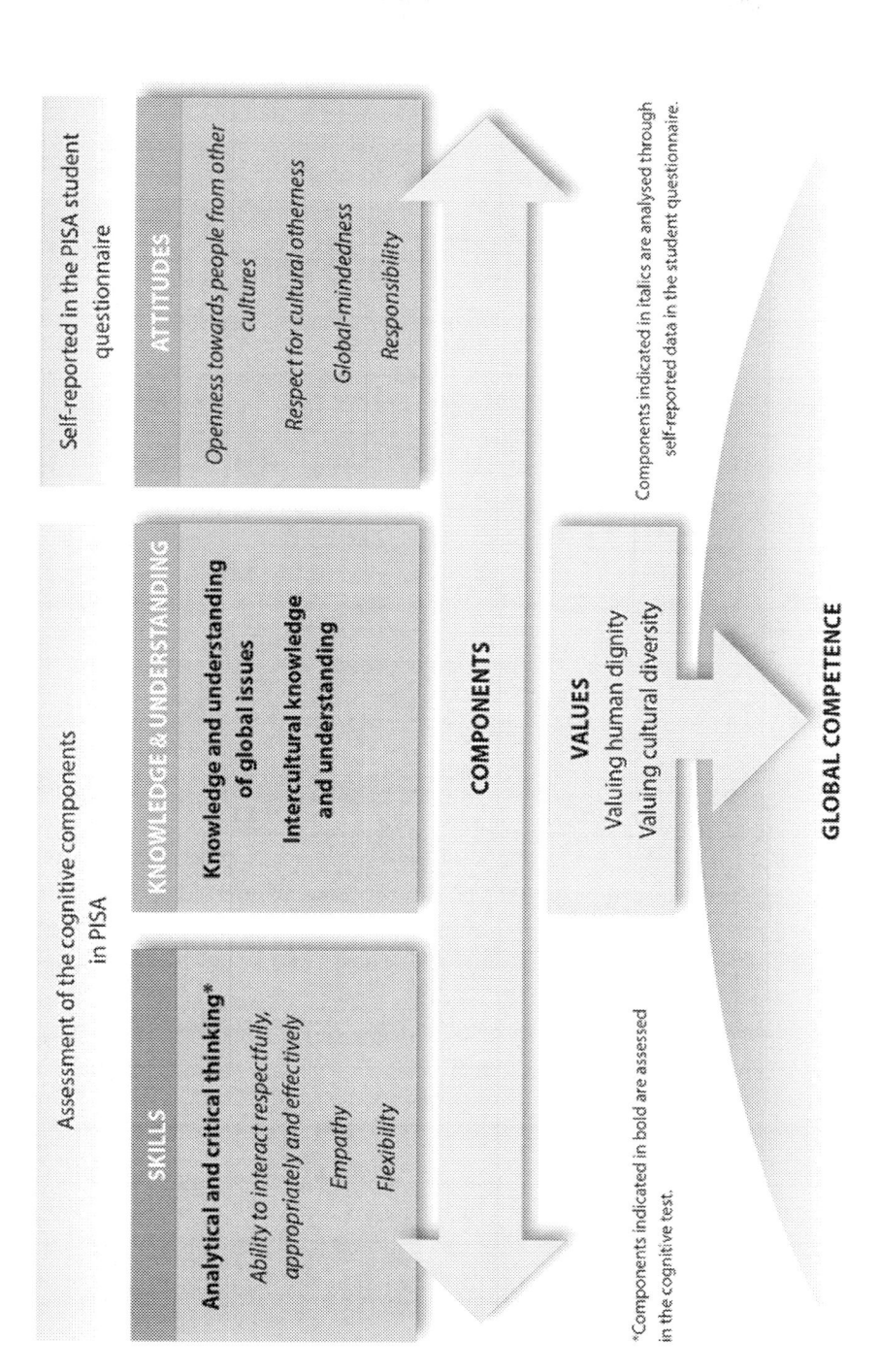

Figure 2.2 Global competences (Ramos and Schleicher 2016, p. 6 OECD)

Table 2.3 Which values are supported by your curricula?

1	Collaboration, cohesion
2	Equality and social justice, gender/trans/diversity/equality
3	Happiness
4	Concern for others, (interconnectedness) cohesion, be willing to adapt
5	Valuing cultural diversity, integration
6	Critical thinking, open-mindedness and problem solving
7	Creativity
8	Emancipation and empowerment, with the belief that that everyone can grow and generate ideas

Lessons learned: about national vision and values and leadership styles

2.1: Devolving leadership (Mode 1 leadership): While devolving responsibility to regions and individual schools is for some aspects of education to be preferred, delegation *could deny teachers the support of substantial nationally funded resources, in particular online knowledge management tools*. Having in place an effective nationwide knowledge management tool, such as Ghana's Icampus (Icampus.gh) or Scotland's Glow Connect online platforms and those in many other countries as mentioned, enabled a swift and agile response to Covid-19 which, teachers have reported, supported ensured continuity of learning.

2.2 Collaboration (Mode 2 leadership): All the governmental advice on pandemic planning that we reviewed urges caution in the closing of schools (EC 2009a, b) because of the disruption: the amount of disruption is severe and significant for children and working parents, affecting the economy as well as education. Having national and local expert groups ready to lead on carefully worked-through plans for each phase and subject could be expected to mitigate some of the damage of disruption. A benefit of such formal professional collaboration may be the development of understanding of pedagogy in politicians and public servants so they are not prey to 'snake oil' merchants and lone ranger charismatic experts who may step to the fore in crises.

2.3 Limitations of centralised national plans (Mode 3 leadership): National plans developed centrally by politicians and their advisers who do not have experience in education, may not work in practice. The national plans on crisis management during a pandemic that we have looked at are missing detail on how the education sector manages specific issues, such as safety; how to ensure equity for children in disadvantaged situations; equal access to resources; expectations for forms of remote teaching and learning; and, managing public examinations/national assessments when children are out of schools.

To be operationalised, any education plan need to be detailed at the school level – to ensure continuity of learning as much as possible. This level of detail requires input from teachers themselves. See examples in the Annexes,

One consequence of this mode is that it is 'inequitable': for some, the plethora of access options to learning materials is too great, and teachers, pupils and parents become overwhelmed with choice. For others there are very limited, if any, options with very limited materials available thus widening the divide between the 'haves' and 'have-nots' and adding to further disadvantage marginalised learners.

2.4 Ad hoc responses (Mode 4 leadership): The coronavirus pandemic of 2020 tested national disaster plans. Teachers' reports from many countries (MESHGuides 2020a; VSO 2020a, b, c), indicated that, too often, individual teachers were expected to carry the load of maintaining education on their own, using their own resources: financial and technical. This ad hoc mode, leaving schools and teachers and communities to sort out the detail, does not take advantage of the systematic approach to knowledge-sharing that is possible with advanced digital technologies but relies on a less coordinated approach from individuals sharing what they know or have found out, leaving the education of children to chance. There may be no quality assurance of materials used for remote teaching and few checks and balances. By way of contrast, materials from TV and radio channels, subject and professional associations, and teacher training departments which are quality assessed by peers can be rapidly harnessed and disseminated.

Planning toolkit: contingency planning and your vision and values

The WHO (2009) and the EC (2009a, b) provided clear advice that governments should have plans in place to support continuity of learning during crises. Some governments did have plans ready (e.g. NZ [2011]), others had ditched plans drawn up by a previous government without replacing them (Leask 2020). These decisions of whether to be prepared or not reflect the values and priorities of those making decisions. The planning toolkit in Table 2.4 is intended to support contingency planning, and the answers to the questions posed are influenced by the vision and values of those making the decisions.

Table 2.4 Planning toolkit: aims and values

Decision 2.1 What vision and values underpin your decisions and your system	
Questions to resolve	What is your vision for education? What values shape your decisions? What is the impact of your values on the already marginalised: those from poor families, those in remote areas, those with special needs and disabilities?
	a. **Equity:** How will you manage equitable access to schooling for all learners including those in impoverished homes, rural areas and those with special needs? How will you

(Continued)

Table 2.4 (Cont).

ensure continuation of support services to those receiving, for example, free meals, support for special needs, psychological support and so on. How will you ensure equity of access to knowledge?

b. **Access:** How will you consider needs to cover access to any technologies required and any specialist services? How will you ensure access to the technologies you use to support continuity of schooling?

c. **Curriculum/assessment and teacher empowerment:** How can teachers be supported at a local level to adjust the curriculum, expectations and assessments to meet the needs of their pupils? How can teachers be trained to use a range of pedagogies, for example, online, 'free-choice learning' (Falk and Dierking 2002; Dierking 2005) and intergenerational pedagogies, drawing on parents and grandparents to support learning?

d. **Infrastructure:** What infrastructure is needed to support your plans specifically to support equitable access to continuity of schooling and learning?

e. **Communications:** Do you have designated risk management/disaster recovery staff who provide the link between government communications and local communities and schools? What alternative means of communication do you have in place if existing communication channels are blocked? Are all stakeholders involved aware of these channels?

f. **Community/volunteer engagement:** What resources – human, networks, organisations, individuals) and materials – are available in communities to help in times of crises? Do you hold up-to-date contact information for these resources?

g. **Evaluation strategy:** How will you evaluate your activities and plans to ensure that no child is left behind? How will you check that teachers are able to work as effectively as possible?

h. **Leadership:** What can you do to ensure confidence of the population at a national level?

Solutions	These will depend on your context – what is acceptable in one country may not be acceptable in another.

Decision 2.2 What is important in the curriculum? What can be discarded?

Questions to resolve	At times of crisis, it is unlikely that the whole planned curriculum will be available to learners. To maximise continuity of learning, what are the essential skills, concepts, knowledge and attitudes to be developed in each area of the curriculum? What can be discarded? At the time of Covid-19, practical subjects were constrained because of requirements for social distancing to limit transmission of the virus. Subjects such as computing (with virus transmission via keyboards) and practical music, art, design, science, technology were affected because of the sharing of tools.
Solutions	This chapter suggests a focus on core skills could provide an engaging curriculum. The ICET/MESHGuides report (2020) highlights the dissatisfaction of learners where remote teaching was taken to mean directly transferring the structure of the school day and the content of lessons. Again, the decisions made at a time of crisis in one country, or region or school, are not likely to apply in other contexts. Decisions about the curricula relate to job opportunities and national development priorities and values. Chapter 8 outlines alternative pedagogies.

Futurecasting: the impact of vision and values on the continuity of education during a crisis

This chapter illustrates how the vision and values of those making contingency plans for disruption of schooling can impact on access to all to the best education possible during a crisis. The ICET/MESHGuides (2020) research found excellent as well as poor practice across low-, medium- and high-income countries, and the chapters following in the rest of this book provide more detail about which strategies worked well in supporting continuity of education and which worked less well.

 # Notes

1 EAGLE Report https://eagleresearchgroup.org/wp-content/uploads/2020/08/How-can-schools-reopen-safely.pdf
2 Back to school pressures www.telegraph.co.uk/news/2020/08/27/go-back-work-risk-losing-job-major-drive-launched-get-people/
3 Alice Springs School of the Air www.assoa.nt.edu.au/the-school/our-school/
4 The previous Secretary of State for education says he thinks going for a car drive to test one's eyesight is normal www.youtube.com/watch?v=irRjqXe9Epg
5 Moral duty to reopen schools www.gov.uk/government/news/prime-ministers-statement-on-returning-children-to-school

Section 2

Leadership and management – lessons learned during Covid-19

3 | Teachers' experiences

Introduction and context

> *Education systems provide the foundations for the future wellbeing of every society. In addition, teaching is the one profession that makes all other professions possible.*
>
> Younie et al. 2021b

This chapter reports experiences of teachers during the Covid-19 pandemic and the demands placed on them as schools closed, opened, closed and opened again. For most teachers, the expectation was they would continue teaching, but some lost jobs and secondary sources of income. As mentioned in the Introduction, the chapter draws on research from the series of global webinars and international surveys, organised by MESHGuides/ICET/VSO in 2020 with participants from more than 30 countries who were teachers, school leaders, researchers and educators from NGOs.[1]

The Covid-19 pandemic created unprecedented challenges for education with implications for significant changes in how we think about and practice the work of teaching and learning. UNESCO's International Teachers' Task Force (UNESCO 2020a, d, e) estimated that by the middle of 2020 'around 63 million primary and secondary teachers around the world were affected by school closures in 165 countries due to the pandemic'. This placed teachers 'on the frontlines of the response to ensure that learning continued for 1.5 billion students worldwide'. In rising to this challenge, many teachers had to shift rapidly from accustomed ways of teaching in physical classrooms to teaching online/remotely. In contexts where this was difficult or not possible, teachers had to figure out unconventional ways to reach vulnerable and marginalised learners. The closure, with little notice, of schools, colleges and universities led to an immediate switch to online teaching and learning in some countries, but with little or no teaching in others.

DOI: 10.4324/9781003155591-6

Overall challenge: for teachers

Ensuring continuity of education when schools are closed at very short notice was a significant challenge: even for those schools where all students had their own learning devices, robust online connection and were motivated to learn. There was considerable willingness and deep commitment by teachers, college lecturers and university academics (along with any number of well-informed others, including businesses) to adapt existing learning materials to make them available online and to suit distance learning or to make paper-based packs and deliver these to students. In some low-income countries, tourism venues allowed schools to use the Wi-Fi during the day.

To provide continuity of teaching and learning teachers turned to TV, radio, telephone, mosque and temple loudspeakers, putting posters on walls of shops and community noticeboards, online and paper-based resources, SMS messaging and internet 'classroom' type software in a mixed pedagogical approach across countries. Where necessary, teachers in high- and low-income countries, took to delivering paper-based packs to homes and to local shops for collection. In one South American country, the local egg seller, who went door to door, delivered learning materials.

 # Specific challenges: pedagogies for remote learning

The 2020/21 Covid-19 pandemic faced teachers with a number of specific challenges:

* Rapid professional development: teachers needed to upskill quickly in new ways of teaching remotely.
* Increased workloads: in some countries, some schools remained open for specific children (usually children of key workers and vulnerable pupils) thus requiring teachers to manage some face-to-face learning while also providing remote learning through paper-based packs, online or telephone for the other students.
* New partnerships with parents and communities: a range of new practices developed from enforced home education by parents who may also have been working from home as lockdown ensued and places of work were closed. Teachers had to contact families directly to find out which students had personal access to technology at home and which did not. Teachers also had to set up and train families in the use of internet-connected devices.
* Initial teacher training placements were stopped in some cases as schools took actions to minimise the number of people in a school.
* Government advice was in some countries confusing, late and not appropriate.

These specific challenges are discussed in more detail below.

Specific challenge 3.1 Rapid professional development

At the same time that learners found their lives were severely disrupted, teachers found they had to transform their practice overnight (see the example in Table 3.1). At the same time, the crisis brought extra caring responsibilities for teachers with families. It is easy to forget in retrospect that no one knew how many people would die and how quickly, so teachers were working in the early months with considerable uncertainty.

Initial reports (UNESCO 2020a, c, d, e; Education International 2020) suggested that, while the response of teachers in the first stages of the pandemic has been described as heroic and praiseworthy, it has affected them psychologically and professionally. In many instances, for example, teachers worked during school closures without adequate socio-emotional support. Many functioned in a climate of fear and anxiety around their own safety and that of their families while adapting to working from home. Teachers also had to figure out how to adjust curricula, their pedagogy and practice for online or other delivery, often without professional training or support. As countries moved towards reopening schools, (although the threat of the pandemic was not over) expectations for teacher-work changed again. Not only were teachers expected to return to physical classrooms and continue providing quality learning for all students they were also expected to play key roles in making schools into safe spaces. In some cases teachers were expected to teach online at the same time as face to face because a rolling programme of exclusions of pupils as infections spread meant student groups were sent home to self-isolate. Data from some schools showed staff under strain as colleagues became ill with the virus or had to self-isolate.

The premise that underpinned the ICET/MESHGuides research (2020) was that listening to and documenting the voices of teachers must be a core part of charting the way forward for education during crises. The research gathered and examined the experiences and practices of teachers in response to five key questions.

1   How have teachers' jobs changed since the pandemic?
2   What strategies have teachers found useful?
3   What strategies/practices do teachers want to continue using?
4   What do teachers see themselves doing differently in the future?
5   What do teachers see as challenges for sustaining education during times of crisis?

Examples of the responses to these questions are in the Table 3.1: these form a snapshot summary of teachers' experiences across low-, medium- and high-income countries unless stated otherwise.

Table 3.1 Teacher experience and practices in the time of Covid-19 – what the research says (extract from ICET/MESHGuides Teacher Voice report 2020).

Question 1: How have teachers' jobs changed since the pandemic?

Positive outcomes: a step change in teachers' understanding of digital pedagogies and technologies was achieved with teachers wanting to keep new ways of working (e.g. online assessment and communications). Students who were normally quiet in class contributed more via online chat windows. Online tools helped teachers keep in touch with students and these have long-term application (e.g. for support for students who are ill). Students liked being able to access lesson materials before and after the lesson.

Teacher quote: 'All teachers had to adapt to using technologies for teaching, including the dinosaurs in the staff room of which I am one . . . some new practices we will keep – the use of online resources'.

On the negative side, some teachers lost jobs and additional income from tutoring, and contact was lost with many students.

Question 2: What strategies have they found useful?

Partnerships: close collaboration with parents and the community was reported. One example is where school leaders set up a School Emergency Education Plan (EEP) to create new policies to manage the crisis, including setting up a local 'Covid-19 committee' with representatives from the school's governing body, parents, community leaders, to plan and share ideas and feedback into the school's EEP.

Professional collaboration: Teachers found and shared ideas about online resources to support teaching and want to continue to use these if and when schooling returns to normal.

Question 3: What strategies/practices do they want to continue using?

Use of technology to support learning and to keep alternative/remote provision, including online learning, going for all marginalised students who are unable to attend school and are at risk of high absence, through physical illness or mental health, and are classified as students who are school reluctant or school refusers.

Question 4: What do they see themselves doing differently in the future?

Keeping up-to-date with digital technologies that can be appropriated to support learning and encourage creative pedagogic practice.

Holding more training with technology for teachers and also for parents (e.g. workshops on using online face-to-face video platforms) for communicating and working remotely.

Teachers reported wanting to see an end to stressful external assessment practices, particularly external high-stakes testing and move to more teacher-based assessment.

Question 5: What do teachers see as challenges for sustaining education during times of crisis?

Where a country had a well-established online resource banks for teachers, teachers felt supported in the move to remote teaching.

The core challenges are explored in the different chapters in this book, but government leadership with clear guidance developed in collaboration with those who have to carry it out was one feature of what teachers viewed as supportive government decisions.

Bridging the digital divide is a major challenge. The other major challenges are lack of internet connectivity, lack of affordability of data, lack of access to devices (e.g. in a family of six with parents working at home, children had to take turns, often just learning through a mobile phone). School expectations that parents had electricity, internet, computers, printers and could afford to print out worksheets were inappropriate for numerous families in high- and low-income countries.

Specific challenge 3.2 The digital divide and working from home – for students and teachers

In some countries, politicians pumped funds into online internet-based teaching as the solution – apparently not realising that a large number of the population could not afford to access this form of technology. In Finland, 96% students were said to be internet-connected.[2] In contrast, in England, a country with the fifth largest economy in the world, an NFER[3] survey in July 2020 found that as many as 28% young people had no online connection and that many teachers did not have their own personal devices. 'Although many schools were supplying IT equipment to their staff, over a third of teachers were providing their own laptop or computer, and three-fifths either supplied their own camera/video equipment or had no access to this at all' (NFER 2020, p. 1).

In low-, medium- and high-income countries, teachers reported that online teaching worked reasonably well in independent schools as learners had their own devices and connectivity. However, the reality across all countries – high- and low-income – was that internet access was not available for significant numbers of households. Therefore the assumption by some governments that a shift to online teaching was the priority led to increased marginalisation of learners in low-, medium- and high-income countries who could not reliably access online teaching. Reasons included:

* rural areas experience lack of reliable connectivity and, even in the USA, electricity;
* poorer households lack the money to pay for internet access, data and technology devices;
* internet access for students may be limited to one parent's phone with limited data – under lockdown, with all family members confined to the home, a family would have had to have connected devices for all family members if all were to continue their work and learning during daytime hours;
* some schools required children to be online at particular times for synchronous remote teaching. It simply wasn't possible if there were a limited number of devices per household for all children to have access at the same time;
* some parents prioritised buying data for certain subjects and for certain of their children over other subjects and over their other children;
* some religious groups do not allow their children to use technology.
* teachers reported not having appropriate spaces to work at home as they managed their personal lives as well with children, partners working at home and caring for elderly relatives. Privacy for teachers and learners was a concern as video cams showed home environments.
* teachers also reported that they were on call 24/7 and found it difficult to keep work and home-life separate.

Specific challenge 3.3 Teacher training

Teacher training was disrupted in a number of countries.

Trainee teachers on existing placements found, in some cases, their placements were terminated. In others, the trainees were treated as staff members and took part in adapting teaching to remote teaching along with other staff. An unexpected but logical outcome of Covid-19 is a shortage of placements for teacher training courses going into 2021 (Hazell 2020a).

Teachers reported concerns about any non-essential adults being in the school. In countries where government had not taken responsibility for school safety, anxieties were reported that the responsibility for risk assessment may rest just with the head teacher, who is not medically trained.

Formal lectures can of course be covered online and university input into initial teacher education was converted to online teaching as university academics also had to adapt to remote learning when campuses were shut down as part of the national lockdowns.

Remote observations were reported as providing a solution to removing the risk of tutors observing students visiting schools; these were already being used in many countries. The IRISConnect tool (www.irisconnect.com) provides an example of this approach. See also the *Journal for Education on Teaching* special issue 2020 on initial teacher education provision during Covid across a number of countries for adaptions that were made to teacher training.

Specific challenge 3.4 The impact of leadership at government level

In some low-, medium- and high-income countries, teachers reported that their government issued clear and sensible guidelines. Some reports linked this with officials coming from educational backgrounds and understanding how the system worked.

In others, teachers reported a vacuum in leadership from the government, with teachers and schools left to solve the challenge of remote teaching. For example, guidance which had been issued was then changed with rapid U-turns. This happened with respect to the wearing of face masks in schools, the reopening of schools and with managing the outcomes of cancelling national examinations.

A key challenge is ensuring clear and robust leadership on education matters from government. Without this, teachers, school leaders and education unions quickly stepped in to create Covid-19 strategies for managing schooling during the pandemic. However, this put a strain on the profession and school leaders, who had to rapidly create contingency plans and take on the strategic management of learning when schools were suddenly closed. Teachers reported a sense of abandonment and neglect when government advice was not forthcoming, timely or reliable.

An issue worrying teachers was who would be responsible if schools reopened and pupils and teachers died because they were required to return to work or to study. (In England, there were reports in August that parents would be fined if their children didn't return to school.)[4]

As an example, Tables 3.2 and 3.3 outline the chaos that teachers experienced from government in England in the period March to August 2020. When the pandemic is over, it will be hard to believe these accounts of the chaotic experiences of teachers in England and the lack of national leadership.

Table 3.2 Notice of imminent closure of schools

In England, an announcement was made by Prime Minister Boris Johnson at 5pm on Wednesday 18th March that schools would close (except for provision for the children of key workers and vulnerable children) at the end of the school day on Friday 20th March. Teachers had only a weekend to prepare for remote teaching as they were already teaching on Thursday and the Friday in school, prior to school closure on Monday 23rd March. Schools were without pandemic policy plans and the ministry (the DFE) did not have any guidance documents for continuity of learning and assessment. (The government in power in 2020 had removed the national school pandemic planning advice when they closed all the government-funded online education resources in 2010 [World Bank 2017; Leask 2020; Blamires 2015; Younie and Leask 2019]).

Eventually, a group of teachers asked for and received money from the ministry to set up an online school for England from scratch when the ministry refused an offer from the Council for Subject Associations, whose members had thousands of existing resources produced by teacher members, and when the ministry already had in the national archives, as a search of the archives shows, resources that had been developed for teachers, costing tens of millions of pounds, which they had taken offline when taking office (World Bank 2017; Blamires 2015). (Source: Connell 2020b: ministry letter to chair of Council for Subject Associations).

Table 3.3 Case study 'A struggle for trust' – the teaching profession in England in June 2020

The following is a quote from a headteacher who reported the situation for the teaching profession arising in England because of the lack of clear government guidance for schooling during the Covid-19 pandemic.

In the vacuum created by a government not exercising effective leadership or providing clarity over many aspects of education, teachers had to step in to create crisis policies and strategies to cope.

This felt like the first time that the profession has been given the freedom and autonomy (and therefore trust by default) to educate in ways of their choosing. By way of example, and as a result of this situation, teacher assessments were requested by [government] at short notice as replacements for [public] examinations.

Headteachers and school leaders have been frustrated at changes in government guidance over school reopening measures (almost on a daily basis) and lack of timely, coherent guidance overall. This led to a lack of trust.

There was little support for headteachers and school leaders to make well-informed decisions about what is best for their students, which has been disheartening and teachers and headteachers are being encouraged by one another on social media to make sure they have the support of a strong union behind them when making decisions about their school, their pupils and their staff because government U-turns leave schools open to challenge.

Lessons learned: from teacher experiences

3.1 Worldwide step change in teacher, parent and learner understanding of education technologies: The rapid upskilling of the teaching profession in low-, medium- and high-income countries has led to a desire to integrate the strengths of online resources and communication into regular teaching practice.

3.2 Teachers lack home equipment: It cannot be assumed that teachers have the equipment, the connectivity or the personal funds to support online learning from home.

3.3 Teacher workload: Teacher workload becomes exceptionally high in crisis situations.

3.4 Teacher training: Continuity of teacher training programmes is clearly desirable and, where the technology is available, online university lectures and remote video tutoring of trainee teachers can mean that the additional health risk to trainees, school staff and pupils can be minimised.

3.5 Teacher-tested government guidance: Teachers and parents need leadership and clear guidance based on knowledge of educational practices from ministries of education in the event of school closures if national lockdowns are issued.

Planning toolkit: decisions to be made to maintain continuity and quality teaching

Table 3.4 presents some ideas: you need to adapt and add to these to suit your context and circumstances.

Futurecasting: learning from teachers' experiences

Critical to the success of planning for and managing continuity of education during crises is the development of policies guided by the first-hand experiences of teachers.

Table 3.4 Planning toolkit: decisions to be made to maintain continuity of teaching and quality teaching

Decision 3.1: Infrastructure, resources, staff and learner well being	
Questions to resolve	What is the state of infrastructure and training for teachers for delivering internet-based content and learning?
	What strategies are in place to support teachers identifying learners who are at risk of becoming marginalised, through being disengaged with learning?
	How can teachers be supported in their monitoring of learner engagement and learner progression?
	What strategies are in place to monitor teacher workloads?
	What processes with respect to 'duty of care' are in place for monitoring staff health and safety and well-being, when they are required to a) work from home, or b) work in a school that has remained open during a health pandemic?
Solutions	Solutions are dependent on local resources and schools cannot solve problems of lack of national infrastructure although there are solutions allowing students to access resources offline. Some schools loaned teachers and learners devices, some required teachers to teach remotely from their classroom in school.
	Mitigation of teachers' workloads. Teacher workload as well as the learner experience has to be considered at every stage of contingency planning. For example, expecting the whole teaching day to be replicated online means teachers cannot attend to children during the school day who do not have online access or who are in school because they are in a priority category.
	Tokuhama-Espinosa's (2020) advice for checking readiness for online classroom teaching may help in assessing online curriculum delivery (free online https://thelearningsciences.com/site/taking-your-course-online-think-before-you-leap/?lang=en)
Decision 3.2: Initial Teacher training	
Questions to resolve	How will you ensure continuity of experiences for trainee teachers as much as is possible if schools close?
	Can remote video tutoring and observation play a role, whereby a trainee can deliver a lesson remotely to students via a camera or alternatively, if in school, be supervised and observed remotely by their tutor? Can a recording be kept for the mentor to access in helping support the mentee/trainee in their development?
	Is your education system recruiting trainee teachers who are likely to teach and live long-term in deprived or disadvantaged regions (e.g. remote rural/coastal areas, inner cities)?
	Are there incentives to attract new teachers to areas considered more disadvantaged?
Solutions	Locating trainees fully in schools like a member of staff.
	Using remote videoing to reduce the need for outsiders to visit the school.
	Using remote teaching modes as for correspondence schools or online universities.
	Recruiting new student teachers from areas where there is a shortage of teachers.

This view is supported by the call from UNESCO'S International Teacher Task-force (UNESCO 2020d, e) to include teachers in developing Covid-19 education responses at all steps of education policy-making and planning.

It speaks to the notion that teacher voice is a critical element in any successful approach (Doucet et al. 2020, p. 2) to delivering quality education in the time of

Covid -19 and indeed in times of any future global crises. This is so because it is teachers who know their students and know where they were academically when schools shut down. It is teachers who have monitored their students' learning, their social-emotional and mental health (ibid 2020), communicated with students, their parents and tried to support their students' transition to online learning.

In situations where online delivery was problematic and students could not be reached, it was teachers who noted and monitored the increasing marginalisation of their students. It was teachers who strategised and led the search for ways to connect with students. It is also teachers who experienced having to function without proper support. It is thus teachers who are best positioned to offer insight into the types of professional learning opportunities and training they need to function effectively now and in the future.

Any futurecasting events *must* include experienced classroom teachers and experienced school leaders if the plans made are to be capable of implementation.

Notes

1 For a detailed record of teachers' experiences across 30 countries during Covid-19 see the freely available ICET/MESHGuides Network report 2020, www.icet4u.org; (www.MESHGuides.org)

2 UNESCO mobile week 2020 Keynote Presentation https://en.unesco.org/mlw

3 NFER research report www.nfer.ac.uk/news-events/press-releases/new-report-looks-at-pupil-engagement-in-remote-learning-during-the-covid-19-pandemic/

4 Parents threatened with fines www.theguardian.com/education/2020/oct/09/parents-in-england-refusing-to-send-their-children-back-to-school

Learners' experiences and marginalisation – Carol Hordatt Gentles

Introduction and context

> *The COVID-19 pandemic has created the largest disruption of education systems in history, affecting nearly 1.6 billion learners in more than 190 countries and all continents. Closures of schools and other learning spaces have impacted 94 per cent of the world's student population, up to 99 per cent in low and lower-middle income countries. The crisis is exacerbating pre-[1] education disparities by reducing the opportunities for many of the most vulnerable children, youth, and adults . . . to continue their learning.*
>
> (UNESCO 2020a, p. 2)

In stark contrast to UNESCO's mandate of Education for All, the reality for learners during Covid-19 has been loss of access and ultimately loss of learning for all. For many learners, this loss has been forecast to be irreparable with serious repercussions in the future:

> Learning losses also threaten to extend beyond this generation and erase decades of progress . . . Some 23.8 million additional children and youth (from pre-primary to tertiary) may drop out or not have access to school next year due to the pandemic's economic impact alone
>
> (Ibid. 2020a, p. 2)

The pandemic has also compromised the capacity of education systems to achieve the UN's SDG 4 goal to:

> Ensure inclusive and equitable **quality** education and promote lifelong learning opportunities for all.
>
> (UNESCO 2020a, p. 2, authors' emphasis)

DOI: 10.4324/9781003155591-7

This chapter considers the experiences of learners that led to such unprecedented loss of learning. It examines how known ways of learning changed as schools closed and teachers and students were mandated to switch to online, remote or distance teaching. It suggests that across the globe, most learners, regardless of context, suffered marginalisation to varying degrees. This points to the need to focus on ways of mitigating this marginalisation in the future by examining the positive and negative experiences of learners and teachers and futurecasting ways of working that support learners and teachers at times of crisis. This requires plans that facilitate the move from school to home and community-based education *for all*, so that in the future, when crises occur, marginalisation of groups of learners can be minimised and continuity of education can be maximised.

Overall challenge: continuing learning

For learners, the challenge they faced during the Covid-19 period was to continue their learning.

A major finding from the ICET/MESHGuides (2020) research is that learners from remote areas, poorer families or with disabilities, from both developed and developing countries, were marginalised by government policies where these were not based on the practical reality of schools and home life nor on the value of inclusion (i.e. that governments had a responsibility to educate every child). Consequently, in comparison with their well-off peers, these young people experienced major loss of learning opportunities. One consequence of Covid-19 appears to be a widening of the gap with disadvantaged students being disproportionately affected leading to further falling behind in their learning. At the same time, the transition to online teaching and learning during a lockdown, was for most – teachers, students and parents, a journey into the unknown. It brought to the forefront how little was really known, by many, about education in virtual spaces. Consequently, for most learners, including those who were not disadvantaged, the quality of education delivered was often substandard because their teachers were unprepared for online delivery and thus lacked the competence and capacity to teach effectively online. Although it was recognised that the impact of the shutdown amidst fears and anxieties due to the pandemic might be traumatic for learners, somehow there was a misconception that the transition to online learning simply meant a change in location. Thus, the true impact on students was misunderstood and miscalculated. This is captured by a report in the Canadian media:

> Unprepared for the shutdown and thrown completely off-kilter, educational leadership slapped together 'emergency' home learning programmes. Perpetually optimistic technology-driven educators found 'silver linings' amidst the dark clouds, progressive educators focused on responding to children's 'fears,

anxieties and trauma' and global thought leaders rhapsodised about a 'better normal,' where 'Maslow triumphed over Bloom'.

(https://policyoptions.irpp.org/magazines/july-2020/
the-educational-experience-has-been-substandard-
for-students-during-covid-19/)

It is important to note that not all reports of learners' experiences were negative. Many did benefit in that the shutdown and school closures led to:

* an outburst of creativity and imagination from learners and parents who were thrown into thinking about how to use home time constructively;
* a sudden increase in awareness and engagement with online, distance-learning materials of both an informal and formal kind across communities;
* an immediate embrace of technology for communicating, collaborating and for just staying in touch, informed and entertained, as well as for teaching;
* a growing widespread awareness of the potential liberating, opening up of opportunities for anyone to learn anything that captures their interests, enthusiasms and passions, at any time, at their own pace and in their own environment, and in collaboration with others if they wish;
* more intergenerational activities: online face-to-face technologies (offering video conferencing platforms) were embraced across the generations as the need for intergenerational online contact for grandparents to remain in touch with children, grandchildren and other family members and friends grew with lockdown isolation;
* more family time as parents worked from home during the lockdown.

In some countries the crisis stimulated innovation as well as returns to low tech ways of reaching learners such as through radio and television and take-home packages.

Specific challenges: faced by learners

The Covid-19 period will be one that is remembered by learners as life changing but for many different reasons. This chapter summarises positive and negative experiences which were reported as part of the ICET/MESHGuides (2020) research. The impact of the digital divide on life changes has been exposed during the Covid period as this was the key determining factor in whether learners could continue to learn or not. We have not come across data which documents how those learners who missed out feel, but we expect that they are not likely to forget the impact of school closures on their hopes and aspirations.

The following specific challenges relating learners' experiences are covered in this chapter:

* Variation in learners' experiences
* Disappointments with exams and endings
* Learner well-being and mental health.

Specific challenge 4.1 Variation in learners' experiences

Varied learning experiences provided by different countries

A policy brief from UNESCO (2020a) shows marked differences across countries in learner access to schooling during the pandemic:

* *An estimated 40 per cent of the poorest countries failed to support learners at risk during the COVID-19 crisis, and past experiences show that both education and gender inequalities tend to be neglected in responses to disease outbreaks. (p. 8)*
* *The ability to respond to school closures changes dramatically with level of development: for instance, during the second quarter 2020, 86 per cent of children in primary education have been effectively out of school in countries with low human development – compared with just 20 per cent in countries with very high human development. (p. 5)*

Varied learning experiences provided by schools and 'virtual' attendance issues

Learners' experiences also varied a lot depending on what and how their school could provide for their continuity of learning. Factors such as leadership; school type (whether privately or publicly funded); school community culture and support; resources; school location; teacher capacity and competence; and degree of external support from government policies and funding determined the type of experiences their learners had.

For some students, learning continued their normal timetables, where students were sent home but then were expected to attend the 'virtual school' during the usual hours. One teacher said pupils at their school did not miss a single lesson. 'We coupled face to face sessions between students and teachers in the morning with independent working and self-reporting later in the day (e.g. students who were set a task to read a book, took photos of key sections and wrote an analysis following the teacher's guidelines).' This type of experience was reported in many countries particularly by private fee-paying students and some public-school students. In some countries, like Australia and England, schools remained open to accommodate the children of essential health care workers. In other countries like Guyana, where education in its vast hinterland has relied on the preparation and distribution of paper-learning materials, nothing much changed.

This, however, was more the exception than the norm. For millions of children, schools were unprepared to provide proper support for remote or online teaching and learning. Consequently, schooling was either non-existent or extremely limited. An NFER survey in July 2020 (NFER 2020) in England found: 'Over one quarter (28 per cent) of pupils had limited access to IT at home. This is a particular issue for schools serving the most deprived pupil populations.' Many of the teachers interviewed for the MESHGuides/ ICETGuides (2020) and VSO (2020a, b, c) surveys shared their experiences that pupil attendance was low when they taught online. For example, in the Caribbean, teachers reported attendance percentages as low as 10 per cent over periods of several weeks. There were similar reports from England that attendance records for online lessons were not kept or checked and that, where records were kept, teachers reported that attendance online was only about 30 per cent of students for many reasons.

Specific challenge 4.2 Disappointments with exams and endings

In addition to cancelled exams and end of year assessments, in those countries where the school year ends in June/July learners had no time for end of school year celebrations and for those leaving school, there were no leaving rituals. These are significant times in the lives of young people and the psychological impact on all, including particularly those at major transition stages, has left memories they may carry all their lives.

In some countries, end of year examinations took place as normal but with adaptions[2] and apparently little dissatisfaction. In other countries, there was considerable dissatisfaction and protest. For example, in the Caribbean, the Caribbean Examination Council, which sets common syllabi and school-leaving examinations for 16 countries, modified its Examination Administration Framework in response to the pandemic.[3] As a result, students did not sit all the papers that they had prepared for and the weighting for components using School Based Assessments was modified. When the results were released, there was a large public outcry across the region about the results and alleged discrepancies.[4] Many students expressed disappointment and sadness about the experience which was so different from what they had expected. They also worried about the effect of uncertainties around the reliability of the results on their chances of gaining admission to quality higher education.[5]

In India, students demonstrated on the streets[6] and petitioned the courts about the risks they would incur in taking the competitive National Eligibility cum Entrance Test (NEET) and Joint Entrance Examination (JEE) university entrance exams which are high stakes – giving access to medicine and engineering degrees.[7]

A particularly sad result was in England where, in place of examinations, an algorithm was applied to teacher-assessed grades which privileged those from high performing schools and disadvantaged those from schools in poorer areas;[8] this resulted in young people demonstrating on the streets.[9] Universities allocated places based on these grades to the successful students. Within a matter of days, the government performed a U-turn allowing teacher-assessed grades to be used.[10] But on competitive university courses, such as medicine and dentistry, the places were already allocated. For the students, who one week later gained the required grades (from using teacher-assessed grades) rather than the lower algorithm grades, it was too late. This perpetuated a system where disadvantaged students are underrepresented on what some consider prestigious courses and in what are considered by some to be top universities in England.

Specific challenge 4.3 Learner well-being and mental health

One of the most difficult and growing challenges created by the Covid -19 pandemic is its effect on the well-being and health of learners. This has been both positive and negative. Learners found that they missed the social interaction with their friends and with their teachers during lockdown, emphasising the importance of schools as social meeting places as well as places where learning occurs. They also found some elements of online learning difficult and stressful:

Negative experiences included:

* expectations that they would sit in synchronous online lessons all day following a normal school timetable (this was very tiring);
* uninteresting lessons, reported as 'boring', leading to learners feeling 'switched off' and disengaged from learning;
* micro-technical issues (e.g. responses to questions could not be written on materials sent on a pdf document)
* disadvantaged students were unable and could not be expected to be able to print off materials at home should that be required for completing a pdf worksheet sent by teachers;
* teachers saying such a resource was on the school online platform without giving the link and students unable to find the learning resources easily and then giving up;
* not getting feedback from teachers for work completed and submitted;
* teachers not showing up for online classes or being inadequately prepared to teach;
* learners who were struggling with the work set but lacked confidence (low self-esteem and self-efficacy) and possibly lacking technical skills too, to email the teacher to ask for help;
* not being able to understand or navigate digital tools and online-learning platforms.

In some countries where the language of online instruction differed from the language spoken between teachers and students, they struggled to cope. For example, in Caribbean countries with students and teachers who communicate orally in creole or patois, there is no written form to use for responding online. This hinders learners in answering questions or performing written tasks.

However, some learners with stable home backgrounds were happier during lockdown than prior to lockdown because they have done more together as a family. As O'Reilly (2020), citing research in England from the University of Bristol, reports, some teenagers felt less anxious during lockdown. It was found that this was because there were no longer the day-to-day pressures of school life and difficult peer relationships. This was also the case for Canadian teenagers who missed school and seeing their friends but did not miss going to school (Angus Reid Institute 2020).

Positive experiences included:

* being able to work through automatically assessed mathematics examples at their own pace, alongside other curriculum subjects that utilised online-learning programmes, which included formative assessment and monitoring of learning progression;
* being able to listen to recordings of teachers' lessons;
* personalised projects (project-based learning and family-learning projects, see Chapter 8);
* being away from school bullies;
* not having the significant stress of national exams and high stakes testing;
* not having the pressure of school attendance (and legal action, including fines for non-attendance) for students experiencing 'school refusal', where children feel overt distress at being forced to attend school, due to anxiety/depression and other mental health issues (Bodycote 2019);
* students involved in other youth organisations were able to engage in extracurricular activities which involved gaining wider experiences and accreditation through badges, for example, with the Scouts and Girl Guide associations. Also, in England, alternative qualifications such as BTECs or Duke of Edinburgh awards were offered through youth programmes linked to the Armed Forces in the UK (Army cadets, air cadets and sea cadets), for example, taking short courses in cyber security, aviation communication. Whilst these are also available during non-crisis times, some students reported that, with school closures, they had the opportunity to undertake the online-learning programmes offered through their organisation and could attain, for example, a BTEC in engineering, which they would not have been able to undertake if they had been at school with their 'normal school workload'.

The pandemic also affected physical well-being. When families were put under strict lockdown in areas of Spain and Italy and in Wuhan in China, people were permitted to leave home only for emergencies and food. Exercise in parks was not permitted. In England, families had to stay indoors and take only one hour's exercise outside per day. Children and young people had very different experiences at this time. Those with gardens had some freedom, those without gardens created a range of alternative forms of indoor exercise, some with the use of online exercise videos and YouTube PE lessons.

A serious concern was reports of an increase of violence and abuse against women and children because of increased tension due to quarantines, social isolation, financial and health challenges. There have been reports of teenage girls getting pregnant during the shutdown. Although the impact on learners is not well documented it must undoubtedly have a negative effect on their capacity to continue learning (WHO 2020). This highlights the fact that, for many learners, schools provide a safe space from the threat of violence and a place in which to escape the harsh realities of poverty, degradation and particularly in low-income countries, being forced into labour. Millions of children in both high- and low-income countries rely on meals provided at school for daily sustenance. In high- and low-income countries, maintaining continuity in supplying and delivering meals for learners in their homes has been a priority for teachers.

Varied learning experiences due to home circumstances

Learners have had to manage much change during the pandemic including their relocation to home as the designated space for learning. This has meant extending their reliance on teachers to include parents and caregivers for support with learning. The quality of support has depended on a variety of factors such as parents' financial status, level of education, home environment and what is offered in terms of quality of space in which to do learning tasks. Critical to learners' success with learning at home was the ability of parents to provide devices for online learning and data to access the internet. Disparities in parents' capacity to support learners created much inequity and stress for everyone, particularly in poorer homes with several children. This created challenges for parents who could not afford to provide a device for each child or who could not afford to buy internet access.

In some countries there have been reports of parents rationing their children's use of data for learning online. For financial reasons, parents had to choose which child to support based on gender, age, perceived potential for success.

Many parents faced the challenge of having to do two jobs: working from home themselves and homeschooling their children. This was difficult and anxiety provoking, if the parent worked full-time in the home and had children who were at the early years and lower primary stages where the learner needs more structure and guidance through work set by teachers and is less able to learn independently. Some parents had to leave the home to work despite quarantines. This meant the quality of supervision was poor with learners not managing to devote adequate time to schoolwork. In Canada, a survey of children aged 10–17 years brought to our attention by a colleague, found that almost half worried about 'missing out on work' this school year. Most 'attending' school online (60 percent) were unmotivated, not very busy with the work, but still 'keeping up' with the reduced academic expectations. The vast majority spent their time glued to small screens, dominated by watching TV/Netflix, YouTube (88 per cent), and playing video games (74 per cent) and over half of teens ages 13 to 17 years reported needing more help with their work (Angus Reid 2020).

Lessons learned: what we know and what we do not know

What we know

4.1 *Positive and negative experiences*: The experience of learners across the globe has been both negative and positive in its impact on their ability to continue learning. Overall, though, the fallout from the pandemic has been tremendous loss of learning and marginalisation for most. For some learners, especially in LIC, learning was almost non-existent. Although there were exceptions, for millions of others, opportunities for quality learning were provided but often diminished to varying degrees due to reasons including the failure of governments, education officials and schools to offer decisive planning and funding for continued learning, inadequate support from the home, loss of nutritional support, poor preparation among teachers, school leaders and governments for online delivery, failure of schools to prepare students to manage online learning; lack of access to resources needed for online learning.

4.2 *Health and well-being*: The pandemic has also impacted the health and wellbeing of learners and, in some cases, increased their risk for physical, sexual and emotional abuse. For others, school closures have offered a respite from the anxieties associated with attending school particularly among teenagers. In countries and cultural contexts where schooling has been burdensome for parents, the situation has led to its reprioritisation with students dropping out to join the workforce, to get married or to work in the home or on the farm. This increase in drop-out rates is alarming, and it is anticipated that, after COVID, millions of children may not return to school.

4.3 *Learner marginalisation*: Finally, it is instructive to recognise that school closures served to reinforce and widen disparities in opportunities for learning that were already there. The new normal for education simply shone a spotlight on pedagogical, cultural and political issues around learner marginalisation which were evident but conveniently ignored or given lowered priority in mainstream school systems. Teachers who have embraced the challenge of building their competence for online teaching and support of online learning report they appreciate how this has led them to changed mindsets in regard to ways of improving access and quality which they had previously resisted.

What we do not know

4.4 Maximising learners' experience of online learning: A key lesson with respect to learners' experiences is that there is much we do not know about the impact of transitioning to spaces of virtual learning. Although there are lessons to be learned from schools that are set up as online institutions, for most children online learning is a new experience with many unknowns. Thus, for example, research suggests limited screen-time is best for small children, but when schools shut down and there is no other option for learning, will children's capacity to learn from a screen evolve or adapt?

4.5 Maximising student engagement online: Another grey area is how to manage student engagement in the online environment. One teacher contributing to the ICET/MESHGuides international survey (2020) pointed out that:

> all learners are at risk of becoming marginalised when they disengage from their learning.
> When students are no longer in front of teachers, it is hard for the teachers to assess when children are becoming disengaged.

Many teachers reported that when they teach online, they believe their students may be multi-tasking and not fully engaged, but they do not know how to change this or manage the situation. They were also unsure how to manage the online environment which looks and feels so different from the physical classroom. Navigating the changing student-teacher relationship is challenging for learners and students: accustomed structures and protocols for learning were gone.

Planning toolkit: planning to ensure continuity of learning

Table 4.1 provides key questions to aid your strategic planning for ensuring continuity of learning for your students. These are drawn from the challenges discussed in the preceding section. The table presents some ideas, which you need to adapt and add to, to suit your circumstances. You may wish to gather examples of your learners' experiences to inform your planning for any future school closures due to

Table 4.1 Planning toolkit: planning to ensure continuity of learning

Decision 4.1 How will you ensure continuity of learner experiences as much as is possible?	
Questions to resolve	Examples:
	What technologies (radio, TV, computers [laptops, tablet/mobile devices] memory sticks) and other community and home resources (people and materials) are available for your learners; paying particular attention to disadvantaged learners, including SEND, students with EAL needs, and so on?
	Do learners have access to internet-enabled devices for online learning? for how many learners? all/some/none?
	What blend of synchronous or asynchronous online learning will you opt for? What blend of Modes 1, 2, 3 learning will work for your learners? (See Chapters 8 and 9)
	Have you trained your learners to be skilled in using internet-connected devices for learning?
	How do you need to adapt your pedagogy strategies for learning outside school (e.g. to be project based, to have an intergenerational focus)?
	How do you need to adapt your assessment strategies (e.g. to support self-assessment against success criteria to maintain teacher assessment, both formative and summative)?
	What elements of the curriculum are essential, what can be left out or replaced?
	How many children are not going to be catered for through your strategy?
	How will you identify those learners that are or may become marginalised during school closures?
	What happens when learners become de-motivated with online learning if it is perceived as dull and boring for a number of physical, socio-emotional, and cognitive reasons?
	This is also the same for all remote learning, when students disengaged and become hard to reach – what strategies are best for dealing with marginalised learners? (We note that all learners are at risk of becoming marginalised when they disengage from their learning.)
	How will SEND/disadvantaged students/any other marginalised learners be enabled to carry on learning?
	How do you support accessing the curriculum if learners have special needs?
Solutions	Examples:
	In the specific context of your school and your learners, a range of solutions are possible. These are best conceptualised and operationalised at the local level. Be mindful, however, of the diversity of factors affecting learners' experiences.
Decision 4.2 How will you motivate and engage learners?	
Questions to resolve	Examples:
	What remote teaching pedagogies keep learners motivated and engaged?
	How will you monitor engagement?

(Continued)

Table 4.1 (Cont).

Solutions	Examples:
	Teachers and learners reported:
	* short achievable tasks can be motivating
	* personalised project work can be highly motivating as the project can be on a topic of personal choice
	* collaborative projects, including family learning projects can be motivating in a home learning environment
	* well-planned lessons which use a variety of digital tools may be well received.

Decision 4.3 How will you minimise dropout and marginalisation of learners?	
Questions to resolve	Examples
	What factors prevent your learners from engaging in remote learning?
Solutions	Examples:
	Experience from Covid-19 for hard to reach families and learners (i.e. those who don't engage with the school [because of language or disliking of authority]), is that personal approaches to families may be necessary to explain how to keep engaged in learning and the importance of doing so. This was successfully undertaken by teachers conducting home visits (socially distanced from the front door) and by regular phone calls to home, to parents and pupils. Telephone tutoring supported by printed materials may work for many hard to reach learners. Lessons from Covid-19 indicate that home visits may be required to check the health and well-being of learners too.

a pandemic lockdown or any other crises that require teachers to support remote learning. The following questions may also help you gather data on the Covid-19 experience and its effects on your students' learning.

Futurecasting: to develop resilient learners

The key to futurecasting in the light of Covid-19 lies adopting a new different approach to what it is that children and young people need to learn and know about themselves as learners, so that they can remain in control of their own learning to a greater extent than has been the case during Covid-19.

One possibility is to commit to sustaining innovations and changed mindsets around pedagogies that have worked best in times of crisis. To act on this, asking these questions might be useful.

What if:

I continuously prepare students with skills and mindsets to transition in future crises, in calm and sensitive ways, so that 'being prepared' is normalised?

I continue to be as creative, equitable, inclusive, and flexible in my approach to planning and teaching as I have been during Covid-19?

I create communities for learners that are more inclusive of parents and learners in developing curricula and learning pathways to mitigate marginalisation?

I prioritise constructing an understanding of learner experiences through their eyes?

Notes

1 UN Sustainable Development Goal 4 https://sdgs.un.org/goals/goal4

2 How European countries managed high stakes public examinations during Covid www.theguardian.com/education/2020/aug/12/school-exams-covid-what-could-uk-have-learned-from-eu

3 'In Face of COVID-19 Pandemic, CXC Offers Revised Exams Process'. https://today.caricom.org/2020/03/26/in-face-of-covid-19-pandemic-cxc-offers-revised-exams-process/

4 'Petitions of protest Over CXC results'. http://jamaica-gleaner.com/article/lead-stories/20200925/petitions-protest-over-cxc-results

5 'Barbados Minister calls on CXC to 'swiftly' investigate 2020 results'. www.looptt.com/content/barbados-minister-calls-cxc-swiftly-investigate-2020-results-4

6 Indian students demonstrate against the holding of exams during Covid. www.aljazeera.com/news/2020/8/27/indias-students-concerned-over-entrance-exams-amid-covid-19

7 Indian students petition the courts over examinations during Covid. www.dw.com/en/coronavirus-indias-insistence-on-holding-exams-torments-students/a-54948495

8 See the English government explanation: www.gov.uk/government/publications/coronavirus-covid-19-cancellation-of-gcses-as-and-a-levels-in-2020/coronavirus-covid-19-cancellation-of-gcses-as-and-a-levels-in-2020

9 UK students protest on the streets against exam grades fiasco. www.bbc.co.uk/news/education-53744426

10 See the *New York Times* comment: www.nytimes.com/2020/08/17/world/europe/england-college-exam-johnson.html

School leadership for inclusion

Introduction and context

School leaders faced severe challenges with little support.

> *The pessimist complains about the wind. The optimist expects it to change. The leader adjusts the sails.*
>
> William Ward[1]

School leaders had to react quickly to support teachers and learners to make the transition to remote teaching, in many cases just with the support of peers. In high-, medium- and low-income countries, teachers reported they found governments were paralysed or in denial or simply didn't have the knowledge of how schools worked and what could or could not be done (ICET/MESHGuides 2020).

This chapter reports the key strategic decisions school leaders found they had to make to ensure continuity of learning and assessment for *all* children whilst maximising the safety of adults and children during the Covid-19 pandemic.[2]

Overall challenge: providing continuity of learning and assessment for all learners and safety

For school leaders, the core challenge was creating, implementing and monitoring a school plan for continuity of learning and assessment *for all* while keeping learners and adult staff as safe as possible. The Annexes provide examples of detailed plans schools drew up.

DOI: 10.4324/9781003155591-8

Teacher reports (ICET/MESHGuides 2020, VSOa, b, c) show that countries took different approaches to meeting the challenge of continuing learning and assessment for all in the pandemic, with some providing very clear national leadership and providing national solutions. Teachers from countries such as Mexico, India, Portugal, Bangladesh, Pakistan, Somalia reported that NGOs and governments moved to harness radio and TV as major modes of supporting remote learning. SMS-messaging and telephone-school options were also in place in some locations with government support.

By July 2020, teachers in the Caribbean were reporting that governments were being supportive but were relying too much on schools to figure out what to do for reopening or partial reopening. In England, headteachers wrote to the government asking for national leadership. (Weale 24 August 2020) and schools took legal advice about who would be responsible if staff or children died or were disabled (Hazell 13 July 2020b).[3] In September 2020, when in the UK school leaders were required to reopen schools to all, teachers found themselves teaching online and face to face at the same time as whole year groups of children and staff were sent home to undertake self-isolation for two weeks. Some students found themselves sent home for two weeks when someone in their year group tested positive for Covid-19 only to find on their return to school that after a day they were sent home again as someone else had tested positive. Teachers were left teaching large classes as staff self-isolated. We heard no reports of attempts to bring back retired teachers whereas in health, retired staff were encouraged to return.

The learners who missed out on education during the Covid period seem to be those not necessarily with existing special needs who, in a number of countries were able to continue attending school as a priority group, but those from poor backgrounds or rural areas who were not able to access online learning or, where it was available, remote learning through radio and TV.

Specific challenges: for school leaders in providing continuity of learning and assessment for all learners

The whole-school response to managing the Covid-19 crisis included school leaders making decisions about risks; resources; making decisions about modes of remote teaching ensuring all children can be included; managing and supporting teachers and other staff (i.e. in new ways of working, workloads, planning, monitoring student progress and assessment, mental health and training). The challenge was for all involved – staff and students – to manage home challenges along with work. School leaders found they had to, as well, manage communications both *from* politicians and ministries and *to* parents and communities and of course they needed to show leadership in dealing with the aftermath in their school and local communities.

The following specific challenges are covered in this chapter:

* Risk assessment
* Models of remote teaching
* Keeping a school open in lockdown for vulnerable children
* Rapid change and workload during pandemic phases
* Communication
* Giving teachers a voice and listening.

Specific challenge 5.1 Risk assessment

This section focuses on risk assessment for schools.

In the Annexes are examples of school working risk-assessment documents prepared by primary and secondary schools. These are examples from England and will need adaption to your particular setting, but they show the extensive nature of factors to be considered. Early years and special school settings bring additional risks associated with much more physical contact, food and feeding, medication, toileting and lack of understanding of social distancing.

If risk assessment is your responsibility, then we suggest that you, your team and key stakeholders spend time to go through these working documents and adapt the ideas to your context.[4] The Annexes show the complexity and level of detail needed for schools which enable everyone to know who has to do what, when, why and how and what resources are needed and available. Every school is different and plans must be adapted for the individual context. As Sherwood (2020) pointed out, in many settings, basic hygiene facilities were insufficient or entirely lacking:

> Precautions against Covid-19, such as regular hand washing, are more challenging in countries with poor sanitation. According to the report (Christian Aid June 2020 Building back with Justice: dismantling inequalities post Covid-19[5]), three billion people – about 40% of the global population – do not have access to a basic hand-washing facility at home. In Ethiopia and Democratic Republic of Congo, Africa's second and fourth most populous countries, fewer than one in 10 people can wash their hands at home.
>
> (Sherwood 2020, p. 1)

In high-, medium- and low-income countries, teachers reported a lack of hand washing facilities. But while there are health and safety concerns in keeping schools open, there is also a major health and safety risk in school closures. Sherwood (2020) states that nine out of ten school students across the world have lost part of their education. Many – especially girls – in poorer countries may never return. 'Experience from the west African Ebola epidemic shows school closures led to higher rates of permanent

Table 5.1 Extract from Annex 2: ASCL's Risk assessment template (ASCL 2020, Section 3)

Government response stage [requirement to act]	Trigger Points	Measures to consider	Responsibility

dropout for girls, and to a rise in child labour, neglect, sexual abuse, teenage pregnancies and early marriage' (ibid.).

The risk assessment advice given to headteachers by the Association of School and College Leaders (ASCL) in the UK in March 2020 – as the virus was leading to school closures and lockdowns – is included as Annex 2. The advice remains relevant through the cycle of schools reopening and re-closing. We draw your attention to Section 1: Ten steps to plan and prepare; Section 3 – the Risk Assessment template (summarised in Table 5.1) and Section 5: Suggested actions in response to specific issues specifically the entries on marginalised learners (vulnerable pupils, staff and families, and pupils with SEND – Special Educational Needs and Disabilities).

Specific challenge 5.2 Models of remote teaching

For both school leaders and class teachers, decisions have to be made about how to adapt the curriculum and assessment and the modes of delivery for remote/ home-schooling including for marginalised learners. Table 5.2 provides a planning pro forma to use in allocating main areas of responsibility, including identifying and then supporting vulnerable children including those already marginalised and those who could become marginalised. In the following, we identify three main options for different modes of delivery. What has been provided for learners during Covid-19 has been a mix of modes depending on the human and material resources available in the local context.

Mode 1 Individualised learning provision: teaching tailored to the individual child through student/parent/community guided learning, personalised project-based-learning, supported by printed packs of materials, or online materials, SMS texting, radio, TV, with phone and online personal tutorials or materials distributed

Table 5.2 Planning tool for remote learning

YEAR GROUP_____SUBJECT:_____LEAD TEACHER_____					
	Who is responsible for:				
Scheme of work	Leadership and co-ordination	Content/ resources for each lesson	Assessment	Record keeping, monitoring learning and attendance, QA	Special cases – adaptions for individual learners/groups

by memory stick. We had reports of teachers making materials rapidly (this was very time consuming) and teachers paying for the materials to be printed and delivered to learners at their home addresses. Keeping in touch with learners by telephone and home visits was reported from a number of countries.

Mode 2 School-led synchronous or asynchronous provision: this might be lessons using television/radio/internet/SMS/phone/memory stick, backed up by resources on the schools' websites or non-interactive 'talking heads' (e.g. recorded on YouTube). These might be at a set time of day or repeated at different times. See Table 5.2.

Mode 3 Other providers: synchronous or asynchronous lessons and learning resources from commercial providers or local communities, or specialist groups, with subscription payments or offering private paid-for-services, using local radio and television channels, internet, YouTube, and so forth.

Specific challenge 5.3 Keeping a school open in lockdown for vulnerable children

Whilst a national mandate was issued to close schools in many countries, in some, the government also required schools to remain open during the national lockdown for children designated as either children of 'key workers' or 'vulnerable'. In those countries, this meant that, in every area, some schools remained open.

The list in Table 5.3 provides an example, from England, of the additional work required of school leaders during March – July 2020 in providing both remote teaching and in-school teaching for the vulnerable children and children of key workers.

Table 5.3 Tasks for school leaders in keeping schools open for some while also providing remote teaching for most of March–July 2020 England

* Draw up rotas of staffing to come into school each day during Covid-19 national lockdown
* Ensure that the staff rota included every day a first aider and a DSL (designated safeguarding lead) who had to be on site each day for the children
* Ensure the health and safety of the school site, with respect to hygiene, installing new hand sanitiser stations throughout the school, putting in place social distancing measures with marking tape, and so on
* Provide remote learning for all other students who were offsite
* Mobilise pastoral teams of staff to check in with the most vulnerable pupils who were not attending school, by regular weekly (or even daily) phone calls home
* Direct form tutors/class teachers to be monitoring and checking in with all their tutor group students/pupils by undertaking phone calls home or home visits.

- Manage the teachers in providing data for every student who would have been sitting national exams; this data had to be submitted to exam boards in the cases where national exams were cancelled (year 10 GCSEs and year 12 A Levels) and then senior leaders had to collate the school 'centre-assessed grades' for every student for every subject, and return this data to the national exam boards

- Allocate disadvantaged children free food vouchers during the lockdown. However, the administration of the distribution of the food vouchers to each child was given to schools, which meant the vouchers were delivered to the school to then distribute, rather than being sent direct to the home, which initiated more administrative burden on schools or, where there were issues obtaining vouchers, delivering food packs straight to pupil's homes. (A number of schools reported staff visiting and delivering lunches directly to disadvantaged children).

- Provide laptops and internet access. Access to laptops for each child was also designated a school responsibility, with the government sending the laptops to the schools directly so that they could provide disadvantaged children with a laptop and also a router if there was no internet access in the home. However, again, this incurred an administrative burden as, when the laptops arrived into school brand-new, they needed to be opened out of the boxes and set up with new software put on them, alongside schools writing guidance for the students on the use of the laptop at home. The school was also required to upload software that tracks home use of the internet to identify any inappropriate access or downloads, such as to sites containing pornography, terrorist propaganda, or sites encouraging self-harm, eating disorders and so on. This software then sends an alert which is registered at the school to then monitor and investigate, with teachers identifying what sites and information constituted low-level to high-level risk, for example, the latter being suicide sites; this then became the responsibility of the school to monitor and not the parents' responsibility. This meant an increased workload for senior leaders and teachers regarding the monitoring and investigation of the software filter alerts that were triggered back at the school. In the case of primary schools, very few laptops were available.

- Decide which families would get a laptop and which wouldn't. The government provision of laptops to the most disadvantaged children was 700,000, but four months after school closures, only 200,000 had been distributed; these were financed and issued from central government, but delivered to regions and then onto local schools, proving a lengthy and fragmented process, which failed to deliver the capacity of equipment needed to support the continuity of learning for the most marginalised learners living in poverty in England.

In England, the senior leadership team had to manage the continuity of learning in a time of crisis as well as also having to manage the additional, specific requirements of the crisis with respect to ensuring the health and safety of the school site that remained open. This meant additional risk assessments with respect to the health and safety of the staff and students who were in the school during the lockdown and also, later, for all staff and students with the reopening of schools once all students were returning. Senior leaders were also responsible for the close monitoring of all the teachers returning their curriculum subject grades for their students undertaking national examinations. Additionally, throughout the crisis, senior school managers had to ensure that all teachers were effectively delivering online and remote learning for all students.

Specific challenge 5.4 Rapid change and workload during pandemic phases

As the Covid-19 crisis continued through 2020, school operations were moving quickly, back and forth, through several different types of operation.

Type 1: the school is open/re-opened to all pupils, in accordance with national/local lockdown needs

Type 2: the school is closed completely, to all pupils

Type 3: the school is closed for all, except vulnerable children and children of key workers, given face-to-face teaching with social distancing, with remote learning being offered to all other students.

Type 4: total closure, though short/temporary for deep cleaning

Type 5: partial reopening, with some individual classes/or year groups being sent home and quarantined for two weeks if a child tests positive for Covid-19

Type 6: individual classrooms are closed and deep cleaned.

Specific challenge 5.5 Communication

During Covid-19, misinformation, misconceptions and myths, including conspiracy theories, circulated regarding the origins of the virus and how to manage and limit its content agent and infection rate. These were potentially dangerous.

School leaders found that communities were relying on them for information. Schools with strong existing two-way communication channels between schools and learners' homes could ensure messages were clear and concerns were addressed. This included accurate information and scientifically valid knowledge on Covid-19 (see, for example, the MESHGuide [2020] on Covid-19, which has a science strand explaining the facts and debunking the myths and misconceptions).

This role is important, when during the pandemic, confused world leaders without an understanding of science, spread falsehoods (known to being scientifically untrue), such as the American president, Donald Trump, suggesting injections of disinfectant or using a strong light source to kill the virus.[6] Also, there were other world leaders who dismissed or downplayed the severity of the disease, referring to it as a 'mild illness'.[7] Other falsehoods included using lemon juice to kill the virus and another that it was caused by 5G connectivity, among others. If education is about anything, it must be about teaching scientific truth as we know it at this particular moment in time, based on research evidence. Whilst new research may throw further light on to the ways the virus behaves and we gain new knowledge, school leaders must at the same time be clear about dismissing known misinformation. Also, in times of crisis with heightened insecurity and increased uncertainty, there is a tendency for conspiracy theories to circulate. Research indicates that those willing to believe such conspiracies are more likely to be uneducated and from poorer backgrounds (Georgiou 2020).

Specific challenge 5.6 Giving teachers a voice – and listening

The importance of hearing what teachers have to say and incorporating this into both current and future pandemic planning is reflected in UNESCO's toolkit for school leaders to support teachers as schools reopen. It emphasises that:

> School leaders need to ensure teachers are empowered to make decisions about teaching and learning – [and they should accord teachers] a key role in recognising learning gaps and formulating pedagogical responses [and adjusting] curricula and assessment based on revised school calendars and instructions from central authorities. School leaders should also support teachers to reorganise classrooms to allow for accelerated learning and remedial responses, while adhering to regulations on physical distancing.
>
> (https://en.unesco.org/news/supporting-teachers-back-school-efforts-after-Covid-19-closures-toolkit-school-leaders)

One common misconception among policymakers is that the views and voices of teachers are easily captured in large stakeholder meetings where plans and projects are rolled out for dissemination and discussion. Unfortunately, many teachers who attend these refrain from voicing their genuine concerns. Ultimately, policymakers think erroneously that they have the consensus of teachers and are surprised and disappointed when teachers resist or fail to fall in line with what was planned. This happens because they do not understand the specific challenges with eliciting and hearing Teacher Voice. Many falsely assume that asking teachers to speak up and getting them to say something is evidence that teachers have expressed their opinions. While this may be so for some teachers, for many it is not. It can be argued that this is so because Voice is more than an oral expression. Wink (2010) explains it as 'the use of language to paint a picture of one's reality, one's experience, one's world' (p. 70). Wink argues that voices express who we are, what we believe in and what we have lived and experienced. McLaren (2014) defines voice as 'the cultural grammar and background knowledge that individuals use to interpret and articulate experience' (p. 180). For him, there are a lot of aspects which constitute Voice: culture, history, symbols, narratives and social practices (p. 245). For McLaren (2014), Teacher Voice 'reflects the values, ideologies, and structuring principles that teachers use to understand and mediate their students and professional lives, the histories, cultures, and subjectivities of their students' (p. 180).

The competence and confidence to have a Voice and to use it is not something teachers are taught to do. It is not part of most teacher education models or programmes. To the contrary, in many countries, traditional and/or authoritarian approaches to teaching and teacher preparation often socialise teachers to be conformist and acquiescent to the mandates and views of those in positions of power and authority. The expectation that teachers will support whatever is mandated reflects this traditional training. The problem is that often teachers do not agree, or from their vantage point in real classrooms are able to recognise the flaws and problems inherent in top-down policies and projects. Consequently, they do not openly challenge but instead practice resistance. This means they do not always work in ways that support the success of school policy initiatives.

A specific challenge therefore for encouraging and ensuring the continuity of learning and assessment is to help teachers construct a Voice and the capacity to use it. This will need to be done deliberately and with recognition that it will take time. Although it is more common now for teachers in some countries, to be included in school-leadership decisions and for administrators to act on their recommendations (www.edglossary.org/voice). Arguably, the scope and reach of its inclusion remains limited. For example, the Center on Education Policy in the USA (2016) reporting on a national survey of teachers found '[l]arge majorities of teachers believe their voices are not often factored into the decision-making process' (p. 4). This supports the view that teachers have traditionally been positioned as technicians/semi-professionals with little say in planning for schooling or curricular matters. Drawing from critical theory this has silenced teachers' voices and limited their capacity for agency with implications for being able to teach in culturally /contextually relevant ways (Giroux 1988).

In many countries, national responses to the disruption of education due to the pandemic, suggest a failure to account for what teachers thought about their experiences. What did they have to say about the move to teaching online, teaching remotely, trying to mitigate loss of student learning, reaching or failing to reach marginalised learners, and the reopening of schools? Media and education reports showed teachers around the world did not think their views, their fears or concerns were being heard (ICET/MESHGuides 2020). Hordatt Gentles, Haynes-Brown and

Cole ran a webinar with the title *Coping Personally and Professionally as a teacher in times of Covid-19* which was broadcast to the Jamaican public on a Friday afternoon in July 2020. The webinar drew on stories of teaching during the pandemic, shared by graduate education students (who were themselves teachers). It had over a thousand views. Those who logged into the chat room said they were so grateful for the focus on teachers' experiences. Some said they had been waiting to see when their voices would be represented. Some were disappointed that the webinar only lasted 90 minutes. Others asked that it be repeated to continue the dialogue. This small example conveys the sense of marginalisation that teachers have felt during the pandemic in Jamaica and makes us reflect on what teachers in other countries may think too. The issue of Teacher Voice during Covid-19 is an area for further research and Hordatt Gentles, chair of the International Council on Education for Teaching (www.icet4u.org) is leading an international study on this.

Lessons learned: about school leadership for inclusion

5.1 Schools cannot solve all problems: National educational leaders/politicians cannot expect teachers to take sole responsibility for planning and strategising for schooling to include all learners during a pandemic. While it is critical that teachers and school leaders participate in decision making in a fulsome manner, they should not be asked to do everything or make do with little or no guidance or technical infrastructure and the technology to use it from government leaders.

5.2 Mode 1 Individualised learning provision: Some countries were better than others at providing radio, TV, SMS, telephone teaching. Online resources will not reach all children in low-, medium- and high-income countries as connectivity and access to electricity and data is not universal even in the USA. There needs to be emergency funds for printing and posting learning materials. Distribution systems should be incorporated into disaster plans which use existing delivery systems and access points, such a national postal service, local shops. We had a report of teachers in India who put learning materials on the walls of the local shop and another from Argentina where the local egg seller who went door to door also delivered school packages to learners' homes.

5.3 Mode 2 synchronous learning provision. Any system requiring all children to have access to a device to connect to lessons at a particular time of day will exclude many children. In large households and multigenerational households, it was reported that children have to compete with other siblings and adults in the household for access to radio, TV, internet, telephones etc.

5.4 Privatisation of knowledge: The examples reported to us as providing access to high-quality resources were where national governments worked with other national organisations or NGOs to provide quality assured resources accessed online or through radio (solar radios in Somalia), TV, telephone, SMS. There were many examples of private providers making free offers which turned out to be closely linked to paid-for resources. There is a moral issue it seems around access to knowledge. What is stopping national governments through UNICEF or UNESCO pooling resources to provide open access to quality assured resources to all?

5.5 Paralysed national leadership: Confused and rapidly changing messages from national governments were experienced by school leaders in some countries. Much of this may have been inevitable as knowledge about the effect of the virus on humans emerged over time. In the early days of the virus, it was not known how rapidly it would spread and what the level of deaths among all age groups would be, so being fearful and cautious was a natural response. Evidence about viral transmission and impact on different groups emerged steadily during 2020.

5.6 Teacher workload and new roles: Teachers were quick to adapt and change their regular working practices to meet the demands of the pandemic when schools closed and they were required to shift into remote teaching. Teachers were assigned tasks which were added to their allocated workload, such as adapting their face-to-face lesson materials for remote learning. Protocols for operationalising school crisis plans could be helpful in protecting teachers from overload. We cannot allow teachers' willingness to step up to the plate during a crisis to be taken for granted and allowed to be seen as a 'new normal' role for teachers. Teachers report working longer hours and more than 12-hour days, some reporting 16-hour days. We observed teacher unions and professional associations stepping up to protect teachers in this regard and also to advocate for a 'safe return to work' once schools reopened with respect to social distancing, hand hygiene facilities, requesting face coverings for protection.

5.7 Marginalised learners, engagement in remote learning and attendance: UK research shows the parents of marginalised students were more likely to be reluctant to return their children to school than wealthier families, the students were less likely to engage with school materials and while they were more likely to have access to television and radio, they were less likely to be able to access online learning. A teacher contributing to the ICET/MESHGuides research (2020) reported that five of his students became pregnant during lockdown.

Planning toolkit: decisions school leaders have to make

Table 5.4 provides key questions to aid your strategic planning. These are drawn from the challenges discussed in the preceding section. The table presents some ideas which you need to adapt and add to, to suit your circumstances. For each of the decisions, you will need to note who does what, when and how and what resources are needed and available to support the actions.

Table 5.4 Planning toolkit for senior leaders planning for continuity of learning through a whole school approach

Decision 5.1 Risk Assessments

Questions to resolve	Examples:
	What areas do your risk assessments have to cover?
	What guidelines and templates can help with your school response plan?
	Who has to do what?
	What is the legal context you are now operating in? Are virtual meetings and decisions taken even legal? What is your scheme of delegation and what can be delegated if colleagues cannot meet?
Solutions	Examples:
	For risk assessment guidelines and examples of templates to use, see examples in the Annexes. There are also many private providers of information but this raises the moral issue of restricting access to helpful knowledge during a pandemic with serious life-threatening risks to health; the better prepared school leaders are for managing their school, the lesser chance of risk there is, as children mix with parents, grandparents and wider community members.

Decision 5.2 Considering inclusion of all learners and models of remote teaching

Questions to resolve	Examples:
	What modes of remote learning are you using?
	Who has to do what – see the questions in Tables 5.1, 5.2.
	How will you engage marginalised learners?
Solutions	Examples:
	Schools should not have to do everything on their own. National educational leadership can play a leading role in harnessing resources, in drawing in key knowledge holders and in maximising continuity of learning and assessment for children or conversely, a lack of leadership means opportunities are lost.
	National solutions which support continuity of learning and assessment include telephone, radio and television broadcasts which are accessible to many. Online solutions had varied uptake, as in many countries, even in strong economies such as the UK, there are still great disparities of access to connectivity and devices per child (e.g. rural/urban, rich/poor, cultural/religion).
	Wide access is possible – for example, the Australian School of the Air models and the Scottish GlowConnect models, both developed to cope with remote schooling, provide models for governments to learn from. In the UK prior to a change of government in 2010, all schools were expected to have part of their website (a learning platform) where work is made available and used as a repository for subject teachers to post work. Schools which maintained that provision and had a digital learning strategy were in a strong position to support remote learning.

Decision 5.3 Managing rapid change, workload and resources

Questions to resolve	Examples:
	How will you manage the uncertainty and stress experienced by all involved?

(Continued)

Table 5.4 (Cont).

	How will you manage the increased workload of teachers as they adapt and move to new ways of working remotely?
	How will you make sure traditionally marginalised learners do not miss out more, and that teachers are addressing this need?
	How will you manage learners who are becoming marginalised during the pandemic school closures and help teachers in their identifying of these students?
Solutions	Examples:
	Solutions have to be found on a school-by-school basis as circumstances vary considerably between schools. A first step may be to bring into operation a School Rapid Response committee led by senior staff. The workload can be expected to be considerable because of the short notice given for any changes as any crisis unfolds.

Decision 5.4 Communications

Questions to resolve	Examples:
	What communication channels do you have and do you need?
Solutions	Examples:
	As well as existing media channels, new ones may emerge. In some countries local media supported schools in communications; in some, local shops have had a role to play.

Decision 5.5 Giving teachers a voice

Questions to resolve	Examples:
	How will you engage teachers in supporting the plans and in undertaking what will be, for many, extra work.
Solutions	Examples:
	Suggestions are given in Specific Challenge 5.5, which engage teachers in meaningful ways.

Decision 5.6 Dealing with the aftermath (returning school after long-term closures)

Questions to resolve	Examples:
	What resources, support systems are necessary to mitigate the loss of learning and impact on well-being; this may include missed social interactions with classmates and participation in school activities, to more serious cases of possible/PTSD/raised anxiety among children from the pandemic, also some will have suffered bereavement due to Covid-19 deaths and may be struggling with the social stigma of having the diagnosis of Covid-19 in the family (potential social shunning and bullying).
Solutions	Examples:
	Solutions have to be found on a school-by-school basis as circumstances vary considerably between schools. The School Rapid Response committee may have a role here.

Futurecasting: for school leadership for inclusion

An outcome of the pandemic is teachers were identified as key workers, where schools that remained open had teachers as front-line emergency response workers. We note that in countries where it is normal for both parents to work, if the children aren't in school, the economy falters as parents' ability to be available to work is hampered. So in any national emergency planning, recognising this key worker role for teachers should enable more effective responses to be brought into play at times of crisis.

At the time of writing, November 2020, the second wave of the pandemic is developing in a number of countries and localised lockdowns and random school closures as the virus spreads happened.

For many issues, solutions have to be found on a school-by-school and country-by-country basis as circumstances vary considerably between local context and nations, with widely varying rates of Covid-19 infection across countries.

Any solutions must be supported, however, by formal provision of time and spaces for teachers to provide input so that solutions proposed can be reality-checked. If a country wants the best provision for learners, teachers' contributions have to be acknowledged, valued and validated in systemic ways so as to give credibility to national pandemic plans.

As the World Health Organisation advises (WHO 2009) School Emergency Response Protocols are best developed and tested beforehand so that staff can easily switch into the modes of operation required for a crisis. Having plans and protocols in place for a School Rapid Response committee to lead on crisis responses, led by senior staff, will ease the switch from normal schooling to remote schooling. Engaging young people (e.g. senior students) in the annual updating of the details in the plan (such as resources stocktaking, updating advice, updating the remote learning resources list or the list of community resources available) was reported as one way of sharing the workload while also providing a valuable experience for young people.

 # Notes

1 W. Ward (1970) *Fountains of Faith*. Anderson, SC: Droke House.
2 We noticed a strange phenomenon in many early media reports on whether schools could reopen or not and what the risks of transmission were between young people and what the risks for young people were if they contract Covid-19. Missing was the mention of the fact that there were many adults in school and the realisation that schools act as community hubs with young people linked

with all of the parents and grandparents in a community – so it would seem schools provide the major meeting points for many members of a community and thus provide a likely hub for transfer of viruses. This was corrected later. www.bbc.co.uk/news/uk-53875410

3 That individual groups of schools were left to get legal advice on their own on this issue demonstrates a lack of political leadership. This raises the question, should taxpayers money be spent on schools paying for lawyers as, in the case of England, because of the newly created fragmented academy system, individual schools/MATs were having to pay for legal advice when the government could have dealt with this issue as a national priority regarding 'responsibility' and dealt with this at a national level – not left to individual schools to sort out. We argue this is a moral issue regarding access to knowledge, particularly when that legal knowledge relates to a national crisis, public health issue during a pandemic where lives are at risk.

4 Private companies also provided risk assessment templates which schools had to pay for. In our minds, this raises issues about the clash between public service values and commercial values. When a product is for the benefit of all children in a society and all communities, should access be restricted to those who can pay? In the interests of public health in a pandemic, should knowledge be a privatised commodity or freely available for public good? This is a moral issue and one that we argue has systematically failed to attract any national traction in the media during the Covid-19 pandemic in the UK.

5 Christian Aid Report www.christianaid.org.uk/sites/default/files/2020-07/building-back-justice-covid19-report-Jul2020_0.pdf

6 President Trump on ingesting disinfectant to kill the virus. www.nbcnews.com/politics/donald-trump/trump-suggests-injection-disinfectant-beat-coronavirus-clean-lungs-n1191216

7 Bolsonaro on coronavirus being a mild illness. www.theguardian.com/world/2020/mar/23/brazils-jair-bolsonaro-says-coronavirus-crisis-is-a-media-trick

Leadership and governance

National, regional and local community

Introduction and context

At all institutions, the National COVID-19 Taskforce mandates a set of protocols for operating schools. These include on campus screening stations, where temperature checks are conducted and recorded, as well as other requirements related to social-physical distancing, mask-wearing and hygienic hand cleaning. At large-sized educational institutions . . . the environment is one in which teachers are faced with working in a shift system. Additionally, across many schools (including private institutions), teachers and students have to work within a bubble as part of the restrictions due to COVID-19.

(Teacher respondent ICET/MESHGuides [2020])

In analysing the data for the ICET/MESHGuides Report (2020), Hordatt Gentles and Leask found three countries (low- and medium-income) whose teachers expressed support for the clarity of direction from their governments. The preceding quotation is from one of those teachers. In other countries, teacher leaders spoke of being left to cope without clear national support or guidance.

This chapter focuses on leadership modes, responsibilities and challenges at times of crisis at the national, regional and local community levels.

Chapter 2 makes the point that the philosophy and values of national leaders provided a framework informing and constraining their decisions during the Covid-19 crisis. However, the research showed that some close-knit rural communities were especially mutually supportive at this time with teachers often providing local leadership and headteachers being looked to by their communities for advice about what

DOI: 10.4324/9781003155591-9

to do during the pandemic. We had examples from rural communities with adults and older children organising to teach the children when the schools closed, of the use of temple, mosque and village loud-speakers, of teachers posting school tasks in shops and village noticeboards, of outdoors socially distanced teaching in small groups, of teachers going to the villages and teaching from the back of a truck.

Overall challenge: for leadership at national, regional and local community levels

Some teachers mentioned the value of national and regional rapid-response disaster planning committees which are a standard and well-tested mechanism for disaster preparedness and for managing crises with a chain of command from the national to the local level. Such systems require stakeholders at different levels of the system to work together with the backing of a national system which makes clear who does what at a time of crisis.

Countries with an advantage in ensuring continuity of learning were those where there was clear national leadership with delineation of roles (national/regional/local) and clear communication channels between central and regional/local government coupled with the flexibility to develop locally sensitive responses. Too many teachers reported that government directives did not take into account the local setting.

England was an extreme outlier in the research. The application of free market philosophies had been applied to education, leading to the breakup of the national/regional/local channels of communication, and this seemed to create, at the local level, a lack of effective co-ordination and resource sharing, exacerbated by local competition between schools for prestige and pupils. The deep fragmentation of provision meant there was no effective, systemic knowledge management in the education system at the local level (see Whalley and Greenway (2021) and the case study in Table 6.1).

Specific challenges: for national, regional, local community leaders

While ensuring continuity of learning and assessment during crises ultimately depends on the actions of individual teachers and schools, prior national investment in online/radio/TV resources as well as national communications infrastructure can have a dual benefit. For home learning in times of crisis as well as in non-crisis times, such resources can provide reference and learning materials which may benefit those who have missed out on schooling or who have missed key parts of their schooling. In addition, funding a national bank of education resources, in non- crisis times, has been demonstrated to provide teachers with CPD opportunities (Leask and Younie 2013; World Bank 2017; Younie et al. 2021a).

Countries with national online educational provision were demonstrably at an advantage during the Covid crises when schooling was disrupted. As mentioned in Chapter 2, we found examples of effective national online provision in Scotland, Kenya, South Korea, China, the Netherlands and Germany. During the Covid crisis, normally 'paid-for services' of educational value were made freely available by some companies to support remote learning. It is clear that online/TV/radio systems with educational content which provide value in non-crisis times can provide a lifeline to providing continuity of education during crises.

The following specific challenges are covered in this chapter:

* Chains of command and effective knowledge management
* National leadership: roles and responsibilities
* Regional leadership: roles and responsibilities
* Local community/NGO leadership: potential roles and responsibilities.

Specific challenge 6.1 Chains of command and effective knowledge management – who does what?

Our analysis indicates that effective management of the challenges posed by Covid-19 was dependent upon clear and consistent leadership within *and* across the multiple major stakeholders. Effective leadership was dependent upon effective knowledge management and knowledge being shared across national, regional and local levels.

Knowledge management (i.e. systematic sharing of knowledge alongside a clear communication framework) enabled a coherent response to the crisis. For example, at a national level, some countries acted quickly with decisive political and scientific leadership, with politicians and scientists on the 'same page'; as a result, systems such as South Korea, New Zealand and Australia had relative success with containing the virus early in the pandemic. The consequences of leadership choices during the Covid-19 pandemic have been stark – effective leadership has led to far fewer deaths in some countries than others (Baska 2020; Hatami et al. 2020).

Prof David Heymann, of the London School of Hygiene and Tropical Medicine argued 'a "lack of political leadership" has hampered many countries where "public health leaders and political leaders have difficulty speaking together". In such a climate the virus has flourished' (cited in Gallagher 2020). For example, in the USA, former president Trump and the leading infectious disease public official, Anthony Fauci, were 'on different pages, if not completely different books during the pandemic' (ibid.). In the UK, the messaging from the government was not always clear, with the infamous, confusing statement from Prime Minister Johnson on the evening of Sunday 10th May,[1] for enactment on the Monday morning, leading to comedians creating parodies around the phrases 'go to work, don't go to work'.[2]

Inconsistent messaging from governments on the public wearing of face masks, caused confusion, and in the USA, the non-wearing of masks became a political issue encouraged by the president. At first mask-wearing was dismissed particularly in some European countries, but later in the pandemic, governments brought in compulsory use in shops and public transport; by October/November, use in schools in increasing numbers of countries became compulsory. South Korea, Japan and Singapore had a tradition of mask-wearing to prevent the spread of viruses and had clearer national mandates and consistent messaging about the importance of wearing masks from the beginning.

The preceding examples outline variations in the national strategies for limiting transmission of Covid-19 in public settings. With respect to the education sector, a similar wide range of responses from national governments was observed.

In a number of countries (e.g. USA, Australia, UK), decisions about education were devolved to states or, in the case of the UK, to England, Scotland, Northern Ireland and Wales. The World Health Organisation provided global advice, however, on the ground decisions taken by nation states varied as did the level of collaboration and knowledge sharing across regions. For example, teachers in Malaysia, Pakistan, the state of Victoria, (Australia) and in Wales (UK) reported that clear guidelines were issued to schools. In England, teachers reported that the central government advice was at times confusing, contradictory and sometimes changed before schools had a chance to implement it (Guardian 12 May 2020, 9 June 2020, 2 July 2020). The phased reopening of schools in June 2020 in England led to poor uptake of school places by parents; one large school network (MAT) across London reported an average of 21% pupils attending, which reflected a wider pattern across England. The reasons cited were a lack of confidence from teachers and parents in the decision to reopen with still relatively high rates of transmission of Covid-19 and confusion about whether it was safe for children to return to school or not. Possibly one reason leading to confusion in England was with respect to risk: where was the risk carried? Statutory instruction from a government does not remove the responsibility for the duty of care to children and staff held by school leaders. Teachers wanted evidence to demonstrate that the increased risk from spending extended periods of time in a classroom with 30 children was acceptable in relation to general population risk.

Space to socially distance pupils (recommended as 1.5 metres or 2 meters apart) was a challenge for many schools. Some head teachers felt they could not safely reopen and maintain social distancing for all year groups. In many countries, schools, with more open space and playing fields and good weather, were able to teach outside to enable physical distancing: tents were reported as being used to provide more school space in Jamaica and the UK.

Specific challenge 6.2 National leadership: roles and responsibilities

Whether and how national and regional leaders work with teachers depended on their ideology and values. In Chapter 2 we identified four modes of leadership leading from different value sets. These approaches lead naturally to different policy choices.

* Mode 1: devolved responsibility – to individual regions, communities, schools
* Mode 2: collaborative – working with teacher unions, NGOs, professional associations
* Mode 3: authoritarian – central diktats and mandatory instructions
* Mode 4: ad hoc – centralised and partly localised (chaotic and fragmented).

Our analysis indicates that, in a number of countries, teachers reported positively on what could be classified as Mode 2 leadership: Belize, Jamaica, Mexico, Pakistan, Scotland, Wales with government, professional associations, teacher unions, parent organisations and/or NGOs working together (not always comfortably). Trump, as president of the USA, wanted to impose opening of schools (Mode 3), but was prevented by federal law as these decisions were delegated to state level (Mode 1). In England, teachers experienced Mode 3 and 4 as government tried and failed to directly manage 30,000 schools and school networks. On ideological grounds, they had removed local and regional governance as much as possible stripping out the opportunity for local responsiveness. See the examples in Table 6.1.

This 'lack of system' was created in 2010, by Secretary of State for Education Michael Gove. Whalley and Greenway (2021), who work within the system, speak of the chaos and lack of coherence. Another example of Mode 4 chaotic and fragmented national leadership was, in England, the failure to systematically supply laptops to the most needy and deprived children. With 700,000 earmarked for distribution, by June (four months after school closures) only 200,000 had been dispensed; these were financed and issued from central government, but the distribution through regional channels to local schools proved fragmented and problematic (EAGLE report 2020). A national diktat on the reopening of schools in June 2020 too rapidly proved problematic (Guardian 12 May 2020, 9 June 2020, 2 July 2020). This forced the adoption of a Mode 4 model. See Table 6.2 which illustrates the need for central governments to support local responsiveness during crises.

Table 6.1 Case study: fragmentation – leading to wasting of effort and resources in a crisis

Case 1 – In England, most schools now belong to Multi-Academy Trusts (MATs) (i.e. school networks): some are extensive, some are small; some are based on geographical locations and some are not. For example, in one major city, one school in an MAT was designated as staying open for children of key workers and vulnerable children for all the MAT, but children from the closed school across the road could not attend the open school, as it was in a different MAT. In this case, children for the first MAT were bussed in from across the city and the children from the school across the road were bussed elsewhere, to the school designated open in their MAT chain. This required extra transportation in buses during a pandemic in which the virus is more contagious in contained spaces.

Case 2 – In England (before academisation and Govian reforms post 2010), local authorities managed all schools in their region and could take decisions about resource deployment. The current fragmented, academised system (Whalley and Greenway 2021) meant local coordination leading to efficient decision-making and resource deployment was lost, so more schools were kept open than necessary.

Table 6.2 Case study: coherence between national and local roles: lessons learned about data sharing and miscommunication

Shifting modes of leadership can be a strength if based on effective knowledge management and evidence which is shared and understood by those implementing the policies – otherwise, shifting modes of leadership can feel like gaslighting (see www.psychologytoday.com/gb/blog/here-there-and-everywhere/201701/11-warning-signs-gaslighting; www.nytimes.com/2020/06/03/opinion/dominic-cummings-coronavirus-lockdown.html).

Case Study – policy making at the national/local level – incoherence

England's Covid-19 response, in March 2020, started with a national coordinated approach to the pandemic with a nationwide lockdown for its citizens and the closure of all schools for children as of Monday 23rd March (with the proviso that children of key workers and vulnerable children could attend school). This meant that, within a family of schools, one school had to remain open for those children and was operated by a reduced skeleton staff. This model continued until the easing of the national lockdown and the gradual re-opening of schools in early June, with primary schools returning first, the priority being for years 6 and 1 and EYFS /reception, nurseries and then secondary schools prioritising year 10 and 12. This was the partial reopening of schools, with a national strategy of prioritising those year groups considered to be most affected by the school closures, namely in secondaries those that were exam year groups (year 10 with GCSEs coming up; year 12 with A Levels the following year) and for primaries, those year groups that were transitioning from primary to secondary and needing to 'finish' their primary education and year 1 and EYFS. The policy of the 'phased return' was informed by lengthy documents from the DfE providing the guidance for the safe reopening of schools, which was configured around the notion of 'bubbles', whereby learners could be put in small groups of between 8–15 children, which allowed for 'social distancing' within each classroom, with enough space between desks and children to 'contain transmission' as much as possible.

The policy of a national phased return still required contextualisation and local interpretation as the priority was keeping children safe, and by extension their families. For many primary schools, having the return of their Early Years Foundation Stage (EYFS) year group and ensuring social distancing, there was not the physical space to have year 6 returning too. This was predominantly the case in small/rural primary schools with limited numbers of classrooms, such as one-form entry schools.

The national strategy for easing lockdown and returning to schools was attenuated by a regional/localised strategy, which saw local responses when a Covid-19 spike in cases was reported, as was the case in Leicester in mid-June. The spike led to a lockdown of the city and the schools, which had only been reopened for two weeks. A map was produced of the lockdown area, which had a red ring around the designated area of containment, which included all the schools within it and some surrounding suburbs. This was further complicated by teaching staff who lived in the city, but were teachers in county schools, which were still open; these staff were deemed key workers who could leave the city to teach in county schools. However, the children in the city, who attended county schools, were in lockdown and couldn't leave to attend their school.

The timing and move from national to local policy for managing the pandemic was informed by data, namely the number of positive Covid-19 tests where a spike in transmission required a re-introducing of lockdown measures. This policy was reliant on testing policy. 'Pillar 1 tests' were those carried out in hospitals and the data was shared with the government, Public Health England and local authorities. 'Pillar 2 testing' was community testing undertaken by a private company whose contract was with the government, whereby a person's medical data was only to be shared with the government and the individual, not the local authorities who then were not in receipt of this data in a direct and timely manner. Only once the data were shared at regional level could patterns be seen and specific areas identified that could inform local policy decision-making. When the local authority, in this case, was finally given the data from government, they were able to make the link between marginalised communities in low-paying jobs being made to work in unsafe conditions (in Leicester, in textile factories), which then led to local closure of schools meaning more loss of schooling for children in marginalised communities.

As mentioned in Chapter 4, many countries experienced challenges with high stakes public examinations which needed resolution at the national leadership level. In England and Scotland the mode of assessment was changed to teacher assessment after initial results were published which were based on a computer algorithm using data about typical performance of students at the school – thus advantaging those at schools which typically achieved high grades. Countries, such as Norway, which trust teacher assessment escaped this chaos.

National co-ordination proved essential on matters such as tracking and tracing virus hotspots, on instituting a fair replacement public examinations system, on the coordination of national resources for remote learning, on resources for supporting marginalised learners and on funding the costs. Why some countries managed more effective responses than others is worth further research.

In contrast to the case study in Table 6.2, in Scotland a Mode 2 – collaborative approach – provided a more systematic and coherent way of managing the crisis. This led to the setting up of the 'Education Recovery Group', which consisted of government, the teaching profession, councils, and parents, who met regularly from April 2020. This provided a collaborative forum, giving voice to key stakeholders and the opportunity to develop a more comprehensible response to the pandemic across schools in Scotland. For example, schools will be 'issued with new flow charts to help them address issues quickly' (Watson 2020). As Thewliss, from the professional association School Leaders Scotland, stated, such an inclusive strategy to managing the crisis meant that 'at least [we've] been party to the decisions that have been taken' (ibid.). Arguably this is in sharp contrast to the situation in England (Table 6.2).

Specific challenge 6.3 Regional leadership: roles and responsibilities

The Covid-19 pandemic tested existing structures and revealed deficiencies, for example, with respect to who had authority to make decisions about school closures and openings as well as the standards and actions necessary to maintain health and safety in schools.

Many countries have the structure of national government linked with regional/state/local government with clear delegations of powers (e.g. over education), and existing processes for communication and resource allocation as well as *regional rapid response disaster planning committees*. Such committees include major regional stakeholders who are responsible for crisis plans which can be implemented within minutes. The quote at the beginning of the chapter is from a teacher where this system seemed to be working well.

During the Covid period, the challenge for schools at the regional level was in mediating in the space between national government requirements and local school risks. It became apparent during the Covid-19 crisis that decisions have to be taken at the place where there is knowledge of the impact of the crisis and this is at the local level. Regional authorities also normally have access to local public health networks and resources as well as community and school leaders who can work together in planning regional responses which are locally sensitive. In Table 6.3 we continue the example from England to show how a radical restructuring of the education system disrupted the channels of communication needed to ensure business continuity at a time of crisis (Hudson et al. 2021). Table 6.3 describes the complexity of the fragmented system in England.

Table 6.3 A fragmented system: case study from England

In England, for example, a series of political decisions removed local oversight of most schools from their 152 regional/local authorities (Wolfe in Hudson et al. 2021). Many small independent networks of schools – MATs (multi-academy trusts) – were established; all of the new MAT school networks were smaller than local authorities school networks but they report to central government, the DFE. This reorganisation broke the chain of command between schools and local or regional elected councils and national government.

There are now 2391 MATs managed directly by central government in addition to 152 residual local authority school networks. This means that much responsibility and decision-making is centralised at the national level – but not all. Moving the ministry of education to an operational role led to a chaotic, incoherent system with the DFE, which normally provides ultimate oversight of the school system, now being involved in operational management of thousands of small organisations. As Whalley and Greenway (in Hudson et al. 2021) observe, this has resulted in:

a partially deregulated and therefore massively fragmented education system comprising 152 Local Education Authorities (LAs), 740 Multi-Academy Trusts (MATs) and 1,651 Single Academy Trusts (SATs – which include

> *Free Schools). This is a multi-provider, multi-agency system where the biggest MAT is smaller than the smallest LA. The average size of schools that are not academies (most of which are one form entry primary schools) is 279 pupils. The majority of schools that are not academies are faith-based primary schools and they average 189 pupils.*

We did find excellent examples of system leadership at the regional and national level with national training being provided in online teaching for all teachers in Jamaica prior to the start of online teaching. As mentioned, some countries already had online systems supporting and learning online teaching which were deployed across regions and accompanied by online communities of practice for teachers.

Collaborative models of leadership quickly built capacity and expertise in online delivery should future school closures be required or if particular classes or year groups need to be isolated and sent home for remote learning. Charities, schools and local bodies in LIC and HIC countries stepped in to provide devices supporting online learning for learners who did not have their own. One example was from the regional body in England, Greater Manchester Combined Authority (GMCA) which provided some equipment for more vulnerable students within three weeks of lockdown, significantly ahead of the English government's response. In the GMCA regional approach, which was coordinated across their providers, all the laptops were bespoke to a school-online solution and came with safeguarding support and internet filtering as standard. In other regions, teachers reported having to do this work themselves.

Specific challenge 6.4 Local community/NGO leadership: potential roles and responsibilities

Education is always a national responsibility *and* arguably during a crisis, a whole local community responsibility (i.e. beyond schools) to ensure, firstly, a broader understanding of the crisis because poorly educated community members put everyone at risk in a pandemic, and secondly, to draw on wider community resources (human and material) to facilitate the continuity of learning. Within local areas it is possible to identify community organisations, NGOs, charities with resources which can support learners for homeschooling/remote schooling so that no learner is left behind or marginalised.

VSO case studies (VSO 2020a, b, c) in Myanmar, Nigeria and Uganda show that individual communities and families responded to school closures in very different ways – in some communities parents and older children taught younger children when there were no teachers, in others, the children went to work with parents – in the fields, in care and household duties.

Lessons learned: about chains of command – national to local

6.1 Systems which increase marginalisation: Marginalised learners identified as vulnerable require effective localised support. In some areas, selected schools were kept open for key workers and vulnerable pupils. However, the availability of schooling to vulnerable pupils was inconsistent. Children already disenfranchised from the schooling system with respect to attendance in their local school are not likely to make more effort to go on a bus to attend a school further away as was required in some areas. Routes to school have implications for children's safety for both genders and it cannot be assumed that parents will feel safe letting their children travel to different locations.

6.2 Modes of governance and their impact. National leadership and governance Modes 1 (devolved) and 2 (collaborative) enable national leaders to work with education professionals at a regional and local level on a shared mission to support continuity of learning and assessment. National leadership Mode 3 (Authoritarian) may lead at times to Mode 4 (mixed) with results chaotic and inconsistent. Modes 1 and 2 support sensitive localised solutions which are most likely to have a positive impact on marginalised learners.

6.3 Limitations of centralised control – the example from England: The ministry for education (DfE) was not equipped with the personnel, finances or infrastructure to operate as a body organising education at a sub-regional level. Because of fragmentation, not only does the DfE no longer control the English education system, during the pandemic, it didn't have the historical or attendant knowledge to understand it or mitigate any unintended consequences of its suggested actions. Expecting to devolve planning to local authorities (LAs) was also a weakened strategy because the LAs regional education departments had been defunded.

6.4 Regional leadership and governance: Where existing processes were robust and effective for regional governance, teachers reported that the response to Covid-19 was coherent and efficient across local areas. Risk registers that were regularly updated and risk management processes that had contingency planning in place, could be enacted in a timely manner and multi-stakeholder communications facilitated the running of regional actions. Whereas a more fragmented system for regional governance led to less coordinated responses, as illustrated in the case studies.

6.5 Drawing on community resources: Lessons from Covid-19 about how to draw on community resources to support continuity of learning and assessment during a crisis included the need to:

* Identify who is to lead in ensuring local community readiness and who leads the response to support continuity of learning and assessment and to include

marginalised learners. This is a question that prior contingency planning needs to address and record in local community response teams.

* Consider, does the local community need to set up a local Emergency Education Continuity Committee (EECC) to identify the network of stakeholders and resources who can support continuity of learning and identify leaders and roles?

This Emergency Education Continuity Committee would:

* Find and identify community organisations, NGOs, charities with human or material resources who can support homeschooling/remote schooling so that no learner is left behind. What material resources can be harnessed including halls and other buildings, open spaces, equipment to give access to remote teaching through radio, TV or internet?
* Map local community resources to supplement school resources.
* Identify available human capital, the 'people' resources that the local communities have, for example, those out of work because of the crisis, retired teachers, grandparents and parents. Which, if any school staff, remain in the local community when schools are closed? What other human resources are available? How might they be used to support continuity of learning and assessment and to include marginalised learners?
* Address what funding might be available. How might this be accessed and deployed?
* Locate what local media can be used (e.g. local radio).
* Special cases – are there any?
* As with the containment of the Ebola virus in West Africa, consider mobilising staff from areas not yet affected to support staff in areas when challenges are hardest.

The planning toolkit that follows provides a framework for checking readiness to provide continuity of learning and assessment in your local context.

Planning toolkit: readiness checklist – for continuity of learning and assessment

Table 6.4 summarises the preceding information and highlights problems and solutions for leaders at national, regional and local levels to consider.

Futurecasting: knowledge management processes to support chains of command

A major lesson from the pandemic crisis is the need for effective knowledge management systems that are co-ordinated across national/regional/local levels; such

Table 6.4 Planning toolkit: leadership – national, regional, local

Decisions to be made	Problems to be solved and questions to resolve	Solutions and future risk mitigation needed practices, tools and techniques
National	The main problems to be overcome in ensuring continuity of learning and assessment are: to establish transparent and trusted processes for decision making, employ clear modes of communication, implement rapid decision processes on resource management to ensure safe operations, include marginalised learners and risk management. The different leadership and governance Modes 1–4 outlined previously provide an indication of the choices to be made.	A government adopting a Mode 2 (collaborative) leadership and governance approach should be able to work positively with major education stakeholders in the education sector and so be more likely to achieve the goals of ensuring continuity of learning and assessment coupled with inclusion of marginalised learners than a government that adopts any of the other three modes. Crises, by their nature, require effort by all stakeholders for resolution. Ensuring that rapid response Emergency Education Continuity Committees (EECC) operate at the national and regional level should mitigate risks if they function properly (i.e. preparing for disruption of schooling).
Regional	The challenge at regional level is mediating in the space between national government requirements and local school risks. The different leadership and governance Modes 1–4 outlined provide an indication of the opportunities for and constraints on regional actions.	Regional governments are constrained by the Modes of leadership and governance but having, as a minimum, regional rapid response Emergency Education Continuity Committees (EECC) which meet regularly and update crisis plans so they can be operationalised within minutes seems a basic condition of preparedness.
Local community	The problem is how to manage the multi-stakeholder collaborations needed to allocate human and material resources necessary to provide continuity of education.	National and regional leadership and governance modes have a direct impact on the extent to which community resources are harnessed in times of emergency. For example, the right-wing free-market government in England chose to grant millions of pounds worth of contracts to private companies (often supporters or contacts of the governing Conservative party) rather than engage the energies of existing NGO, community, voluntary or charitable associations such as church, sporting and cultural groups, and professional associations. The Council for school subject associations offered to support the ministry in providing online resources for learning – but a grant was given to a newly formed organisation in April 2020, Oak National Academy without transparent procurement processes, (Connell 2020b).

knowledge management systems could include a learning resources repository. This could be made available internationally, thereby supporting those countries that are low- to middle-income (LMIC) to manage and support continuity of learning during a global crisis.

For leaders at all levels – national, regional and local – futurecasting requires careful analysis and evaluation of lessons learnt from the Covid-19 pandemic. This is more than managing a 'risk register' to pass on risk. For effective crisis futurecasting, knowledge management processes need to be in place and be operational. Knowledge of human and material resources at different levels and of alternative modes of operation is central and any supporting knowledge bank needs to be evaluated by potential users with knowledge collated, stored, updated regularly and shared for future use. Such knowledge management structures are valuable not just for pandemics and other crises but can support effective operation of the whole system during normal times. A knowledge bank would contain current thinking on the solutions and learning from the key questions that had to be addressed during the crisis. Different levels of leadership and their roles and responsibilities and their needs would be defined. Human capital and material resources, including financing and training would be analysed and recorded. Repositories of resources, records of known losses, risks and challenges will engender better futurecasting at all levels.

As discussed previously, policy options are influenced by values and the mode of leadership that is adopted, and there are different consequences following on from the different modes. For example, a more collaborative coordinated approach has the potential to bring greater breadth of ideas and different perspectives to futurecasting which may improve coherence of strategy and the likelihood of implementation. An authoritarian and ad hoc mode has the potential to create greater inconsistencies and disparities, leading to possible disturbances and civil discontent.

Chapter 1, on planning, highlights the importance of building pandemic plans on existing structures. If open access national banks of updated educational resources are available – such as the existing Chinese, South Korean, Scottish, Kenyan, Ghanaian, Australian, German and Dutch resources – there are multiple benefits to the whole nation: at the time of crises a switch to homeschooling is facilitated, in non-crisis times teacher professional development in their subject area is facilitated, and for the wider community, those out of education can still access summaries of the latest knowledge about key developments in curriculum areas. However, the experience of teachers from Sweden, the UK, Australia and India is that such repositories have been created by one government, only to be closed down by the next or when funding priorities change (World Bank 2017; Blamires 2015), so somehow, such resources necessary in times of crises need to be seen as an important national resource, worth protecting and managing for the benefit of all.

Notes

1 Johnson 'Go to work Don't go to work' www.youtube.com/watch?v=IqHYoV34j0w
2 Comedians mock Prime Minister Johnson https://news.sky.com/story/corona virus-matt-lucas-video-mocking-boris-johnsons-speech-to-the-nation-goes-viral-11986438

Section 3

Teaching – during Covid-19

7 Curriculum and assessment

Introduction and context

The teaching approaches adopted for remote learning depended on whether the goal of the teacher was for the student to learn facts or for the mind to be stimulated: the first approach lending itself to memorisation, the second to the setting of open-ended projects also known as 'rich tasks' which draw on knowledge from a range of disciplines.

> the mind does not require filling like a bottle, but rather, like wood, it only requires kindling to create in it an impulse to think independently and an ardent desire for the truth.
>
> Plutarch[1]

The 'lighting of a fire' in a learner (i.e. their motivation to learn), as teachers know, often comes from interactions and discussions – teacher to students, student to student – pedagogical approaches which were too easily forgotten as governments moved to remote delivery of the curriculum often using 'filling of the mind' pedagogy through online/TV/radio programmes during the Covid crisis.

It seems that during crises, we (school leaders, teachers, parents) should assume that school closures will occur on an ad-hoc basis depending on the level of illness/disruption in the surrounding community. Experience from the Covid-19 crisis is that teachers can expect to have just a few days' notice (if that) that learning has to continue out-of-school. Pre-Covid-19 published advice on the content of national, regional and school 'business continuity plans' did, on the whole, assume the ability to continue face-to-face teaching after only a short while (WHO 2009; EC 2009a, b). However, what happened with Covid-19, was that schools were closed suddenly and then there was little pattern to what followed: some opened for children of key

DOI: 10.4324/9781003155591-11

workers and vulnerable pupils, some closed entirely, some opened but only took half the pupils per day, others opened only to close because of local lockdowns or outbreaks (see EAGLE Report for Leicester June 2020, and New South Wales, Australia, examples[2]).

Later in 2020, schools and nurseries, in the UK at least, moved to a model of placing leaners in 'bubbles' and sending home all those in the bubble when one tested positive for Covid-19. Cases were reported to us of learners being in school for a day and then being sent home for two weeks, then back for a day, only to be sent home again. By late November the virus was spreading fast across Europe and national lockdowns were in place in many countries (Belgium, Germany, France, Austria, UK) while in countries such as Taiwan, South Korea, many Pacific Islands, Australia and New Zealand life was carrying on as normal but with external borders closed. In England, with 1 in 80 of the population having Covid-19[3] in November 2020, it is of no surprise that there was disruption in schools. Clearly, providing continuity of learning in such chaos was impossible and curriculum and assessment adaption was essential.

The aim of this chapter is to highlight areas for consideration when planning for delivering the curriculum and managing assessment when schools close. It is not meant to be a definitive guide, but rather a supportive set of suggestions to aid schools with their continuity planning during crises. This chapter considers the challenges and solutions for curriculum continuity and for teachers' formative and summative assessment of what is learned.

Overall challenge: adapting the curriculum and assessment

For learning and accompanying formative and summative assessment to continue, a robust system supporting remote/out-of-school learning and its assessment needs to be available, accessible and understood by teachers, learners and parents/community members alike. Planning such a system includes allocation of roles, responsibilities, resources, so as to make clear *who* does *what, how, where, when and why*.

Ensuring the curriculum is accessible to remote learners from home demands different pedagogical approaches to those employed in the classroom. Examples of pedagogical approaches are covered in Chapters 8 and 9 where examples of three modes of remote/out-of-school teaching are discussed. These were blended by teachers during the Covid-19 period to meet the local context and are discussed under Specific challenge 8.2.

Assessment for remote learning can be problematic. In the words of one deputy head: 'The difficulty we have with summative assessment is that we have no way of knowing how much input pupils had from their parents – it can become a competition as to who is doing the best home-schooling!'

With respect to identifying gaps in learning when schools reopen again, formative assessment to diagnose gaps in knowledge is the main tool that teachers have.

We received reports that schools designed a 'recovery curriculum' to cover what might have been missed. The same deputy head explains her school approach: 'On return to school, teachers used reading running records and diagnostic comprehension activities in English. In Maths, staff used the government (DfE June 2020) guidance produced in June, alongside NCETM Mastery tracking questions (Askew et al. 2020) to look for gaps at the start of each new topic e.g. through class quizzes.'

The challenge of managing high-stakes public summative assessments during Covid-19 was highly controversial and, in any case, is outside teacher's control as it is a responsibility of national leaders. Examples of what happened are included in Chapter 4.

Specific challenges: for curriculum and assessment

This section focuses on four specific challenges teachers faced with respect to curriculum and assessment. A fifth challenge – pedagogies for remote teaching and catch up – is covered in Chapters 8 and 9.

* Motivating learners
* Access to resources
* Curriculum content: what can be covered and what has to be cut
* Assessment and feedback.

Chapter 4, school leadership, considers school level issues such as: infrastructure (for out-of-school learning), monitoring (of learning and teacher workload), inclusion (of marginalised learners and any special cases) and funding (to support the changes, including additional health and safety measures).

Specific challenge 7.1 Motivating learners

Without motivation, education stops.

In secondary schools, student motivation generally comes from a desire to please the teacher, avoid punishment and achieve good examination grades. Younger adolescents are less under the influence of their parents than they were at primary school but have yet to reach an age where material concerns, such as achieving the entry requirements for further or higher education or to access preferred career paths, are likely to have much influence. By early adolescence, pupils are naturally more resistant to the influence of parent or teacher authority figures but usually still too young to explicitly make the connection between their educational success and success in the adult world.

This creates a significant *motivation deficit* in early adolescence with which all secondary teachers are familiar, but in a situation where education can only happen remotely the effect is amplified. Students are thrown back into the home environment at an age when they are just starting to seek new experiences beyond it, and this often breeds resentment which manifests itself in a resistance to education. In the case of marginalised or disadvantaged pupils, this effect is likely to be amplified even further, leading to a potentially debilitating motivation deficit and a complete disengagement from education.

Whilst primary age pupils, encouraged by their class teacher and parents, may initially be excited by the novelty of homeschooling, over longer periods of time the motivation to learn remotely can begin to wane. This could be for a number of reasons: they do not see the adults at home as having the same authority over their learning as their teachers; there is a lack of peer pressure to conform and ensure that children are presenting their best work; or anxiety regarding wider world events, which in some cases can completely hinder any attempts to encourage children to engage. Additionally, as primary pupils cannot be as autonomous in their learning as secondary pupils, schools also need to be concerned with parental motivation. Those parents who initially rise to the challenge, attempting to support their children and work from home, may find themselves burnt out after a couple of weeks and require support from school staff to persevere, whilst others may not have the skills necessary to help their children or may not value education sufficiently (perhaps after their own negative experiences) to begin homeschooling in the first place.

Whether primary or secondary pupils, it is vital this motivation deficit is overcome if marginalised students are not to suffer from a serious if not permanent learning loss, but recent evidence suggests national policymakers are far more likely to concentrate on questions of curriculum content or methods of delivery and simply devolve responsibility for motivating students to individual schools and teachers who have limited tools at their disposal in a remote-learning situation.

Therefore, when remote learning is required, greater thought must be given as to how to motivate pupils to continue to engage with their education; this is particularly true with younger secondary age and more marginalised pupils. Strategies designed to motivate pupils in a remote situation are often considered a problem for teachers or schools rather than policymakers, but recent experience suggests that this is not enough. Without assistance at a regional or national level, schools and teachers are often dependent on the willingness and ability of parents and carers to take on much greater responsibility for motivating their children to carry on learning and invariably, the most marginalised and disadvantaged families are most ill-equipped to do so.

Ways of motivating include:

Financial or material rewards

Confirmed and/or sustained engagement could lead to additional child benefit or shopping vouchers which would simultaneously boost economic activity and motivate parents to support their children. In effect, these material rewards could simply be transferred directly to parents but made contingent on their children continuing to engage fully with their education.

Controls or punishments

Consequences, such as further intervention by local officers could also act as a control, particularly with more vulnerable families. In effect, in England this may happen anyway, but it isn't always explicitly linked to continued engagement in education and may be more often triggered by safeguarding concerns. At a local level, systems could be developed whereby children were required to engage with core questions for the week or be marked absent with concerns reported to (in England) the school's Educational Welfare Officer or pupil marked as 'missing' on local authority pupil attendance returns. England also has a system of fining parents if pupils are absent without an acceptable reason.

In order to reduce or eliminate the motivation deficit, particularly for marginalised pupils, governments need to consider how to institute a national system of remote registration and educational engagement, probably through a combination of online and school-based reporting systems. There are potential issues with legal challenges to such a system, but for many years in England, an Education Maintenance Allowance was used in a similar way to encourage post-16 Education Maintenance Allowance students to stay in education and it worked reasonably well. At the very least a national mechanism for the remote tracking and delivery of rewards and controls would assist schools in addressing the motivation deficit.

However, given the very short timescales that might be involved in setting up remote-learning systems in response to a crisis or emergency and the long period of time it might take to set up a national attendance and engagement tracking system linked to rewards and controls, planning needs to happen well in advance if keeping students motivated is to be possible.

Fortunately, there are many good reasons why such a system would raise standards in education even in normal times and help reduce the achievement gap between disadvantaged and marginalised students and others. For example, the system could be applied formally to excluded students or those who are absent for long periods of time whether because of illness or other reasons. It could also be applied to the many thousands of students who are home-educated. A national virtual school could bring this under its umbrella in much the same way as virtual schools operate on a local level already.

Specific challenge 7.2 Access to resources

Schools normally provide the resources and opportunities for students to access learning resources, but in a remote learning/home location, students are dependent on their parents for this access. Unfortunately, in practice, as mentioned earlier, some parents either cannot or do not provide these resources for their children (particular problems may be faced as a result of parents needing to work from home and requiring the use of the household's technology provision), and difficult home circumstances for marginalised students may reduce or preclude altogether the opportunity to learn effectively and access the resources needed to continue education remotely when required to do so.

For example, students may lack or share access to study resources including digital devices and quiet study areas. Marginalised students in particular may also lack sufficient access to time at home or be unable to access learning at particular times of the day because of other domestic responsibilities they have to undertake, such as looking after younger siblings or attending to household duties, especially when parents are themselves under significant additional strain.

Marginalised or disadvantaged students were found to be significantly more likely to be absent from school for a variety of reasons including sickness, exclusion, safeguarding concerns and carer responsibilities, all of which add up to a significant learning loss over time. Responsibility for maximising attendance is often devolved to schools which may even be held accountable against national benchmarks, but little attention is given to the quality of learning provided when students are absent, and it is rare for schools to have a comprehensive strategy to address this issue. Typically, in the case of absences, work is sent home several days into the absence if at all (with the exception of exclusion in England, where there is a statutory duty to provide it immediately), and because teachers are incredibly hard pressed with other matters, it tends to take the form of an unplanned collection of worksheets and directions to access websites or learning apps. The work may be uninspiring and invariably isn't followed up or even seen by teachers when the student returns. Unsurprisingly, it is usually done badly at best.

Furthermore, there is considerable evidence of learning loss amongst marginalised students during holidays, particularly the long summer holidays typical in most countries. Various schemes to rearrange holiday patterns, for example, by spreading holidays out more evenly across the year, are unpopular with teachers and students and may lead to recruitment and retention issues. Advantaged students tend to continue learning through holiday times, albeit more informally, through their day-to-day exposure to language-rich environments and a more education-ally stimulating home environment. They are also more likely to travel widely and participate in extracurricular activities, such as camps and other organised activities, and less likely to become involved in antisocial behaviour.

Specific challenge 7.3 Curriculum content: what can be covered and what has to be cut

It might seem that in countries or states where a prescribed curriculum exists, content is predetermined, which makes the matter of what to learn remotely fairly straightfor-ward, but for a variety of reasons this is not the case:

Firstly, schools and individual teachers can retain a great deal of autonomy over when topics are taught and in what form. This means that national online content platforms are often of limited value in practice unless they are highly flexible and can be easily tailored to individual circumstances. Teachers may find that, having covered certain topics in a particular way, it would be confusing for students to switch to a generic online platform where a different emphasis was placed on certain ideas and concepts that students were not familiar with. In other words, they are familiar with the topic as it was taught by their own teacher but not so much when taught by another.

The lack of transferability of content which is taught out of context discourages teachers from directing younger or less confident learners to generic platforms unless they have been fully integrated into the learning process from the start. This is not to say that some students are not capable of learning from different sources, but only their teachers know the extent to which they can do so effectively. Older and more confident students are less likely to have this problem, but it will be common amongst marginalised younger adolescent students and primary school pupils.

A simple illustration of this can be given by reference to the teaching of a com-mon topic in the English history curriculum. When teaching the First World War (1914–1918) it is possible that the teacher had focused on the experience of war from the perspective of certain individuals – as opposed to taking a broader politi-cal or military overview – as a technique to engage less able students because the human element might interest those with relatively little background knowledge or a narrower vocabulary. Then imagine that students were required to access nationally designed resources on the same topic which were focused more heavily on political and military events. They might be bored or confused by the sudden presentation of new concepts and terminology or lack the skills or determination to work their way through the new material with the result that they became quickly disengaged. The point here is that learning for both primary and secondary aged students is often quite specific to the context in which they learned it, and this is typical for novice learners. Suddenly switching to a different content base does not always work, particularly for less able or more marginalised learners.

Specific challenge 7.4 Assessment and feedback

Without feedback or effective assessment, remote learning is unlikely to motivate students or have much of an impact, but this aspect of learning is particularly problematic for several reasons.

Firstly, unless there is a common process for submitting work, teachers may be faced with work in a variety of forms ranging from simple word files through to photos, videos and PDF documents amongst others. Some methods of submission may be compatible with access to certain types of hardware or software which neither the teacher nor student share.

Secondly, different forms of submission lend themselves to different forms of feedback which may be more or less suitable depending on the subject, level or task undertaken. For example, automated feedback via apps or interactive tools are ideal for remote learning but they are less well-suited to more complex text-heavy work where subjective overall judgements play a significant part.

Consequently, mathematics and science lend themselves well to automated feedback, particularly at primary and lower secondary level, while many elements of English or history, such as essay writing, do not. Given the obvious advantages of automated feedback for students learning remotely, in terms of access, accuracy, immediacy and improving students motivation, there is a danger that these parts of the curriculum receive greater emphasis, and although for some learners this may even be desirable, especially if they are relatively weaker in these subjects, overall it would not lead to a balanced curriculum.

Fortunately, automated feedback for more subjective subjects is improving. For instance, there are many well-developed tools for assessing reading comprehension online, and although not yet commonly used in primary and secondary education, there are several systems that can assess pieces of specialist writing. Nevertheless, problems with non-automated remote assessment means that, for most teachers, it continues to be much more time-consuming than more traditional methods of marking, making it unsustainable for a long period of time.

Assuming an average class size of 30, it is not uncommon for a secondary school teacher to teach in excess of 350 students in any given week, sometimes more. If each student wrote an essay every two weeks that could potentially mean 700 essays to mark, all submitted in different formats. Even assuming a perfunctory 10 minutes to mark each one, that amounts to approximately 116 hours of marking *after* lessons have been planned or an eye-watering 8 hours of marking a day in a continuous and indefinite loop, on top of time spent teaching. Spending half this time marking would be unsustainable for most teachers, especially if they were also caring for children of their own, which is often the case given the numbers of women working in education and the fact that these domestic duties still fall disproportionately on women. This amount of marking is simply unsustainable.

In primary schools, this would also be problematic with a daily timetable of at least five different subjects. However, there are a number of online platforms available (more than 50 according to a TES survey www.tes.com/news/revealed-50-plus-online-platforms-used-schools carried out while UK schools were still in lockdown) that, along with parental buy-in, allow teachers a little more control in how work is returned. Additionally, the development of self-marking strategies through the use of success criteria, taught from the beginning of primary schooling and in which pupils are very well practised as they need to be able to effectively self-edit their work (in preparation for moderation of teacher assessments), can make the marking of extended activities easier, although still very time consuming.

Teachers and automated assessment

The result is that, without effective automated assessment systems, teachers using remote learning may simply prefer to set tasks that are easily assessed. While this might be acceptable in the short term, it is clearly not good for anything more than a few weeks. At best it narrows the curriculum, at worst it lowers expectations and standards. For example, it might be tempting for teachers to solely set work that requires short response or factual recall, especially if students find this work easier and complete it more often than other types of work. Teachers may take the view that some form of engagement is better than no engagement at all, encouraging them to set tasks they know have a good chance of being completed rather than ones that are more challenging and likely to stretch their students. The object of remote learning can simply become a matter of compliance, where teachers and students claim engagement is happening, but in practice, little is being learned. A curriculum for appearances is not an effective teaching strategy.

Instead, teachers leading remote learning must become directors of assessment strategy rather than assessors in their own right. It is perfectly feasible for teachers to look at and interpret scores or feedback data remotely and intervene more directly where required; indeed this is where the professional expertise of the teacher and their personal knowledge of the student becomes most important. To reach that point, governments need to invest in making highly effective automated assessment systems that are easily accessible to school staff in all subjects and at all levels.

This is far more important than developing vast content libraries or banks of generic online lessons and far more sustainable and effective over time. If teachers in a remote situation can assess effectively, they can teach effectively and have the greatest potential impact on their students. The potential impact of automated assessment systems for enhancing the effectiveness of remote learning is so significant that their further development should not be left to chance. It is no exaggeration to say that if effective automated assessment systems were available to all teachers at all levels, the quality of remote learning in education would be transformed.

Lessons learned: curriculum and assessment

7.1 Motivating learners: Futurecasters need to plan for models of curricula and assessment for remote learning which take account of motivation challenges. Ideas about motivating learners appear in the preceding and in Chapter 8 on creative pedagogies.

7.2 Access to resources: marginalised regions and marginalised learners. If governments wish to close the achievement gap between disadvantaged and marginalised children and others, the learning loss that takes place during periods of disruption of an individual's schooling must be minimised – one effective way to do that is to maintain some form of remote learning. However, that can only be possible if access issues are overcome, and attention will need to be paid to teacher workload if teachers are to provide this.

An effective strategy to reduce or eliminate access issues would have the twin benefit of reducing the achievement gap between marginalised or disadvantaged students and others whilst also ensuring that effective education for all continued in times of disruption in the lives of individual learners, in a national emergency or when individual school closure is required.

The ICET/MESHGuides research (2020) with teachers across 30 countries showed that in all countries there are areas of lack of access to online resources. A more global approach to sharing learning resources and knowledge management tools can be expected to be cost effective. It would be of global benefit for low- and medium-income countries, including small national states, to combine with others to pool resources to develop sustainable remote-learning systems.

There is a great deal that national and regional policymakers can do to help students, particularly marginalised students overcome most or all of these access issues, but they will only be effective if they are built into normal practice for remote learning rather than introduced hastily in response to an emergency or crisis:

Access can be overcome to an extent by:

- making technology devices free to the most deprived students including laptops, routers and headphones (to shut out extrinsic noise);
- making technology resources affordable for more families, for example by offering interest free loans, or tax relief schemes for those who may want to purchase their own devices to support learning outside of school;
- ensuring that learning resources can be flexibly accessed (i.e. at different times) to enable those under pressure at home to build their learning routines around domestic circumstances.

The time required to procure free or low-cost digital devices for marginalised students in response to an emergency may be too long to avoid a significant learning loss. Even a period of one to two months is too long to avoid a large gap emerging between the learning of those with and without access to resources. However, once again, there are many reasons why a coordinated long-term strategy to eliminate access issues for remote learning will also raise standards overall and reduce the achievement gap.

7.3 Cutting curriculum content and design of online content for remote teaching: Remote learning and teaching are not the same as classroom-based learning and teaching. Curricula and the accompanying assessment need to be adapted to the time and resources and local context of the teacher and the learner. Chapter 8 includes creative solutions through adaptive pedagogies.

National governments or commercial providers may take great pride in constructing vast online content platforms only to find they are accessed sporadically or to little effect. They may also find that teachers lack familiarity with the platforms, especially if there are competing versions, and consequently make limited or no use of them. Furthermore, teacher autonomy over content production is more important to their own motivation than might be supposed by well-meaning content providers, and for many teachers, the creative part of designing lessons and resources is one of the most enjoyable parts of the job, which means they might be resistant to these platforms irrespective of how well designed they are.

These problems mean that simply providing content online, however well designed that content might be, will not in and of itself ensure that effective remote education is continued in an emergency, particularly for marginalised primary age and younger adolescent learners. Such approaches fail to understand – or take a rather simplistic view – of the importance of the relationship between teacher and the primary and secondary aged student in directing learning. Context is all important and unless there is a sufficient match between that and the content presented, content platforms will have a limited impact.

However, if teachers are familiar with online content and frequently make use of it in their everyday teaching, this problem is likely to be less. It might therefore be argued that this content familiarity would be more likely if there were only one online content platform but that is unlikely in a liberal democracy with free access to information.

Governments in countries where the commercial sector is well developed are perhaps better to focus their attention on solving more intractable access and motivational issues and leaving the selection of content platforms to schools and teachers. In other countries, the challenge of supportive online materials which enable progression in learning will need to be addressed as part of national planning for continuity of education.

7.4 Assessment: Specific challenge 4.2 outlined some of the challenges with public assessment in different countries during the Covid-19 period. Remote learning requires adapted assessment procedures for different subjects and the suggestion made in this chapter is that national investment in 'effective automated assessment systems' could bring benefits to teachers and to students in non-crisis times as well as during times of crisis.

Planning toolkit: curriculum and assessment

Table 7.1 provides examples of questions to guide your planning and solutions that other educators have used. You will need to adapt and add to this toolkit to suit your circumstances and context.

Table 7.1 Planning toolkit: curriculum and assessment decisions to be made for implementing emergency remote teaching

Decision 7.1 Motivating learners for out-of-school lessons	
Questions to resolve	Examples: How will you motivate learners, particularly marginalised learners, to engage with your programme for continuity of learning and assessment? What rewards can you and the local community offer? What financial or material rewards, or controls or punishments can you operate?
Solutions	Examples to consider: see Specific challenge 7.1.
Decision 7.2 Accessing resources	
Questions to resolve	Examples: Have you the resources in your school/organisation to support your plans for continuity of curriculum and assessment ? How can leaders and teachers ensure access to resources for marginalised learners? Can teachers harness potential new resources that may be available in home education settings (e.g. family history stories, specialist knowledge and hobbies of parents or grandparents).

(Continued)

Table 7.1 (Cont).

Solutions	Examples: Supplying technology devices (laptops) and routers (connectivity to the internet) to marginalised learners; this is particularly important to disadvantaged families living in deprived communities and areas of socio-economic deprivation. Providing print-based resources as an alternative. Offline learning for students in low-, medium- and high-income countries was solved by staff physically delivering packs of paper resources. A UK primary school reported 'this had a massively positive effect on well-being and relationships'.

Decision 7.3 Curriculum content

Questions to resolve	Examples: What in the planned curriculum can still be covered? What can't be covered? How can the human and material resources in the environment local to learners be harnessed for teaching? What pedagogies will help learning and motivation yet ensure the learning planned is accessible to all? How might catch-up be planned for and managed? What would a recovery curriculum need to cover once schools reopen?
Solutions	Examples: Focus on core learning; this may include creativity in pedagogical approaches. For example, particular pedagogical approaches may make the most of the local environment and can make home-learning more impactful and more inclusive through using intergenerational teaching with the help of grandparents. For primary schools: review the curriculum for each year group. For secondary schools: each subject department will need to make decisions for each year group.

Decision 7.4 Assessment

Questions to resolve	Examples: What adjustments to assessment requirements may need to be made? What localised adjustments are required from teachers for formative and summative assessment? What national adjustments are required from public examination bodies? Is it possible to ensure robust systems for equity? Accrediting informal learning: what different forms of assessment might be employed during the crisis to accredit informal learning/intergenerational learning (e.g. pupil diaries – written, audio or video), online show-and-tell, performances and so on. What, if any, formative and what summative assessment is essential for informal learning? When should it be carried out and by whom? How can you involve those at home in any necessary assessments? Have you considered whether the potential stress of assessment is worthwhile? How can you assure fairness in assessment tests?
Solutions	Examples: When schools reopen and a recovery curriculum is put in place: Catch-up through diagnostic tests followed by targeted interventions need to be planned for. A fundamental part of any continuity plan for education is how online and remote-learning pedagogies might recognise and validate achievement in different forms through forms of evaluation and assessment that have a closer fit with the principles of online learning and pedagogies that use the home environment.

(Continued)

Table 7.1 (Cont).

Decision 7.5 Special cases: children falling behind and becoming marginalised with respect to their learning

Questions to resolve	Examples: In your plans, what children will experience difficulties in continuing to learn? Are individual solutions needed in some cases?
Solutions	Examples: One school reported identifying children working significantly below the expected level for their age group. To support home learning, they were provided whole sets of work at their level and parents were invited in to meet (adhering to social distancing) with their dyscalculia and dyslexia specialist teachers to show them activities that could be used. Differentiation can also be achieved through the use of some online personalised learning programmes for some subjects (e.g. the SAM Learning (2020) approach to many subjects).

Futurecasting: for curriculum and assessment

The questions in the preceding toolkit outline areas for your consideration when forecasting and planning for contingencies, so that, as much as it is possible, you can ensure continuity of learning. However, although Covid-19 is a global pandemic, what works in education during a pandemic in one context, region or country may not work in another.

Having agreement on a common core curriculum and taking steps to make sure assessment systems can operate fairly are two core elements of any future planning on curriculum and assessment. Allowing flexibility for local education emergency response committees for school neighbourhoods may help the utilisation of local resources which can support continuity of learning.

As mentioned in Chapter 1, it is not possible to future-proof your system because you do not know what the future will bring, but should a crisis emerge and schooling temporarily stops, parents and teachers will at least know what the core knowledge, skills, attitudes and concepts are for your curriculum. So, with respect to curriculum and assessment the futurecasting process helps you prepare for crises by guiding you to:

* identify and understand key aspects of curriculum and assessment which need to be adapted during crises;
* create multiple 'what if' scenarios of plausible futures for delivering the curriculum and undertaking assessment.

Decide on the most relevant scenarios and develop strategies to act on them developing contingency plans around curriculum and assessment and the deployment of human and material resources to support continuity of learning.

Notes

1 Plutarch (translated by F. C. Babbitt, 1927) *Moralia*. New York: Loeb Classical Library. Vol. I, pp. 201–259. http://penelope.uchicago.edu/Thayer/E/Roman/Texts/Plutarch/Moralia/De_auditu*.html
2 NSW School closures. https://education.nsw.gov.au/public-schools/school-safety
3 UK one in 80 have Covid. www.youtube.com/watch?v=b5zh7dO9s4s

Crisis-resilient creative pedagogies

When school stops, learning must not[1]

 Introduction and context

In response to school closures during the pandemic, pedagogical approaches – the practices of teachers leading to learning – had to be adapted rapidly for remote/home learning. Millions of children stopped going to school.

> *More than nine in ten students worldwide have been affected by school closures prompted by the COVID-19 pandemic.[2] The profound impact on so many millions of young lives is difficult to comprehend, and the potential disruption to learning risks holding back a generation.*

> (Shrestha and Lal 2020)

This chapter reports pedagogies with accompanying learning activities which teachers found effective and ineffective in adapting teaching to what was called 'the new normal' of remote teaching during the Covid-19 period. Examples of teachers' creative pedagogies not requiring face-to-face delivery are included together with approaches which didn't work. The challenges of remote teaching and parents' obligations to undertake homeschooling are considered.

Before Covid, across the teaching profession worldwide, there were teachers fully aware and practicing remote teaching with and without digital technologies. Canada's Telephone School[3] and Australia's virtual Schools of the Air[4] provide examples. Blended learning using resources in school's individual learning environments was well understood in schools that had embraced the educational technologies available since the 1980s with pedagogical practices being well developed if not widely known. (Younie and Leask 2015, 2019; Leask and Pachler 2013).

However, some teachers reported they had not even used email before the Covid pandemic but were suddenly expected to teach online.

DOI: 10.4324/9781003155591-12

The speed of upskilling, over days and weeks, of large numbers of teachers across low-, middle- and high-income countries into completely new ways of working, worldwide, has produced a pedagogic revolution.

This step change in online pedagogy understanding and experience has the potential to provide positive improvements in learning outcomes for all *if* teachers can be supported with digital infrastructure and open access to high-quality resources (Chapter 11 outlines solutions).

Overall challenge: a mandated pedagogic revolution

This chapter discusses how teachers responded to the need for new pedagogies brought by what was in many countries a mandated revolution: teachers were required to move from face-to-face to remote teaching both paper-based, community-based (using community notice/blackboards), telephone/SMS, radio and TV and online. Chapter 9 is devoted to an examination of broader issues around the adoption of digital technologies.

Rapid knowledge-sharing of pedagogies within and across schools was reported as a positive outcome of the need for teachers to adapt. Peer challenge through discussion and collaborative problem solving was reported as providing a fertile ground for innovation with failure being acceptable and seen as a natural part of learning due to the pressure from the crisis (ICET/MESHGuides 2020). In addition, knowledge-sharing internationally took place as NGOs and UN agencies held webinar events. These brought together educators with different perspectives to share knowledge and experiences. During these discussions, many similarities emerged between participating countries – whether low-, medium- or high-income.

Overall, remote teaching took many forms – radio, TV, telephone, SMS, printed materials, online or other media.

Specific challenges: in doing education differently

The following specific challenges are addressed in this chapter:

* Teacher Workload
* Modes of remote learning: using traditional media
* Homeschooling/home-education and marginalised learners
* Access to learning devices at home – knowing what your learners can use
* Politicians' understanding of learning needs

* Creative pedagogies for motivation and achievable learning – adapting curriculum and assessment
* Flexible pedagogies – synchronous and asynchronous learning
* Organising remote learning for primary and secondary school students.

Specific challenge 8.1 Teacher workload

There is a danger that this chapter will set an unjustifiably positive tone.

Spec (2020) reports potential burn-out of teachers through the effort that has been put into transferring traditional materials into remote online schooling environments (and the requirement in some schools that teachers and children sit at a computer all day).

Senior leaders and teachers reported working 12- to 16-hour days to prepare learning materials – online and paper-based for the remote lessons – and to ensure a rapid response to changing conditions. Reports included teachers being required to supervise learning activities in their classroom and remotely, simultaneously. Further to this, the ongoing monitoring and assessing of learning of all students was required to be undertaken remotely.

The different devices learners used to access online learning added further challenges. School surveys of what devices learners could access for remote learning showed some could handle video easily, some not.

Much of the work reported in this book was undertaken by teachers working at home, while caring for their own children, elderly relatives and neighbours and with family, friends and colleagues ill, dying or disabled from the virus. Some teachers reported they could only be in touch with families late at night when parents were home, some students could only be online when no one else in the family wanted the device.

In some cases, some individual teachers and schools went to extraordinary lengths to keep marginalised learners engaged – delivering food and food vouchers, organising laptops and dongles for internet connection, keeping schools open for vulnerable children while also teaching online and producing paper resource packs for others, with regular telephone and SMS contact, personally paying for resources and leaving these at local corner stores for collection. One special needs teacher hired an open truck and took what was effectively a mobile school to young people. In other cases, communities found themselves without any teachers as the teachers returned to their home villages at the beginning of the pandemic.

Specific challenge 8.2 Modes of remote learning and filling gaps

National governments addressed the challenge of remote teaching in different ways. In some, teachers reported governments in paralysis, leaving teachers to cope as best they could. In others, governments stepped into a leadership role working with teachers to harness the power of the traditional media of radio and TV as these were accessible to more families than any other media. Radio (including solar-powered radio) was harnessed, reportedly to good effect, in reaching learners in Mexico and Pakistan. Educators from New Zealand, Mexico and Portugal reported a positive lead from government in the use of television. At the UNESCO's Mobile Learning week (online, 12–15th October 2020) the Ghanaian and German online initiatives were showcased. The existing international European SchoolNet as well as Dutch, South Korean, Australian, Scottish and Chinese national initiatives provided useful online support for teachers. Teachers where internet is missing or unreliable also reported the usefulness of tools which download web resources for offline use for distribution via memory sticks. Chapter 9 provides more detail.

Teachers reported models of remote teaching which fall roughly into three types:

* Type 1: individual or small group remote-learning provision
* Type 2: school-supported whole class synchronous or asynchronous online provision
* Type 3: commercial/NGO/charity/professional association providers, offering synchronous or asynchronous learning. These were a mix of free and private providers, for example, national media providers, BBC or paid-for-services, subscription channels.

Teachers reported a wide range of ways were used to engage with parents and that there was a dramatic shift in relationships between parents and schools and parents' roles in teaching. For those who were normally reluctant to come to school, there were examples from low-, medium- and high-income countries where teachers met parents and children within their world, meeting near to their home, in their community, delivering prepared learning materials and food, and being in touch by telephone (see Table 8.1 for a case study from India written at the height of the pandemic in 2020).

Table 8.1 Case Study of an intervention to support learning in rural India: stories-on-the-phone (with thanks to Jwalin Patel)

This case study examines a non-internet based intervention in rural India.

In India, online synchronous learning is impeded due to limited access to internet communication technologies (ranging from absence of smart phones, limited data packs to a single digital device shared between multiple children). Several interventions have been developed to counter these, including those that leverage SMSs, telephonic calls, radio and TV channels.

The Indian government has rolled out academic content over multiple TV channels, all India radio and an app-based platform named Diksha. Pratham, a large-scale NGO, has developed an interactive voice response storytelling system, a series of SMS and WhatsApp based activities, radio broadcast programmes and community-based educational activities that engage parents and students in the educational process. These materials are available in 20 languages. The Muktangan Education trust and Prabhat Foundation which work with students with special needs have designed flashcards and educational materials which are shared over WhatsApp and/or short video calls with parents.

Meanwhile, several interventions have tried to adapt approaches that aren't as technologically intensive; for example, the NGO TIDE (Together in Development and Education) Foundation has developed graphical/visual, self-directed learning materials. Additionally, several villages play educational programmes on temple loudspeakers. Notably, a group of teachers have set up *vali-shalas* (parent-run mini-schools), whereby the teachers support parents to run mini-classes with students who maintain social distance.

With schools shut and limited technology accessibility (no smart phones and no internet), Balaji Jadhav from ZP School Vijayanagar, Mahrashtra, set-up a conference calling system for small groups of grade 1, 2, 3 and 4 students. Since March, he has been calling students in the mornings and evenings (before and after parents come back from work).

The intervention is divided into six phases which include ice-breaking activities, story-listening, story-telling, story-writing and story-recording sessions. He also converts academic content such as language, science, mathematics and social science into short stories, which is an excellent example of a teacher acting as a facilitator of learning by reaching out to students in a way that makes their learning more accessible and equitable.

Additionally, he prompted students to narrate the stories to their parents leading to a stronger buy-in from parents. To support and track student learning, he conducts weekly home visits and drops off postcards at every child's home and asks them to write him a letter a week summarising concepts they learnt. For more details visit his website www.shikshanbhakti.in

The detail of the intervention is as follows:

* Icebreaking (10 days) – he discussed topics across a wide range of interest areas to engage students
* Story listening (10 days) – he narrated short stories with pauses where he asked questions and paused for comments
* Story telling (10 days) – evening sessions were dedicated for students to narrate stories from the previous sessions or one they made

* Story writing (10 days) – he asked students to write a short summary which he reviewed during his weekly home visits
* Story recording (10 days) – he supported students as they recorded stories on their phones (and collected them via Bluetooth transfer)
* Academic content as stories – he converted language, science, mathematics and social science content into short stories.

We also had reports that none of these strategies worked in some cases so that some children just dropped out of learning altogether.

No single pattern has emerged as suiting all situations. Localised responses were the norm. The challenges teachers and schools faced depend on their localised context and their pupil intake – was it rural/urban, affluent/deprived, large ethnic minority and/or additional language needs, or high percentages of SEN? The learning needs of each particular school intake required nuanced responses to meet their learning needs. Online teaching was reported in as universal in private schools in high- and low-income countries as learners tended to come from families affluent enough to pay for devices and internet connection.

At the time of writing, December 2020, some students in a number of low- and high-income countries had lost nearly a year or more of face-to-face teaching because of the natural disasters in 2019 and 2020 of flood, fire and earthquake and war as well as the Covid-19 pandemic. Successive waves of the virus caused opening and closing, then reopening and closing of schools in many countries. Notable exceptions in the latter part of 2020 were Taiwan, New Zealand, Australia and many islands in different parts of the world.

Specific challenge 8.3 Homeschooling/home education and marginalised learners

Many parents took on the challenge of 'homeschooling'. The terms homeschooling and home education are often used quite interchangeably as there is no agreed upon or definitive distinction between the two terms. However, Devitt (2018), writing on the website www.howdoihomeschool.com, offers the following observation about the terms.

What is homeschooling? Is it simply school at home or is there more to it than that? If you are asking these questions, you are not alone as the definition is murky due to the variety of methods with which a child can be educated at home. While many parents employ the traditional method that mimics the public school setup, others employ a more flexible and natural way of learning.

This reflects the experience of many parents across countries during the Covid-19 lockdown, with some children experiencing school replicated within the home, other children experiencing a rich diversity of both formal and informal learning experiences and some children having no education at all.

Press in the UK reported that during the initial period of school closures due to the pandemic, parents found a home*schooling* pedagogy (highly structured, formal learning) to be more of a challenge than a home-*educating* pedagogy (more flexible, spontaneous and informal learning) (see also Jeffs and Smith 2011). Parents and their children had previously demonstrated that they could be highly innovative, imaginative and creative at seeing opportunities for intergenerational, informal learning both online and at home (Morton 2010). However, during the Covid-19 period, this was not consistently true for every household and many children in low-, medium- and high-income countries did not enjoy either the support and encouragement from parents or other members of their family or access to continued learning provision. This was particularly the case for young adolescents whose motivation is not always intrinsic (internally self-motivated). With little teachers' direct interaction there was no extrinsic motivation (external rewards and drivers) to learn. For disadvantaged and disengaged students this situation may have exacerbated their marginalisation. VSO case studies of marginalised learners in Myanmar, Nigeria and Uganda (VSO 2020a, b, c) showed that some children went to work in the fields once schools closed but in other settings in low-income countries, older children and parents took on responsibility for teaching groups of children (microteaching).

Teacher reports showed there was little or no consensus on what pedagogy is best suited for remote or online learning for children. The Education Endowment Foundation (EEF 2020a) published a Rapid Evidence Assessment: Distance Learning document that examined the existing research (from 60 systematic reviews and meta-analyses) for approaches that schools could use, or were already using, to support the learning of pupils while schools were closed due to Covid-19, but the findings would require further interpretation to be applicable to parents working in a homeschooling environment.

Specific challenge 8.4 Access to learning devices at home – knowing what your learners can use

Schools needed to survey students to identify who had access at home to telephone, radio, TV, internet and when, if at all, children could access these devices. The results of such a survey then had to be used to group the children by the mode of teaching and learning suitable to their circumstances.

As mentioned not all pupils had access to a technology device that could be used to receive, respond to, create or modify learning materials for individual and/or collaborative use. In multi-generational and large households, teachers reported that children found that other family members had priority over them in accessing and using the devices to support learning. The research data suggest that where governments pushed for online learning, the children most in need in any country were marginalised: they were least likely to have internet access and most likely to need high levels of support to achieve success in education (World Economic Forum 2020).

Some creative solutions were found which could be replicated elsewhere: as well as those already mentioned, we heard reports of activities being available through dialling into specific telephone numbers (India) and teachers recording themselves reading stories to children.

Specific challenge 8.5 Politicians' answers to schools' challenges

There is a limit to what schools can do alone. In some countries, governments and NGOs stepped in to provide support for students and teachers. In some countries such need to provide materials in many languages provided additional challenges.

Across countries included in the research there was been discussion about whether politicians should have an educational background in order to be able to make workable decisions. The USA's Teach to Lead programme is seen as a good example of how teachers and politicians can work together and achieve workable outcomes (O'Meara 2020). National direction of the education system by non-educators in ministries for the most part brought derision. Teachers found they had to move from traditional classroom-based methods sometimes, as mandated by politicians, to quite different remote-learning pedagogies, and then as schools opened and closed again during local outbreaks, had to be able to flip between modes to ensure continuity of learning and assessment for all children. In some countries, governments changed public assessment requirements or curriculum coverage requirements to accommodate interrupted schooling, in others, the same requirements were set.

Schools looked for national leadership but teacher leaders reported that the level of detail schools had to consider in adopting new pedagogies for remote schooling was not understood by politicians in charge of national education systems who had no background in education. Unless they accessed expert respected advice, these politicians caused chaos or, as some teachers reported, appeared paralysed. Table 8.2 outlines some of the decisions schools had to take; the Annexes provide more detail.

Table 8.2 Pedagogical decisions for Emergency Remote Teaching

Schools had to adapt their Education Emergency Plans to accommodate the different pedagogical approaches required when switching back and forth from face to face to remote teaching as schools opened and closed. The following list outlines some of the issues they had to consider:

* Was there a shared definition and understanding of the pedagogical model to be implemented?
* Had all stakeholders, such as teachers, learners and parents/carers, been consulted and contributed to any adopted pedagogies for online/remote learning?
* Was 'free-choice learning ' suitable – where children work on substantial projects on issues of their choice, which are particularly relevant to what they wish to learn about (Falk and Dierking 2002; Dierking 2005)?
* Were intergenerational pedagogies appropriate?
* What training was needed so that teachers could deliver alternative pedagogies in different learning environments, incorporating learner-centred and learner-initiated approaches, project-based learning, intergenerational learning, including cross-curricular family-based learning projects?
* What training was needed for teachers regarding differentiation of volume of work and levels of challenge according to the needs and abilities of individual learners?
* Was there sufficient up-skilling of teachers, including the use of the range of digital technologies and multiple platforms that teachers identified as workable in a local context?
* Were there sufficient checks and balances that commercially available materials, especially those which use a sit-and-follow pedagogical approach to learning, would work for all learners rather than only work for some learners with a certain level of skill, knowledge and support?
* Had online materials been quality assured?
* Had the pedagogical model been updated in the light of research and evidence into the use of new and emerging technologies?
* Did teachers understand how to ensure progression through teaching online and remotely? Was this regularly updated to take account of advances in technology and the need for digital literacies?
* What records were teachers required to keep? What was feasible?
* How was e-safety to be managed?

Specific challenge 8.6 Creative pedagogies for motivation and achievable learning – adapting curriculum and assessment

Early decisions for educators concerned which elements of the curriculum were worth keeping, what could be trimmed and what elements of the planned learning could be experienced outside the classroom?

In some countries, teachers reported being expected to cover the curriculum as set previously with no accommodation to the needs, presence or absence of learners, thus, they felt, setting the learners up to fail. In addition, teachers expressed their fears that pressing on with the set curriculum in spite of the pandemic meant the basics might not being covered, leaving learners at a disadvantage as they progress through the system.

Lesson objectives are set around concepts, attitudes, knowledge and skills (the CASK approach to lesson planning, Capel et al. 2019) and while some curriculum objectives can be easily adapted for home-supported learning or independent learning, some cannot.

Teachers were challenged to develop pedagogies to meet the same objectives in different ways. Cross-curricular pedagogies, for example, can cover the expected learning outcomes in several subjects through one project or through thematic teaching in different subjects. See, for example, Williams in Leask and Pachler (2013) where he provides a number of examples of this form of pedagogy. For example, he describes a cross-curricular programme for lower secondary on light: in science, light is taught as content knowledge; in art, the technique of creating light in paintings is taught (concept) and practised (skill); in English, a task can be set to create a poem or story linking light with emotions and attitudes or to create a radio programme and so on. Many such activities can be undertaken as an independent learner and some schools during Covid-19 have set creative cross-curricular tasks. Others asked students to send in photographs to show them undertaking the required activities – another example of how those with access to technology gain the edge on learners from less well-off families: the disadvantaged again becoming further marginalised.

Other creative pedagogical approaches taken by schools were ones that attempted to directly involve the family in order to generate positive home-learning experiences, this included creating 'family learning projects'. This was found to be very effective with children of upper primary and lower secondary from age 10 to 14 years. Activities were scheduled across the week from Monday to Friday that encouraged all the family to become involved in the project; a theme for each project was identified, alongside which skills were developed and how these related to each curriculum subject. For example, a project on 'patterns' provided a set of resources ranging from the visual and graphic to poetry and science and encouraged all family members to participate, with older children supporting younger alongside parents and grandparents, with the added advantage that the work could be done remotely or just from the home environment if families were self-isolating due to Covid-19.

Collaborative learning with others, whether it is peers, siblings or extended family members, is known to be stimulating and engaging and highlights the value of this particular pedagogic practice. Online collaboration is the action of working with someone to produce something such as a document, presentation, spreadsheet or data or a rich media project using videos and photographs. Online collaboration for project work is a form of creative pedagogy, which encourages cooperation and dialogic learning (MESHGuides 2020b) Collaboration is a sought-after skill for learning, life and work.

Collaborative pedagogical approaches were reported as being used to support learning during the Covid-19 period, not only in the home environment but also online through, for example, individual countries' online platforms for teachers and students, such as Scotland's GlowConnect or the education platform supported by EU countries through the European SchoolNet (www.eun.org) which supports teacher-teacher collaboration across countries. Around 34 countries fund the European SchoolNet (initiated in1995, Leask and Younie 2001a, b) to support international collaboration between their teachers and learners. We received reports of the value of individual country's online environments for schools, teachers, learners and parents. These include the Netherlands, South Korea, China, Australia, Germany, Ghana. Others had these but closed them down as governmental priorities changed (World Bank 2017). Tables 8.3 and 8.4 provide examples of the provision offered by two of these services: Scotland's GlowConnect platform (https://glowconnect.org.uk/) and Australia's Scootle to their registered teachers and learners.

Table 8.3 Scotland's GlowConnect

'GlowConnect provides online Collaboration Tools (https://glowconnect.org.uk/online-collaboration-tools-in-glow/) and identifies the benefits of online collaboration as follows:

Pupil Voice: Every learner can have a voice to express themselves, can contribute to online discussions, ask questions and offer peer support.

Real time multiuser editing: Learners can collaborate on documents at the same time and see each other's changes happening in real time. These changes are also saved automatically as the user types. This allows users the ability to quickly create, share and edit documents with all changes saving in real time. Therefore, no requirement for email documents, editing and saving changes and then emailing back.

Feedback: when a document is uploaded or shared in a collaborative space online there are opportunities for teacher and peer feedback. This can happen live via chat if the users have the document open at the same time. Alternatively, comments can be inserted and responded to asynchronously.

Reaching all learners: All learners can collaborate online with access to built in accessibility tools where learners can customise the content for their own needs and requirements – for example, increasing the line spacing to prevent visual crowding, having the text read out loud, highlighting nouns, verbs and adjectives, changing the background page colour and accessing the picture dictionary by clicking on a word they don't understand. This may help dyslexic and other SEN learners who may be at risk of becoming marginalised learners, when learning remotely.

Social Media: Newsfeeds and conversation areas look like a Blog or Facebook interface which is an ideal secure environment to learn about Social Media, have discussions around online responsible use and online etiquette.

Beyond the Classroom Walls: Learning and collaboration can happen across Scotland, with all learners and educators having access to a Glow account. This opens up opportunities for joint projects between schools, including transition projects.'

(https://glowconnect.org.uk/online-collaboration-tools-in-glow/)

Table 8.4 Australia's Scootle

Here are just some examples of what this resource provides:

'Digital Technologies Hub

An open and **free** site, the Digital Technologies Hub supports Australian teachers, students and school communities to engage with the Australian Curriculum: Digital Technologies. It offers a range of resources, learning sequences, and case studies.

Student Wellbeing Hub

The Student Wellbeing Hub helps schools to build and sustain positive, respectful and supportive teaching and learning environments. The site provides a framework and resources to enhance student safety and wellbeing. It also features best-practice case studies and interviews with experts.

Browse and save resources

> Browse over 20,000 quality-assured digital learning resources aligned to the Australian Curriculum. Filter your search to uncover a wealth of relevant teaching and learning items. Bookmark resources to come back to later, and build resource collections. Organise, annotate and share your curriculum resource collections with students or colleagues by creating Learning paths'.

NGOs also stepped up to support continuity of learning when schools closed. The example in Table 8.4 is from Purna Kumar Shrestha the Education Expert Group Lead from Voluntary Services Overseas International.

Table 8.5 VSO: Examples of an NGO response to the education emergency[5]

'VSO follows a holistic approach to ensuring ongoing educational development of the most marginalised children when they cannot attend schools physically. This includes:

1 Supporting marginalised children to continue learning at home
2 Engaging families and communities in educational support and sensitisation around the protection of vulnerable groups
3 Ensuring that media used to deliver out-of-school education, such as radio and social media, are responsive the priorities of the most vulnerable groups
4 Mobilising community youth volunteers to provide accurate information about the prevention of COVID-19.

When schools were closed abruptly because of COVID-19 in Nigeria, for example, Enugu State Government started broadcasting distance education through radio programmes. VSO mobilised national and community volunteers and discovered that only one in ten families in Enugu had a radio at home. VSO community volunteers ran classes in rural communities supported by solar-powered radio. Their support included translating the English radio broadcasts and providing sign language materials.

In Malawi VSO, with support from the UK charity Onebillion and the Government of Malawi, provided tablets with apps that allowed children to learn from home. The project initially deployed 500 tablets in the Lilongwe District.'

Shrestha also organised online cultural exchange events engaging children from many countries, some of whom travelled hours to participate. For examples of creative pedagogies see his work with English-speaking children teaching English to Nepalese children through storytelling and song.[6]

So while some countries already had extensive online resources for teaching and national infrastructure to support the development and dissemination of resources to support continuity of learning, other countries had nothing. This leads us to ask the question which we will return to in the last chapter, surely there are enough governments of goodwill in the world to provide mutual support for the low-income countries, small nations and small island states which, alone, have insufficient resources to provide a comprehensive resource bank for their teachers.

One outcome of the pandemic, in response to these disparities and the loss of young people's learning due to Covid, has been the creation of a Global Education Coalition (GEC) by UNESCO.[7] The purpose of the Global Education Coalition is to support countries in scaling up their online and distance learning to reach those who are most at risk in order to support learning for all and potentially addressing marginalised learners' needs.

Specific challenge 8.7 Flexible pedagogies – synchronous and asynchronous learning

In areas where online teaching was possible, it was popularly assumed by many parents, politicians and non-educationalists that live, synchronised lessons were the best lessons, and school leaders reported they were under pressure from expectant parents to do this. In the words of one secondary headteacher: 'Some school leaders caved into this pressure rather than actually doing the best thing. Less experienced or secure leaders are more vulnerable to this pressure and there is a danger they will do things for show rather than have the courage of their convictions.' A lesson from this is that perhaps if future disaster plans spell out how continuity of learning and assessment is to be managed based on lessons from the current crises, then learners and parents could have confidence in the approaches and will know why choices are made.

There was an assumption that the closer remote teaching resembles real teaching, the more effective it is, but this is misleading. This approach tends to encourage the manifestation of teaching a curriculum for appearance's sake if schools come under pressure to deliver a full timetable of synchronous learning via live online lessons. Some schools even tried to replicate their whole timetable in this way, teaching up to five to six separate lessons a day. While this suits some students and may look impressive to parents, it is far from the panacea that some might suppose and was reported by learners, as part of this research, as extremely boring.

Problems with access to technology mean that a fully synchronous approach to remote teaching is much less likely to suit marginalised or disadvantaged learners than other learners and is therefore more likely to widen the achievement gap between the two. In independent schools, where access issues were reported as not being an issue, it may be just about possible to operate successfully this way, but for the majority of schools it is impossible to sustain an entirely synchronous programme over time even if it were educationally desirable.

There is currently little evidence that an entirely synchronous method of delivery is either desirable or effective. The Education Endowment Foundation in the UK has suggested that a blend of synchronous and asynchronous learning is probably more effective and certainly more realistic as form of remote delivery over time. The realities of teaching and learning from home mean that a degree of flexibility in terms of delivery and access are crucial to the long-term success and sustainability of a remote-learning system.

Asynchronous learning may appear superficially less effective, because as one journalist put it, 'students can't see the whites of their teachers' eyes' but that is rather misleading. Leaving aside the fact that in many forms of asynchronous teaching (e.g. recorded commentaries or lessons), students can actually see the whites of their teachers' eyes, the fact that there is no real-time interaction, while not ideal, is far from the insurmountable problem that some might believe. This is partly because, unless the class size is particularly small, there is little actual interaction in most synchronous teaching anyway. Synchronous methods of delivery were found to be most effective with small groups of reasonably committed, older teenage students but less so with larger groups of primary school pupils and young adolescents.

Asynchronous learning was found better suited to overcoming the significant access and motivational problems that are likely to act as barriers to effective remote learning. For secondary aged students because it is easier to access, particularly when they might be coping with domestic responsibilities of their own, this is not necessarily a bad thing. For example, it may suit some secondary students to start their learning later in the morning when they are wide awake, rather than attend a fixed live synchronous lesson at 9am, and they may also prefer to work in the early evening when their younger siblings are in bed. With primary age pupils, it allows parents the flexibility to plan work around their own schedule. The flexibility offered by asynchronous teaching may particularly appeal to marginalised students who have to cope with home environments that are less naturally conducive to effective learning.

Similarly, teachers working from home preferred flexible models of working that didn't necessarily match their normal working day as they themselves had young children to care for when nurseries/schools were closed or other caring responsibilities. In the case of excluded or absent individual students, asynchronous teaching is the only realistic way to deliver lessons remotely because teachers are fully occupied with teaching during the day. In other words, it is a more realistic and sustainable method of teaching remote learners in a variety of circumstances.

Although, asynchronous lacks the immediate interaction of synchronous learning it may also encourage a higher quality of delivery. This is because teachers can plan their delivery more carefully and possibly edit their lessons. They can also use the same lesson again and again, which to a certain extent mitigates against the workload problem created by the burden of effective remote learning.

Specific challenge 8.8 Organising remote learning for primary and secondary school students

Primary pupils and younger secondary aged students are not normally confident, independent learners and cannot be expected to cope alone when suddenly faced with the prospect of online study over a series of weeks or months. Whilst with remote teaching, primary pupils relied on parents to provide a schedule for the work to be completed, the lack of a physically present teacher or organised weekly timetable put a much greater responsibility on secondary aged students to organise their time than they would ever normally have at that age, and the low attendance figures reported earlier indicate a lack of success. There are lessons to be learned perhaps from Australia's School of the Air which has provided remote teaching and learning since 1953.

Primary and secondary school teachers were similarly unfamiliar with how to organise remote learning for their students, which is perhaps why so many attempted to recreate the familiarity of a traditional school timetable in the form of live synchronous lessons.

Table 8.6 outlines a case study of a primary school that illustrates their organisation of remote learning.

Table 8.6 Case Study: Organising remote learning for primary school pupils in England

This case study was reported by a senior leader of an English primary school by way of illustration of the organisation of remote learning for primary aged children.

Although school closures were not announced until Wednesday 18th March 2020, we had been anticipating that this would happen. We did not, as this point, have a school online learning platform. The week before we closed, teachers began to put together home-learning packs across a range of subjects with a focus on revision and with enough work to last the first two-week period leading up to the Easter holidays with the expectation that, after the holiday period, we would be in a position to launch online learning. We also arranged for our ICT technician to show all teachers how to use Google Drive so that they could begin to gather resources within year group folders.

As Deputy Head, I was charged with looking into our options. There were a number of systems available (more than 50 according to a TES survey carried out while UK schools were still in lockdown) such as Purple Mash, Seesaw and

Tapestry as well as Google Classrooms and Microsoft Teams: (www.tes.com/news/ revealed-50-plus-online-platforms-used-schools). We needed a system that would work for both Infant and Junior school pupils. A number of staff had positive experiences of using Class Dojo either while working in a previous school or as a parent. It was also free, which was important at a time when we were incurring unexpected costs – keeping the school open over the Easter and half-term breaks; increased photocopying and equipment to be sent home for our marginalised pupils as well as employing our sports coaches to work extra hours alongside our rota of teachers, to provide care for our key worker and vulnerable pupils.

The initial set up took about a week learning how to carry out all the back office tasks such as importing classes, assigning teachers and inviting parents to set up an account for their children and we were ready to go for the first week after the Easter holidays. Although predominantly known for being a pupil reward system, we made a decision not to use this feature whilst some of our pupils were not connected (87% of our pupils were initially signed up). Instead, we used it to post links to our Google Drive folders and send messages of encouragement from teachers to pupils (as well as to parents who often just needed reassurance that they were doing a great job).

At the start of every week, we posted an assembly, five English and Maths lessons, several guided reading activities as well as work from all other areas of the curriculum. This followed closely the topics and themes that the pupils would have experienced through the summer term had they been in school. In addition, our PE coaches posted twice weekly videos of activities and challenges. Whilst we made the decision not to run any 'live' sessions, staff did post videos of themselves explaining tricky topics, particularly in Maths, that the children could refer to if they needed to. There was no expectation that pupils had to carry out work on set days or at set times. We knew that families needed the flexibility to plan their own timetables. We also tried to ensure a balance between work that would need greater parental support and input (for example, when introducing new concepts) and tasks that the children could carry out independently. These were presented in a similar way to how they would have been in class, using similar materials so that the children were familiar with them. We were also aware that lockdown provided a unique opportunity for parents to spend some quality time with their children and therefore, there was no expectation that every single activity was completed, and we were always thrilled to see examples of some of the less formal learning that took place. We received positive comments on this approach from many of our parents.

Throughout this time, we still provided a mixture of online learning and paper-based work packs (for some children, provision was wholly paper-based and this proved effective for those that needed work differentiating to a greater degree). This was in response to the knowledge that not all of our pupils had access to ICT resources, particularly if parents were also working from home. Whilst not a directive from SLT, teachers decided to hand deliver work to pupils every couple of weeks, using this as a way of keeping in touch. It required a huge amount of drive and dedication from staff; however, they all loved the opportunity to see their children. After we reopened to our Year 6 pupils (on the instruction of government in June 2020 https://schoolsweek.co.uk/schools-will-reopen-on-june-1-prime-minister-confirms/), this became more difficult as all of our teachers were drafted in to work with [year 6 who were in] small bubbles of no more than 13 pupils. Our Emotional Learning Support Assistant would also make weekly calls to any families that were not signed up to our online platform (as well as those of our marginalised pupils) to check that they were all okay and to offer support with any work as necessary.

In terms of assessment, the system did have limitations. It relied on pupils posting photographs of the work that they had undertaken. For some knowledge-based activities it was easy enough to provide parents with answers that they could share with their children. Longer writing tasks were trickier to mark. These relied on well thought-out success criteria with pupils underlining examples of where they had used certain features within their work. Teachers would use the messenger section of the online platform to provide responses to pupils' work. Through discussion with SLT, teachers are able to talk confidently about which pupils have completed work in which areas and are already able to begin to plan for the likely gaps that will have inevitably developed between cohort peers learning. However, assessment is still an area that we need to develop further and may require us to look at another remote-learning provider.

The best way to organise learning seemed to be to set weekly deadlines but allow learners (with primary school pupils, directed by their parents) a degree of flexibility over the order in which they do the work. Some students may still find it easier to stick to their original timetable, especially the more motivated ones, but since this is unenforceable and marginalised learners in particular may struggle to maintain such a schedule, it may be better to accept from the start that this is unlikely to work for all. (Incidentally this pedagogical approach is similar to the Swedish Kunskapsskolan[8] personalised learning pedagogical approach).

Of course, many primary and secondary aged students, and their parents, did not know how to estimate the amount of time that each task would take, so teachers had to give them direction. School leaders then had to give their teachers broad guidance on how much work they should expect their students to undertake each day – just as is done for face-to-face teaching plans. For example, parents needed to know if a learner was expected to spend an hour each day on both English and Maths but schools did not need to specify exactly when this work should take place.

In doing so, schools needed to give due consideration to the fact that remote learning often takes longer than face-to-face learning except for students already adept at concentrating for long periods of time. Without the motivation provided by teacher expectations and the social pressure to conform with those expectations in a physical classroom setting, teachers reported that concentration was difficult to maintain for all but the most dedicated students.

At first, unrealistic expectations were set about how much students were capable of undertaking in a remote-learning environment. Parents reported that secondary aged students lacked the ability to organise or prioritise their time effectively and felt overwhelmed by the sudden demands placed upon them. High levels of stress and demoralisation were reported as being experienced quite quickly. A similar picture was seen amongst primary pupils, where they regarded their parents as having less authority over learning than their teachers. Even parents who were teachers but having to educate their children at home found that those learners who can opt out will, and of course, marginalised learners are far more likely to take this option, lacking as they often do, a calm and structured home environment in which to work.

As teachers became more experienced with remote teaching, understanding grew about what it was both possible and reasonable to expect their students to undertake remotely and what guidance was necessary to give them the maximum chance of doing so effectively. The more familiar schools and teachers are at planning remote learning, the more adept they will become. So, looking to the future, if planning remote work is seen as part of being a teacher, whether for absent individual students, holiday time or whole cohorts of students during periods of lockdown, the more that remote learning is a planned part of the normal curriculum the better practice will become and the better prepared the school will be to support continuity of learning in times of crisis.

Consideration also needed to be made for those who, for whatever reason, did not use the online systems provided, particularly very young children in primary schools. Primary schools needed to ensure a balance between work that needed greater parental support and input (for example, when introducing new tasks) and activities that could be carried out more independently. One of the challenges with mass remote teaching through any medium is that materials, whether online or paper copies, need to be presented in a familiar context to the children (e.g. the lesson a teacher may give on weather would relate the subject content to the learner's environment) and schools may need to make manipulatives available, particularly for subjects such as Maths. Senior leaders needed to decide how any home-learning packs were to be distributed to pupils and how. In primary schools, class teachers used the delivery of these as an opportunity to make contact with hard to reach/ marginalised pupils and to offer support to parents, addressing issues of well-being. During crises, if not at all times, there is a place for primary schools to recognise and celebrate the more informal learning that children undertaken at home, often with other family members – grandparents, for example.

Perhaps, inspection systems can serve a purpose here, by gathering data on the quality of remote learning. This is not entirely unreasonable given that students are normally expected to undertake regular homework anyway, and it is still relatively unusual for schools to do much more than suggest setting homework according to a weekly timetable. This can be relatively ineffective because it imposes a rigid expectation on teachers that a certain amount of homework will be set every week, regardless of whether it is needed or not, with the result that the tasks may be of low quality. The consequent non-compliance of students leads to unnecessary conflict and disengagement from the curriculum, making the setting of homework actually detrimental to progress.

However, if more attempts were made to define what good remote teaching and learning looked like, and schools and teachers were effectively supported to ensure that it could be delivered, then it is much more likely that effective remote learning would be available for all students, including the most marginalised, throughout their school lives. For a variety of reasons, relatively little thought has been given to this aspect of education in recent years, and until comparatively recently, the technology required to support it was somewhat limited, but now the opportunity exists to change that situation and help all students to learn independently more effectively.

It would be unfair and counterproductive to hold schools and teachers to account for making remote learning effective when they don't have the tools to do so. A better approach would be to use these definitions to inform practice and work with decision makers to develop the national infrastructure required to make them a reality.

Lessons learned: crisis-resilient creative pedagogies: 'when school stops, learning must not'

8.1 Payoff for earlier local technology investments: Countries and schools which had invested in sustained technological provision over the years were in a stronger position to provide continuity of learning and 'business as usual'. Localisation was important, both for understanding the needs of learners and the arranging of suitable alternative provision. Continuity of education depended on earlier investments in resourcing in various forms (physical resources or electronic online materials).

8.2 Structuring student learning and teacher development: Schools and educational establishments needed to be agile in their response. Curricula, assessment systems and learning systems were severely tested and some aspects were questioned for whether they genuinely added value to the education of an individual. The ongoing training of teachers and delivery of individualised forms of continued professional development (CPD) necessary to develop teachers' ability to provide remote teaching highlighted the need to move from the previous 'one-size-fits-all' mode of delivery for teachers' CPD to systems supporting the continual updating of their knowledge and skills. Preserving and maintaining relationships provided a global sense of educators being in the same situation. In times of uncertainty, some resemblance of structure is helpful in maintaining a sense of normality.

8.3 Future-aware and creative pedagogies: When planning ahead in an attempt to future-proof teacher and learning strategies that work well in non-emergency and emergency scenarios, there is a need to review existing practices to ensure that teachers and schools employ 'future-aware pedagogies'.

These are also referred to as 'creative pedagogies', but in reality, the 'creative' element is provided by enabling, encouraging and empowering practitioners, pupils and parents to make changes and adaptations to both curriculum content and learning approaches that meet the needs of all learners.

Such personalisation of learning should, in any case, be standard practice during stable conditions in addition to being specially adapted practice during emergency situations. However, the prerequisite for this to happen is firstly that teachers are trusted to make such changes and adaptations and secondly that they have individual knowledge of their students, their needs and how they learn best so that personal learning plans can be put into place quickly when circumstances and conditions for teaching and learning change.

The following list of conditions summarises what might support effective 'creative' and 'future-aware' pedagogies.

* Teachers are trusted and empowered to adapt the curriculum to meet the needs of their learners on a contextual and an individual basis.
* Teaching and learning includes 'reaching out' to learners in terms of their own local language and culture, particularly where this aids accessibility and equality of opportunity.
* Remote learning strategies planned for crises may be used for those learners whose needs are such that it is advantageous for them to learn anywhere, anytime, any way that works best for them (e.g. for those who are ill or experience disrupted schooling).
* All remote learning, including online, should have a clearly defined rationale and pedagogy of its own that includes how learners are supported, mentored and coached differently to face-to-face support.
* Remote and online learning includes access to local, regional and international resource banks of teaching and learning materials (such as GLOWConnect in

Scotland, Scootle in Australia) that have been licensed and certified by national governments and teachers' professional bodies.

* Community-led and family-led learning is recognised as a key aspect of education that can provide supplementary support for teaching and learning to a greater or lesser extent depending on the prevailing educational and environmental conditions at the time and the needs of the individual learner.
* Flexible approaches to assessment of skills, knowledge and understanding relating to curriculum content with moderated teacher-assessments used as first choice for assessing student/pupil achievement.
* Teachers and learners are encouraged to support one another, where possible and appropriate, through communities of learning and interest that offer mutual support, including personal, social, emotional and mental health, and well-being.
* All facilitators of learning whether formal (in schools) or informal (in communities and families) have access to their own communities of practice where they can provide and experience mutual support, including personal, social, emotional and mental health, and well-being.

8.4 Synchronous or asynchronous remote learning? While synchronous learning may have a part to play in remote teaching, it is not worth policymakers or school leaders investing too much time in making this their primary method of delivery. It is certainly not the answer to helping most disadvantaged or marginalised students in primary or the early years of their secondary education and placing too much emphasis on it might actually widen rather than narrow the achievement gap. Asynchronous methods, on the other hand, are more accessible and sustainable over time.

8.5 Publicly available learning materials: To support a national emergency education strategy and associated schooling plans, a national strategy could include ensuring existing resources – radio, TV, online – can be harnessed to support continuity of learning out of school. In all countries, making sure such resources are available in non-crisis times may help improve literacy levels in the population as well as support learners. Working with high-quality media channels with a commitment to public service, such as Open Universities and public broadcasters, seems logical.

We welcome the newly formed UNESCO Global Education Coalition, leading international coordination in quality assured, free resources. The lessons learned from the Covid pandemic coupled with mass affordable adoption of technologies supporting remote education, including radio, TV, telephone and internet, show that we could have a world where every young person could access high-quality education, thereby reducing the number of learners marginalised during crises.

8.6 Opportunities: doing education differently – a new vision for education post-Covid-19: The pandemic gave way to school closures, which enforced a different way of learning for children and young people. This, in turn, stimulated thinking on new ways of doing education differently. A vision for alternative pedagogies where learning could be conceived more holistically emerged from discussions following the webinars listed in the introduction; Hall (2021) outlines this vision. What follows in the rest of this chapter is a summary of Hall's thinking in the context of the English education system.

There has been a general acceptance by society that education, schooling and learning were synonymous concepts. The immediate crisis with the pandemic led to the temporary shutdown of the education system as we have known it for the past 150 years and has replaced it in some places by an unregulated outburst of creative energy from teachers, children, parents and grandparents.

This has raised speculation about what education could look like post-Covid-19 and invites us to consider how education may change as a result of this libera-tion of creativity, energy and dynamic learning. Given this possibility we consider a question –

What if, following the pandemic crisis, we emerge with an education system which:

* is fit for purpose for all learners with less emphasis on a one-size-fits-all approach
* is flexible enough to account for learners who rely on different learning patterns for managing their learning in a 'use first' and 'use as needed' way – phrases that refer to how we subconsciously (or consciously) use our preferred learning patterns to process new knowledge
* puts leadership and learning ahead of accountability
* abandons high stakes assessment and focuses more on process or praxis cur-riculum models and less on either product or syllabus curriculum models
* recognises limitations to any national curriculum which unnaturally compart-mentalises and restricts learning by 'thinking in subjects'
* looks for opportunities to develop pupils in a holistic way, rather than focusing on qualifications as a priority
* actively encourages and empowers parental involvement in a deep, collabora-tive way by eradicating any suggestion of a 'them and us' mentality
* provides sufficient opportunity for learners to take ownership of their learning or to follow their own interests across peer age groups and generations
* creates and facilitates opportunities for learners of all ages to use new technolo-gies to learn in a more flexible way
* embraces the national trend of increasing numbers of parents home educat-ing their children and integrates this into a more flexible attendance policy for schools
* develops more research-based and evidence-based practice in a more systematic way that combines strategic and operational use of research-informed practice

* rejects any form of commercial approach to education and learning or privatisation of knowledge, as is the case in England, by academy chains and reverses the trend of a loss of education as a public service as a result of the policy of privatising government-funded schools
* regulates the uncontrolled use of funds in government-funded schools which in England has led to uncontrolled salaries for school network CEOs.

Planning toolkit: doing education differently

Table 8.7 Planning toolkit: doing education differently

Decision 8.1 Teacher Workload	
Questions to resolve	How can teacher workload be minimised?
Solutions	Preparedness will minimise teacher workload as will well-established school virtual learning environments and the provision of electricity and internet connection to all. This might seem a big ask, but what kind of a world are we inhabiting and creating for the future if, collectively, we cannot look after those with least opportunity to provide these things for their communities?
Decision 8.2 Modes of teaching and learning: homeschooling/home education	
Questions to resolve	Examples: * How does your plan accommodate emerging pedagogies building on effective practice that the current crisis has uncovered? * How is research into what effective pedagogies look like within an online environment utilised within your plan? * What support is offered to parents/carers regarding home education to avoid children switching off? * How are misconceptions and misunderstandings about how to teach addressed, such as structuring learning at home differently from the structure of school lessons and avoiding the counter-productive outcomes from too high a volume of work and not enough rest time for processing what has been learned? * Is information freely and readily available to parents/carers on maximising environmental conditions for learning at home, wherever possible? Issues such as temperature, lighting levels, fresh air can be critical to effective learning. * Have you established what devices students can access to support learning? * What can you do to ensure marginalised learners are not further disadvantaged? * How will you ensure sustained learner experiences for all learners: where possible by providing ready access to devices?
Solutions	Examples: There is a role for professional associations/unions to pool and share knowledge in these respects and to ensure that politicians and public servants develop an understanding of relevant pedagogies so they are less likely to be persuaded by non-experts (with their associated consultancy fees) to adopt a particular product or approach by commercial bodies looking to profit from the confusion of ignorance?

(Continued)

Table 8.7 (Cont).

Decision 8.3 Teacher training that includes pedagogies required in times of crisis	
Questions to resolve	This chapter provides an overview of pedagogies that teachers found worked during the Covid crisis. What should be incorporated into initial and continuing teacher training so that teachers' practice is crisis resilient?
Solutions	Discussions with those training teaching and reviews of teacher training standards would be needed to prepare teachers better to manage continuity of learning and assessment during crises.

Futurecasting: a new kind of pedagogy for a new paradigm

A key prerequisite of any new paradigm if it is to be more than just a new education fad or fashion is to redefine teaching and learning. No longer will it be appropriate to refer to the way that children are taught (in schools) as 'Pedagogy' and to separate this from the way that adults learn, as 'Andragogy'. What will be needed is a new way of looking at learning and teaching within this new paradigm that captures the way that learners take greater ownership of their own learning as they mature, gain increased self-confidence, self-awareness and self-efficacy. One possible way of considering this is to merge the separate concepts of learning for children and for adults into one, dynamic concept of 'Pedandragogy' or 'Pandragogy', a maturity model of learning and teaching in which the learner increasingly takes greater responsibility for their own learning as they grow towards self-actualisation and self-determination.

Any new paradigm would also need to be built on some new principles for education and learning that define purpose and form. These ideas are designed to start a dialogue that considers what those key principles might be and to attempt to find a shared agreement and understanding to define them.

Key principles for education of the future

The following list is the beginning of an exploration of the principles that might underpin education and learning in the future. Within any new framework for learning that emerges, post Covid-19, these principles will be clearly discernible:

- *Identity and awareness of self:* increasingly greater awareness of identity and self as a learner (metacognition) will lead to interdependent learners who self-organise, self-direct and ultimately self-determine their learning.
- *Evaluation and quality:* in order to validate learning we will need to design quality methods of evaluation of learning and progression that include self-assessment and portfolio-building.

- *Age, culture, diversity, and intergenerational learning:* how we learn best, whether as children, adolescents or adults will matter more than what we learn, and who we learn with best will change according to interest, context and learning preferences.
- *Social, emotional and mental health and well-being as a dimension of learning:* arguably these are the most important dimension of learning because learning is suppressed when, emotionally or mentally, we are not in a good place; yet learning can be at its deepest when we engage with learning at a deeper emotional level.
- *Merging of the valuing of formal and informal learning for many people, young or old:* the difference between formal and informal learning is artificial and is highly arbitrary depending on how an individual learns best.
- *Technology as a tool for learning:* this was highlighted by teachers as potentially the most exciting and, as yet relatively unexplored, dimension of how education could be done differently during the Covid pandemic and post Covid-19.

A vision for the future

Imagine if the education system could change in diverse and dynamic ways so that it becomes possible to do education differently in a way that combines both formal and informal approaches to learning and education, across age groups and generations.

A conceivable outcome of the Covid-19 pandemic is that education could evolve into a new paradigm, captured by the phrase *'doing education differently'* that encompasses three main elements:

1 *Online Learning:* a permanent move towards online/distance learning with open access to free materials for individuals and groups of like-minded learners of all ages.
2 *Home Education:* an increase in the amount of time that children spend learning at home, with parents and grandparents as both home educators and co-learners.
3 *Flexible Schooling:* a more specialised role for schools (or some kind of similar, community facility) that offers maker spaces, meeting places and provides specialist advice and guidance to deepen learning and support for gaining qualifications.

Notes

1 'When school stops, learning must not' Shrestha and Lal (2020).
2 Shrestha and Lal (2020) VSO for this quote www.vsointernational.org/news/blog/when-school-stops-learning-must-not#ref-1

3 The Teacher Mediated option for schooling (TMO) or Telephone School www.edu. gov.mb.ca/k12/dl/index.html

4 Alice Springs School of the Air www.assoa.nt.edu.au

5 VSO   www.vsointernational.org/news/blog/when-school-stops-learning-must-not#ref-1

6 Example of children teaching across cultures https://drive.google.com/file/d/1HI PWFoWS2kPHx_V_9bDogScmWbF7lUjf/view?usp=drivesdk; and, https://drive. google.com/file/d/1Q-KRDprCtVegSXJksTPFVs9anvPgeQ7n/view?usp=drivesdk

7 UNESCO's Global Education Coalition https://en.unesco.org/covid19/education response/globalcoalition

8 Sweden's Kunskapsskolan international school network (www.kunskapsskolan. com/thekedprogram.4.1d96c045153756b0c14d5798.html)

Technology support for remote teaching, learning and assessment – Jon Audain

Introduction and context

Technology provided a bonding service for many during the Covid-19 pandemic through facilitating connections necessary to sustain aspects of education, society and the economy. Face-to-face teaching for the majority of children ended abruptly overnight. Across all countries in our research, teachers were directed to move to remote teaching using online teaching where possible. Many parents themselves assumed the role of home-school teacher as well as managing the complexities of working from home.

This change of role required individual teachers to adapt their practice.

In many countries this exposed a lack of a vision and provision for educational technologies to support teaching and learning at both local, regional, national and international levels.

The lessons about inequity of access to online resources were there to be learned from the past (World Bank 2017; UNESCO 2020c).

So at a time of crisis, in low-, medium- and high-income countries, in spite of the technologies available, teachers and communities also had to go back to basics by providing paper-based remote learning.

Background

During 2020, there were numerous webinar events bringing together educators from different international perspectives to share knowledge freely about how to manage teaching during the crisis. From our data, more similarities than differences emerged between low-, medium- and high-income countries with respect to the situation teachers found themselves in. This chapter considers lessons from the first wave and

DOI: 10.4324/9781003155591-13

Table 9.1 Lessons from the early stages of Covid-19 and school lockdowns

A. When physical contact was removed the need to **communicate** became paramount.

B. Preserving and maintaining **relationships** provided a global sense of everyone being in the same situation.

C. Continuity of education needed **resourcing** in various forms (physical or electronic).

D. **The training of teachers and delivery of individualised forms of continued professional development (CPD)** highlighted the need to move from a 'one-size-fits-all' mode of CPD for teachers to providing opportunities for educators to continually update their knowledge and skills ('just-in-time learning').

E. **Systems were severely tested** and some practices and curricula were questioned for whether they genuinely added value to the education of an individual.

F. Schools and educational establishments needed to be **agile** in their response.

G. In times of uncertainty, some resemblance of **structure** is helpful in maintaining a sense of normality.

H. **Localisation** was important, both from the point of view of understanding the needs of learners and the arranging of suitable provision.

I. Schools which had **invested in sustained technological provision** over the years were in a stronger position to provide a 'business as usual' approach to learning and teaching.

J. Knowing that a second wave could hit focused schools on **forecasting and contingency planning**, moving them from a position of reaction to one of strategic development.

how technologies could provide solutions. Table 9.1 summarises lessons from the early stages of Covid-19 and school lockdowns.

Overall challenge: capacity in building virtual-responsive schools for the future

As lockdowns in countries spread along with multiple school closures, technology provided opportunities to innovate practice. However, in reality, the opportunities came at a personal cost as the forced adoption of technology was somewhat inescapable for many. Despite feelings of 'everyone being in the same boat' which can provide a positive community of practice when building capacity in using new technology, the additional burden of learning to use the technology because of the crisis added to the stresses of the profession. Research has shown that gradual professional development in the use of technology for teaching and assessment builds more secure embedding in practice (Younie and Leask 2013) so current gains in teachers' use of educational technologies may at least, in some settings, be lost when the emergency is over.

Schools needed contingency planning, infrastructure, skills and resources so they could respond to their communities. This support had to be localised.

A number of countries, principally low- and medium-income countries, focused on providing lessons through TV and radio. Many countries – low- to high-income – pushed for online teaching. Some governments and NGOs reached out with emergency measures to support groups who were already marginalised within their education system. In a number of countries the government or NGOs provided laptops and tablets for, for example, in England 'disadvantaged and vulnerable families, children and young people who did not have access to them through another source, to enable access to remote education and social care services during the coronavirus (Covid-19)' (DfE 2020, p. 3).[1] As did a number of countries, the UK government also provided funding for schools to gain assistance in setting up one of two free-to-use digital education platforms: G Suite for Education or Office 365 Education.[2]

Specific challenges: for technology-supported remote teaching, learning and assessment

The following specific challenges are covered in this chapter:

- Maintaining a sustained national vision for educational technologies
- Access to technology
- Creation of content
- Strategies for getting content into homes
- Pedagogies for teaching and learning
- The training of teachers and developing awareness of the role of technology
- Parents as partners.

Specific challenge 9.1 Maintaining a sustained national vision for educational technologies

The need to plan for additional closures and re-openings meant that countries and schools which had sustained their investment in technology and training were in a stronger position than others. World Bank reviews on *Building and sustaining national ICT/education agencies* (World Bank 2017) show provision in different countries has been erratic and liable to be lost overnight as governmental priorities change.

Education systems naturally change and evolve, and systems are subjected to different sustained initiatives or 'pressures'. However, the pressure, due to school closures because of the pandemic, to move from normal classroom teaching to using technology for online learning was layered on top of existing pressures. Teachers and learners paid the price of poor national and international leadership: equitable access to high-quality online education for all supported by technologies has long been possible. In the same way that the WHO had been advising governments to plan for pandemics, UNESCO had been urging governments to ensure high-quality education for all. UNESCO was warning of the impact on all societies of the invisible pandemic of uneducated children with consequent lack of self-improvement knowledge destroying communities and creating migration pressures (UNESCO August 2020a). Table 9.2 outlines system pressures placed on teachers and their meaning in terms of technology during the Covid-19 crisis.

These pressures exist within the normal operation of education systems, but the pandemic stressed these weaknesses pointing, in the case of England, to chronic government underfunding due to a political austerity initiative and a lack of focus on keeping up with the technology. This lack of updating is strange, given the fact that a person inherently understands the need to update their phone or computer hardware as well as software to maintain the system at its best. Sadly, the same cannot be said for the updating of its training and application to education at a national level. One could argue that it is not enough to assume that technology is an integral part of education and that technology in schools will be strong without strategic intervention and financial support.

In the 1990s, Australia and the UK were trailblazers in the use of technology to support teaching and learning. Australia's EDNA online resources[3] were one of the early initiatives showing how the internet could be used to support teachers' lifelong learning. The UK agency, BECTA (British Educational Communications and Technology Agency), a non-departmental public body funded by the Department for Education, led the way in terms of research and information around educational technology (Parkin 2017) before funding was removed in a 'slash and burn' exercise known as the 'Bonfire of the quangos' (Gash et al. 2012; Blamires 2015; Younie and Leask 2019; Institute for Government 2012).

During the pandemic, many of the webinar discussions by those new to the edtech space espoused, as though these were new ideas, the merits of online learning; how technology could support children in different ways; how learning materials could be pushed out to various devices; as well as the virtues of using activities hosted on school's virtual learning environments (VLEs) as a scaffold for learning – and they were correct. However, data, examples and materials for teachers were all

System pressures	Type of pressure	Description	What this meant in terms of technology during the Covid-19 crisis
Changes in government policy or procedures, initiatives	hard	Policy changes which happen at a national level and either are mandated or pushed through without being largely supported by or in collaboration with a wide selection of teachers, education professionals and experts. These changes create hard pressure on a system and can cause chaos through creating unintended consequence which are difficult to reverse.	For example, in the UK, the 2012 removal of ICT from the National Curriculum; the dissolution of the government agency for educational technology (BECTA); the closure of Teachers' TV and all government-funded online resources for teachers, the overemphasis on Computer Science and, subsequently, the chronic underfunding of hardware and digital literacy within the curriculum due to years of austerity meant the focus for schools had been reprioritised away from virtual learning and digital skills. Between 1997–2010, policies had set a foundation for virtual learning which included laptops for students and virtual learning environments for all schools. A change of government in 2010 meant this forward-looking policy support was then not sustained, leaving the English education system in a poor position when faced with the challenges of remote schooling (Blamires 2015).
Changes in local and regional practices	reactive	Changes in teaching practices bring uncertainty when new initiatives are introduced. Getting change implemented consistently across a region is difficult. There are costs associated with training.	As different areas in countries were 'locked down' or reopened, the technology support plan had to be strategic and reactive. For example, during a lockdown, does the school adopt asynchronous Emergency Remote Teaching (ERT) or 40 minutes of synchronous learning followed by activities to complete as follow up? When the school returns, what will the digital aspects of home/school learning look like? How are these changes then communicated to parents?
Changes/updates in subject and pedagogic knowledge	moderate	Initial Teacher Education provides an introductory amount of training. Knowledge can become out of date very quickly; teaching techniques are adapted; new system legislation changes the school provision (e.g. for children with additional needs/inclusion).	Early on in the pandemic, educators needed knowledge about the different approaches using technology that schools could adopt (Emergency Remote Teaching, flipped learning, blended learning, etc). Providing professional development introducing teachers Gilly Salmon's five stage model of e-learning or the types of software to record videos, voice-overs or narrated presentations would have rapidly up-skilled teachers in the pedagogy of online learning. They could then confidently make professional judgements for their classrooms, schools and communities.

Table 9.2 (Cont).

System pressures	Type of pressure	Description	What this meant in terms of technology during the Covid-19 crisis
Fads, fashions and misconceptions and myths	sticky	It is all too easy for education fads to be adopted without an evidence base for practice (i.e. Brain Gym); visual, auditory, kinaesthetic approaches (VAK) gain increased popularity and traction in the classroom. Popularity based on loose or no research is replicated and shared through word of mouth, social media or journalistic 'gaslighting' without being underpinned by a robust evidence base.	Fads with no base in evidence can prevent agile responses. Headteachers reported their communities turning to them for myth busting. In times of crisis, there is a role for technology to be utilised to convey the latest information to educators. Establishing a central, co-ordinated and trusted online space with expert advice aids communication during times of crisis. Strategies such as the **M**apping **S**pecialist **E**ducational know**H**ow (MESH) initiative produce MESHGuides (www.MESHGuides.org) which are concise teacher briefings/research-based synthesis of knowledge. Guides such as 'A Germ's Journey' teaching children about microbiology, hand-hygiene and infection control illustrate how this can be useful. (www.meshguides.org/scientists-teachers-and-teacher-educators-work-together-to-combat-the-spread-of-infection/)
Destruction or construction?	hard	Critical services, people, resources and accumulated wealth of knowledge are suddenly or sharply cut and removed from public access due to redirected funds; or funding cuts leads to the removal of information on websites and electronic repositories are lost or not stored. In a number of countries teachers report online resources funded by governments are suddenly removed. This 'burning on the books' approach occurs when funding for organisations/ resourcing and government quangos is cut (see World Bank 2017 for details).	The sustained removable of resources developed by previous governments means that resources have had to be reinvented. This deconstruction leaves fragments of knowledge littered around the internet, for much of which large sums of public money have been spent on creating the resource/research in the first place. The pandemic provides the opportunity and the need to rebuild these resources so that access to information, activities, knowledge and training is stronger in light of a future pandemic. There is the opportunity to construct a stronger system.

available from research carried out since the 1980s, including, for example, BECTA's own research up to 2010. Initiatives such as the £194m Home Access Programme (BECTA 2009; DfE 2011) providing laptops for students and prioritising provision for children with special needs and disabilities, had vital lessons to teach the English education sector – this knowledge could have informed the pandemic planning process. But the knowledge was archived and the knowledge holders dispersed as part of the restructuring of the English education system from 2010 onwards. The BECTA research files can be found on the University of London Institute of Education website.[4]

Specific challenge 9.2 Access to technology

One of the first challenges for teachers, when the pandemic caused schools to close, was to assess the types of technology to which children and teachers had access. This was problematic. Schools which had a clear understanding of their students and specifically the types of hardware, internet connection they had access to and their family's ability to pay for resourcing were able to shape the teaching to make use of the technology appropriately. Related issues which arose included the following.

* In some areas where online data was expensive or where individuals could not access the internet or any forms of technology, printed materials were provided by teachers sometimes as well as online teaching (i.e. doubling the teaching). In some areas of the West Indies and in Africa and parts of South America, for instance, we received reports that learning resources were left at accessible places, such as shops, so learners could collect resources. However, in high- and low-income countries, in areas of social deprivation, parents and students struggled to access learning as the digital divide widened[5] (BBC 2020a)
* Not all children and teachers have access to the technology that governments were basing their plans for continuity of learning on. Many homes have a mixed economy of equipment and where the use of the internet was favoured as the main method of delivery this led to children who had 'handed-down' technology having compatibility issues with software and the work set.
* Laptops, gaming devices, computers, tablets and phones could provide access. Children who were the most marginalised had, in some countries, some form of technology provided. Although in some countries, this provision was patchy and delayed (Dickens 2020) and access was determined through the criteria used to identify eligibility which didn't include all.
* Some governments focused their support on different forms of media which were more accessible to all, via, for example, radio or television (Mexico, Portugal, some parts of India).

❋ Some marginalised learners were still unreachable due to remoteness and lack of communication technology and electricity: we had reports from high- and low-income countries: USA, UK, Myanmar, Nigeria, Uganda. Some cases were reported where families were reluctant to co-operate with the school authorities. Some reports were received that children out of school simply started working for the family – in farming or household and caring duties.

Specific challenge 9.3 Creation of content: online resource repositories, online teaching or online learning?

For those countries with limited useful online educational resources, content had to be created. Individual repositories have long existed to provide resources, but the crisis also demanded content that could be adapted for busy parents who were homeschooling. As the weeks rolled by, there was certainly no shortage of resources available from individuals and organisations. Boxed content from commercial and charitable providers, websites and resources is unlikely to provide effective learning in all subjects to all children without teachers adapting resources for their classes. In England, providers of free resources included the teachers' specialist subject associations, BBC Bitesize, Oak National Academy SENECA. In reality, there was a flooding of online resources, web-based programmes, games, activities and 'edu-celebrities' delivering content, much of which was not quality assured.

Schools had a difficult decision to make between developing online resource repositories, online teaching (EEF 2020b) or online learning with each of these approaches demanding a different pedagogical approach. Some teachers struggled with the speed of change to virtual working when either they had to learn the capabilities of new video conferencing technologies, such as Zoom, Google or Microsoft Teams, or trying to implement virtual learning environments which are not without their challenges (Gillett-Swan 2017; BECTA 2004). The following points were observed in terms of creating content.

❋ Consideration of access to the internet, speed of that access and the age of the device and operating system needed to be known by schools. If content was too media-rich then children struggled to access content. Children without internet access were provided with paper copies of lesson resources which were then delivered to homes. Administratively, this placed an additional burden on the workload of schools.

❋ What was the content intended to provide: online resource repositories, online teaching or online learning? All three need different approaches.

❋ In Ghana, the Ministry of Education produced a large site of resources with the Ministry of Communication. A second wave of support harnessing television was prioritised to support the core subjects of Maths, Science and English. As radio was more widespread, programmes were developed for that medium. Other web initiatives mentioned earlier are available to teachers in Germany, Netherlands, South Korea, Australia, New Zealand, Bangladesh. Similarly in Mexico, the government harnessed radio and TV to provide continuity of schooling as schools closed until 2021. The English example in Table 9.3 describes how following the closing down of online teacher resources costing over £100M in 2010, the government was forced to find funds quickly when teachers put pressure on for some national support.

* In countries where there was no national provision, teachers had to search for quality content to fit their teaching purposes. They needed these resources to be flexible and adaptable. Sadly, many digital resources were rigid and needed to be revised in order to fit the intended learning outcomes.

* The accessibility of content for students with additional educational needs often is poorly considered and is dependent on the type of content provided. As one teacher commented during a webinar, *'Just because you provide stuff through technology doesn't mean there is access. There is a need to address what to do where technology isn't hitting the mark, such as for visually impaired learners when close captioning isn't provided.'*

* Teachers are working more hours than before because of the content creation.

Table 9.3 England-based Oak National Academy: generating national resources at speed during a pandemic – a case study of one initiative.

The normal response during a humanitarian crisis is to provide aid where required. However, how does this translate when applied to digital artefacts for the classroom? Strategically, this is about ensuring that the libraries of curriculum resources are curated. Consider the financial investments that have already been made over decades to ensure schools have resources which are evidence-informed and based on sound professional educational wisdom. (See the World Bank report (2017) for lists of reports from different countries.) However, aspects such as budgetary cuts during periods of austerity and hard types of system pressures (Table 9.2) resulted in the English government ineffectively starting from scratch during a time when rapid response was required to provide high-quality resources that are centred on teaching and learning.

Having closed down all the government funded online teacher's resources in 2010 in which over £100M had been invested (Blamires 2015), the English government's solution at the time of Covid was the creation of Oak National Academy (www.thenational.academy) an online classroom and resource hub as a quick response. Funds were allocated to a non-representative group of teachers without reference to subject associations (NGOs which bring together committed and experience subject specialist teachers and researchers).

'Built at speed' (Crawford 2020) and with millions of views of resources and lessons in its first couple of months, it demonstrated that content can be produced at speed along with an amount of government expenditure (a non-competitively awarded grant of approximately £4.5M plus the unpaid time of many teachers). However, subject associations and curriculum-based organisations working voluntarily do the same work for their members and would have made their resources freely available (Connell 2020a, b). With respect to the Oak Academy, many contributing teachers were not paid while others were.

This was one individual country's response, but the following observations could be noted:

* Content creation at speed is flawed and this was quite rightly recognised by Oak Academy's principal (Hood 2020) and staff (Thomas 2020; Wespieser 2020) in their tweets and blog articles. One size does not fit all, schools have to tailor content or not use it if it does not align with their own curriculum plans.
* The time spent on designing activities for online learning is different from face-to-face teaching. Parents and end users had to adjust their expectations of the resources provided.
* Oak Academy's content of videos, quizzes, lessons and resources are restrictive by design. Something to which most software companies will testify.
* The focus during a pandemic is on maintaining the quality of learning, whether in the form of synchronous, asynchronous or blended learning. Therefore the design of any online classroom hub has to be different from merely the conversion of learning resources.

Specific challenge 9.4 Strategies for getting content into homes

Getting content into homes was dependent on the type of technology to which students had access. These were represented in the following delivery strategies (Table 9.4).

Specific challenge 9.5 Pedagogies for teaching and learning

Teachers know how to communicate their subjects.

Table 9.4 Strategies for getting content into homes and the financial considerations

Method of delivery	Considerations during the pandemic	Financial implications
* Online resources or internet-connected devices such as game consoles. * Access to online repositories of resources or software companies.	* Thousands of electronic educational resources exist on the web. Resources needed to be adjusted to tie into the country's school curriculum so as to aid teachers in their lesson planning. * Tech companies made available time-limited access to resources until the end of term. * Content that was already available behind paywalls was subsidised by regional, local authorities or governments. * Teachers in rural locations in some low-income countries reported that some tourist resorts let teachers and learners use their internet connection during their non-busy times.	* Wi-Fi provides quick access but access is dependent on the home connection and the age of the device. This impacts on whether the content can be run. * Mobile 4G dongles can provide a solution but families also have to be aware of what in their home can drain data. For example, during lockdown, one parent received a dongle from the school to give internet connection, but the data provided was used up after their child connected to their gaming device so they could connect with their peers and talk about their work.
* Television – national televised programmes/classes	* Greater access to more homes. * Dependent on the number of televisions in a household. If families have children of different ages, scheduling becomes challenging or programmes need to be recorded and viewed at a later time sometimes outside the hours of the school day.	* In some countries, a greater percentage of the population can't afford cable services if these are used for delivery so there are learners who are outside that service.
* Radio/Audio equipment	* Even radio reception is difficult to access in some parts of the country. * In some countries, places of worship such as temples and mosques, used their equipment to broadcast programmes.	* The cost of the equipment can be relatively small if a physical device has to be purchased. * Access to radio is often subsumed within smartphone devices requiring an internet connection and, therefore, data. * solar-powered radio for students to receive lessons on was reported as a successful strategy in a number of countries, for example rural Somalia.

(Continued)

Table 9.4 (Cont).

Method of delivery	Considerations during the pandemic	Financial implications
⁂ Teachers video themselves and then the lesson is broadcasted on national TV	⁂ Producing video contents takes longer to create and technical skills, and training may be required by some teachers. ⁂ Video production can be relatively quick, but the editing process takes more time. ⁂ There has to be a consensus around the quality of the video that can be produced.	⁂ Cost of time to produce the video. ⁂ Do teachers have the necessary equipment to produce the video?
⁂ Text message/ WhatsApp messaging	⁂ In Nepal, educators supporting girls' education in remote areas have used devices that are able to send text messages. This has created a culture of learning in the community. Teaching via SMS messaging is reported also from Pakistan and India. ⁂ If countries restrict apps, then this inhibits certain learning pedagogies from being used. ⁂ Emotional support is provided to teachers through a text messaging service. The UK Chartered College of Teachers and Behavioural Insights Team's project 'Teach Together' (https://chartered.college/2020/03/25/teachtogether) is based on 'a pilot in the US and Canada which saw teachers, as well as 911 call handlers, receive a weekly message. The service was found to have reduced burnout and halved resignations.'	⁂ Some schools already have text messaging opportunities as part of their School Management System. ⁂ The cost of messaging can be relatively low and applications such as WhatsApp can be used across an internet connection.
⁂ The telephone school	⁂ This is a similar strategy to the text messaging service. Small community networks or hubs are established in a chain-like way. When a message or work needs to be communicated, it is passed down the line. Communities of practice are developed so that all members of the school community can be reached. This might even include local businesses as part of the hub.	⁂ The cost of text messages but a subsidised version would support communities, as costs could add up, depending on the length of a lockdown and the frequency of messages sent.
⁂ Basic resourcing (i.e. printed worksheets) to be posted or collected by students.	⁂ For example, school staff may drop off packs of work to a local shop so that when families visit to buy food, they also pick up their pack of work for their children. This has worked well for small communities where access to broadband is problematic. ⁂ Worksheets are dependent on what resources are available within the home.	⁂ Even activities of asynchronous learning can have implications on resourcing (i.e. an art activity that require paints that the student has no access to). See the MESHGuides YouTube videos, Numeracy for all, (2020c) for examples of the use of local resources to teach mathematics.

The view of what a classroom is, is well defined and informed by the school environment, values and practices. Physically, this setting has been established with deep roots in the psyche of educators and learners.

The pandemic rocked that understanding and because of the physical remoteness of students, and with the increased reliance on digital technologies, the question was raised: are we teaching children the right things for the world they are now entering into? With more companies allowing people to work from home and occasionally visit the office, do our children need to experience these different modes of working?

Some of the teaching and learning considerations when teachers use educational technology which were highlighted by educators during the pandemic are included in Table 9.5.

Table 9.5 Teaching and learning considerations expressed by educators during the pandemic

Platforms and set up

* There was a mixed economy in the use of different platforms (Google, Zoom, Kahoot, Skype)
* One teacher commented, *'At the beginning of the pandemic, those children who could get online quickly, got online with their learning swiftly. Those who didn't, suffered. Some schools, like ours have been able to get iPads to children in remote areas. Those with iPads are catching up with their learning doing extra hours and we have specific teachers dedicated to support these children'.*
* Extra administrative duties were placed on teaching staff as they tried to establish connections with their classes by telephoning parents to check understanding of the homework tasks set.

Student skills and experiences

* In some cases, children's digital skills and understanding were more advanced than those of their parent or caregiver. Some parents struggled to provide the increased support now expected as families worked from home.
* Some of the students with brothers and sisters at home struggled to concentrate on their studies.

Digital safety and health

* Screen time increased for children as they spent more time on computers.
* Schools are normally held accountable for safeguarding students by ensuring that the correct filters and blacklists are applied to school devices

(Haskell-Dowland and Vasileiou 2020). During the pandemic, this was an additional concern if parents did not have the appropriate protections in place.

Marginalised learners: students with Additional Educational Needs (AEN) during the Covid-19 crisis

* Learners with Additional Educational Needs are already a cluster within the marginalised group, so the starting position is not equitable.
* Teachers reported that some students with extreme anxiety and/or complex needs are preferring the learning from home.
* Levels of anxiety were exacerbated in two ways – one because there is a crisis and the general anxiety level of a nation rose, and two because social media and the use of technology can contribute to poor mental health in a time when daily physical interaction is beneficial for wellness. So students with Additional Educational Needs needed further support.

Specific challenge 9.6 Emergency remote teaching: training teachers and developing awareness of the role of technology

Teachers are naturally adaptive as a profession. With the crisis presenting challenges, teachers suddenly found themselves having to work with technology without the necessary training, software, information or equipment. In addition to this, those challenges were personal in terms of resilience and mental health with teachers subject to 'additional pressures because of their professional role in supporting children' (Müller and Goldenberg 2020, p. 26). The changing nature of workload whilst still teaching children of key workers and providing online work for those children at home were all cited as contributing factors.

Technical terms such as blended learning, flipped learning, synchronous/asynchronous learning and developing hybrid models of teaching (half the children in school and half at home online) were reintroduced. These are step changes in a school's approach to learning and one, like any curriculum development, that needs discussion, planning, support and training. As a result of the pandemic, what schools implemented was something akin to what Hodges et al. (2020, p. 1) refers to as *Emergency Remote Teaching (ERT)*, a temporary shift of:

> instructional delivery to an alternate delivery mode due to crisis circumstances. It involves the use of fully remote teaching solutions for instruction or education that would otherwise be delivered face-to-face or as blended or hybrid courses

that will return to that format once the crisis or emergency has abated. The primary objective in these circumstances is not to re-create a robust educational ecosystem but rather to provide temporary access to instruction and instructional supports in a manner that is quick to set up and is reliably available during an emergency or crisis.

To foster a pragmatic sense of resilience during the crisis, Duffield and O'Hare (2020) identify three key areas of activity professionals should engage in together and with their students: fostering a sense of belongingness and connectedness; promoting help seeking; continuing to support development and learning. Table 9.6 explores how these three areas relate to technology.

Table 9.6 The three key areas of resilience activity and how these relate to technology

Fostering a sense of belonging and connectedness

Teaching online is often intense and requires both good teaching skills as well as technical expertise to troubleshoot when things are not quite right. The technology needs to be used to make the student feel connected to the group despite being separated remotely. Developing icebreakers for students when online and allowing for activities during synchronous learning to take longer go a long way to strengthening a sense of connectedness. Connection was fostered through teaching inputs being shorter and more time being given to develop online communication skills so that students could fully engage.

Promoting help-seeking between professionals

The first question for colleagues to ask each other is 'What do we need?' and how can technology help us make the curriculum accessible to different learners? Schools and educators needed to reflect and audit the skills they currently had. This process supports strategic thinking and therefore builds resilience in developing a 'problem solving' approach to finding out the information.

Managing expectations: the value and importance of young people being independent learners is an essential quality when working remotely, but this does not happen overnight.

Teachers who had established networks, either physically or through social media, had a supportive community of practice for help and support during lockdown. This was useful at the early stages of the pandemic when teachers were looking for ideas and platforms to use for online learning. Specialist subject associations play a role in networking subject experts.

Continuing to support development and learning

During the pandemic, the pace of learning changed. Some staff had time to learn new approaches with some teachers had to push themselves outside their comfort zone because they could not hide from using the technology.

Lockdown provided continuing professional development (CPD) opportunities, especially for student teachers who had placements cancelled, to extend their own professional development. Many were looking for examples of CPD around online learning or other educational themes to demonstrate to future employers ways they spent enhancing their own learning during the lockdown time.

Specific challenge 9.7 Parents as partners

The pandemic reinforced a sense of community which was not without its challenges in terms of technology as parents found themselves assuming the roles of teacher, technology provider and technician at the same time as sustaining their own employment, as many worked from home as well as home-schooling their children. Parental engagement is normally nurtured by schools: the Covid-19 crisis changed that engagement to include the community aspect as well. Heads reported that they were perceived as community leaders and were relied on by parents, for reliable information. The lockdown also introduced different pressures to parents around the use of technology, as Table 9.7 outlines.

Table 9.7 Lockdown pressures around technology experienced by parents

* Families had to parent in challenging economic circumstances. The use of technology for teaching added to the increasing inequality of the digital divide (BBC 2020a, b) in high-, middle- and lower-income families. Even with the various interventions by schools and governments, 'digital poverty' is a significant problem.
* Not all parents are able teachers and some struggled with how to progress learning. Parents were used to supporting homework tasks, but families also needed guidance with maintaining quality and consistent learning at home. If they are not supported, then there is a risk that very little learning will take place.
* The lockdown focus for some parents who were struggling was on using technology to keep children occupied during this time rather than on progressing learning.

Lessons learned: about educational technologies

The lessons learned around each of the specific challenges are complex and they are integrated in the preceding discussion around each specific challenge. In the following, we identify the major stumbling block to all learners experiencing continuity of learning and assessment at times of disruption of schooling whether the disruption is to the whole system or to the individual learner's access to education: the stumbling block is national will, vision and resourcing.

9.1 National will, vision and resourcing for educational technology: Through our research and the contributions of educators around the world to webinars, we identified countries where governments made a significant contribution to supporting continuity of learning and teaching through website repositories, teacher support materials and learners materials. Other governments did not make such commitments, and the research data has many examples of the pressure teachers were under where there was the lack of such a backup resource with its accompanying networking.

9.2 Technology pedagogy: Table 9.8 outlines some of the strategies schools also used during the lockdown.

Table 9.8 Technology pedagogy: advice and strategies which teachers reported using during the lockdown

Organisation

* If software allows, schedule work at different times so that children do not have access to all the work at once.
* Decide whether your learning will be live or whether you will pre-record sessions.
* Work with colleagues where appropriate. Team teach and/or share resources to lighten the workload.
* Explore whether your system allows 'breakout' rooms. This helps to facilitate smaller discussions and can encourage children to join in more than they would in a larger group.

Pupil engagement

* Set quiz questions for pupils to answer as a different way of engaging with content.
* Consider ways of increasing pupil engagement. Ask longer discussion questions or use electronic voting tools or a show of hands if your school allows cameras to be turned on.

- Remember to explore the system settings so you can view engagement data on your children. Look out for students who are spending a short amount of time engaging with your content. Use telephone conversations to parents to assess whether there is a difficulty with the work or whether technical aspects are standing in the way.
- Consider a 'flipped learning' approach by providing content first for children to work through before facilitating a live discussion.

Learning opportunities

- Stream your assemblies. Invite people from your school community to share their experiences so children still see the adults around who are familiar to them.
- Remember to communicate in little ways. Share jokes, cartoons, anecdotes, new learning or other aspects of life.
- Consider the use of personalised calendars to set out the children's work across the week. Use the calendar invite option so that children can join from the calendar.
- Reflect on the week in a talking video journal. Let the children see that, as adults, we too are processing feelings about the crisis.
- Continue to celebrate the things that are going well. Celebrate a birthday or a learning goal.

Social skills and emotional health and well-being

- Remember that online learning takes longer in terms of timings and for children to become comfortable sharing and finding their voice.
- Remember to plan in opportunities for 'small chat' to find out about the children's experiences so they feel connected.

Planning toolkit: implications for digital technology for schools and the wider system

As mentioned earlier, in preparation for pandemics, the European Commission's advice (EC 2009a, b) provides a framework for developing plans. The advice is to have plans 'which strengthen current systems'. We use this framework, as shown in Table 9.9, to encourage decision-makers to explore the implications for digital technology for schools and the wider system.

Table 9.9 Planning toolkit: A Covid-19 framework for decision-makers considering the role of digital technology for schools and the wider system

European Commission's framework for developing pandemic plans	Technology implication	Action/Proposed Solution
1 Pandemic preparedness, response and evaluation **should be built on generic preparedness platforms, structures, mechanisms and plans** for crisis and emergency management.	◦ The use of technology concerns multiple stakeholders. This can lead to disjointed communication surrounding the provision of equipment, resourcing to students and training to up-skill the profession. ◦ The technology varies in terms of different suppliers of software. How do we coordinate other services together to help support schools?	◦ Establish an emergency working group with multiple stakeholders including teachers and senior leaders to coordinate the use and messaging around educational technology during a pandemic. In the UK, there is already a model for this type of development with the 2014 UK National Curriculum. Subject Expert Groups were established with a lead organisation and deputy lead to ensure that structures and guidance are put in place. ◦ Appropriate finance and communication channels to be established so schools receive information that is both relevant, clear and timely. ◦ A central webpage 'hub' should make the collection and dissemination of information easier.
2 To the extent possible, pandemic preparedness should **aim to strengthen existing systems** rather than developing new ones.	◦ Schools, if they are not doing so already, should undertake periodic audits to assess the levels of technology learners and schools have access to. This assists in ascertaining the current strength of the software and hardware provision available. ◦ This information should be fed back centrally so a national picture of access can be realised and interventions put in place to support marginalised learners.	◦ Yearly data should be collected for schools to understand the range of technology children have access to in school and at home. ◦ Based on the preceding responses, commission a working group of the subject associations and educators to form a 'State of the Nation' report so the 'strengths of the existing systems' can clearly be identified.

(Continued)

Table 9.9 (Cont).

European Commission's framework for developing pandemic plans	Technology implication	Action/Proposed Solution
3 New systems implemented during a pandemic **should be tested** during the inter-pandemic period.	◦ Many software companies provided free access to resources or systems to support Virtual Learning. Funding should continue to subsidise heavily the adoption of the most useful. ◦ This should include access to technical support to ensure schools are able to implement solutions.	◦ Ensure that a post-pandemic task group reviews and feeds into the 'State of the Nation' report. Clear recommendations should be set for the future for when another pandemic occurs.
4 **Adequate resources** must be allocated for all aspects of pandemic preparedness and response.	◦ Assessment and analysis should take place across the four key areas of technology school development: a) *Hardware* – Are the computers and devices adequately capable of supporting the learning? b) *Infrastructure-*what is needed to ensure the school has a system? c) *Software* – what do students need access to? Including software to complete tasks at home. d) *Training* – What training is provided for staff and parents to ensure they are supported?	◦ In the light of the first pandemic, consider the key areas of technology school development. Identify gaps and where funding is required in order to provide adequate resources.

5 The planning process, implementing what is planned, testing and revising the plan in order for **key stakeholders to familiarise themselves with the issues at hand**, may be even more important than the pandemic plan itself.

6 Pandemic response requires that **business continuity plans and surge capacity plans be developed** for the health sector and all other sectors that could be affected by a pandemic to ensure sustained capacity during a pandemic.

7 The **response to a pandemic must be evidence-based** where this is available and commensurate with the threat, in accordance with the IHR. Planning should be based on pandemics of differing severity while the response is based on the actual situation determined by national and global risk assessments. (EC 2009a, p. 1).

◦ Schools should be supported in putting in place a technology pandemic plan.

◦ Provide planning templates for different approaches to online learning and strategic planning to support schools in their own thinking process.

The technology pandemic plan should present different models based on pandemics of differing severity so that schools can be agile in their response. This needs to be based on the actual situation determined by local and national assessments. So if a school were to enter lockdown they could make the decision of the appropriate pedagogy to drive the learning forward.

Futurecasting: this pandemic has shown a glimpse of what is possible with educational technologies

Those who cannot learn from history are doomed to repeat it.

George Santayana

Will school leaders and governments learn from history and follow the EU's advice to maintain online knowledge services for teachers during times of stability so that when a rapid transition to Remote Emergency Teaching is needed again, teachers, learners and parents are supported in making the transition? Implementing a solution using technology, especially at scale is problematic if a sustainable solution is not considered.

Key components to be considered when creating an effective system to support continuity of learning and assessment at times of crisis include: the pressures on teachers; young people's skills and knowledge about the use of technology; actual technologies available and everyone's access to internet and data; or alternative ways of accessing online content through offline access options.

This pandemic has shown a glimpse of what is possible.

It is up to stakeholders, organisations and policy makers to create a vision and sustain its implementation in partnership so that technology helps schools and education to be agile in times of disruption in schooling.

Notes

1 In England, over 200,000 laptops and tablets and over 50,000 4G wireless routers were supposed to be provided to children who were care leavers, or aged between 0 to 19 years with a social worker, or disadvantaged Year 10 pupils. This equipment was given to local authorities and multi-academy trusts who then owned the devices. However, like any large technology project, this was not without its difficulties (Dickens 2020).

2 Eligible primary schools in England received £1,500 and secondaries received £2,000. Funding for academies within multi-academy trusts was capped at £1,000 per school. Analysis/comment needed here.

3 Regrettably, much of the research, the documents, the presentations and the reports that emerged during the 15 years of EdNA's development and operation were not archived and have now been lost to posterity. However, there is much to learn about archiving electronic resources and non-commercially published

digital materials and resources. The preservation and storage of national digital education resources may be an area for future national collaborative endeavour (White G. and Parker, L. 2016).

4 BECTA repository https://libguides.ioe.ac.uk/c.php?g=482245andp=3299063

5 'Pay the Wi-Fi or feed the children': Coronavirus has intensified the UK's digital divide www.cam.ac.uk/stories/digitaldivide

Section 4
Moving forward

 # Reopening schools

Introduction and context

Decisions on reopening will require countries to quickly gather critical information on how schools, teachers, students and communities are coping with closures and the pandemic. Rapid response surveys of school and local leaders, teachers, students and parents can help provide this information. Decision makers must then assess how learning and wellbeing can best be supported in each context, with special consideration of the benefits of classroom-based instruction vis-à-vis remote learning, against risk factors related to reopening of schools, noting the inconclusive evidence around the infection risks related to school attendance.

(UNESCO June 2020b, p. 2)

The preceding chapters outline lessons learned in different areas of operation for schools during the Covid period from March to December 2020.

This chapter considers the context schools in which schools in badly affected countries found themselves in the latter part of 2020 as they coped with the aftermath of what was called the first wave of Covid-19. This was followed by the reopening of shops and schools and then the closing of schools for deep cleans and the sending home of students and staff as the virus spread again. In some countries, schooling was suspended until 2021. In New York and Austria in late November, all schools were closed again as national infection rates rose and as it became apparent that teenagers spread the virus at the same rate as adults. There were still questions about the extent to which younger children spread the disease.

In most countries, schools were closed during initial national lockdowns as outbreaks developed for the first time. China was the first country to lockdown a

DOI: 10.4324/9781003155591-15

major area – Wuhan in January 2020 – with Italy being the first European country to lockdown large areas in early 2020. Across the world there was a wave of national lockdowns (but not, for example, in Sweden) followed some months later by gradual easing of restrictions while the virus was still circulating. How to reopen schools – or not – to *all* children was controversial, because no one could be sure what the impact on the spread of the virus and the lives of those associated with school would be.

In years to come, it may be that the fear of the unknown and the disruption to everyday life in 2020 will be forgotten except in the history books.

In early 2020, schools were operating in a society where, in the initial stages of the pandemic, no one could say for certain how infection took place between individuals, what groups in society would be most affected or whether the virus would kill randomly across the age groups or perhaps kill more men or people with preexisting medical conditions. No one predicted that in Western societies proportionately more adult black and minority ethnic members of the population would die. No one knew how many children would die and how quickly they would catch the disease and become ill. What might that mean for children returning to school? No one could answer how long would the virus live in still air, moving air, on cardboard (parcels), paper (books), metal (door handles), footballs, tennis racket handles, computer keyboards, soft toys, in sand, on tools, on taps, on plastic bags, on the outside of masks, on the inside of masks, on fingers. Data on these issues started to become public in the latter part of the year.

The media recalled previous pandemics – influenza 1918–1920 (which started on a farm in the USA and spread via World War I group ships carrying US troops to the battlefields in Europe), polio, smallpox, bubonic plague – which were indiscriminate in their killing.

With Covid-19, the coronavirus pandemic of 2020, there was uncertainty over how to diagnose it and how to treat it. Routine hospital appointments were cancelled, retired health service staff called back into service, emergency hospitals set up in stadia and halls. The Chinese built a large new hospital in Wuhan in weeks.[1] In Western countries, there was much controversy over the wearing of facemasks – a preventative measure well established in the Chinese/Japanese societies, dating, it was said, from the flu pandemic of 1917/18 and more recently with the SARs and MERS outbreaks from 2002 onwards. The requirement to wear masks became seen as a freedom issue in the USA initially and spread to other Western societies with people taking to the streets to protest that compulsory wearing of masks was an infringement of their liberty. What did this mean for schools reopening – for vulnerable pupils, BAME staff, local communities? What were schools expected to require?

Politicians were drawn into the mask controversy with politicians, such as Trump (USA), Johnson (UK) and Bolsonaro (Brazil), decrying the wearing of masks and the severity of the virus only to be forced into U-turn after U-turn as deaths rose and the virus spread and they themselves and, for Trump and Bolsonaro, their families, caught the virus. Trump became known for his super-spreader events.[2]

However, with schools closed and parents working from home or finding their workplaces closed down, national economies began to plummet countries into deep economic recessions. A 'new normal' balance was needed between the risks of schools opening, the benefits to the economy of getting parents back to work and the potential of slowing the loss of national income (which in turn affects the health and education systems negatively). These challenges had the potential of creating a spiral of decline in countries. During the latter part of 2020, the return to school of young people became a priority critical to a nation's well-being and economic progress.

Overall challenge: reopening schools while keeping children, teachers and communities safe

How to exit from lockdown following the school closures was a major challenge. Reopening required a carefully considered re-entry plan for every school because the funding and facilities available for safe practice – for deep cleaning, for extra handwashing, social distancing, air flow, and the availability of resources for each individual child – books, art, computer keyboards, cooking and technology tools – varied.

While governments issued guidelines, these were usually generic and needed interpretation at the local level for each school, as the context of space for social distancing and the age of school buildings differs for each, with old schools having extremely limited options. Tents were used in some countries (e.g. Jamaica), but hurricanes and local climate conditions also had to be considered.

Specific challenges: in reopening schools during a pandemic

The following specific challenges are covered in this chapter:

* Complexity of making schools 'safe enough' places
* Managing teacher and pupil absences
* Anxieties among parents and teachers and absenteeism.

Specific challenge 10.1 Complexity of making schools 'safe enough' places

Guidance was published in UNESCO's Framework for Reopening Schools (June 2020b) and UNESCO, UNICEF, World Bank (April 2020) which was the outcome of collaboration between UNESCO, UNICEF, the World Food Programme and the World Bank.

> Across countries leaders are grappling with difficult and uncertain trade-offs as they consider easing lockdowns. This framework serves to inform the decision-making process on when to reopen schools, support national preparations and guide the implementation process, as part of the overall public health and education planning processes. Contextualisation and continuous adaption is necessary in order to respond to local conditions and meet each child's learning, health and safety needs.
>
> (UNESCO's Framework for Reopening Schools June 2020b, p. 2)

The Framework is a clearly set-out tool but is directed largely at national governments. It recognises the need for school by school contextualisation. In the following, we supplement this guidance for schools on reopening. Examples of risk assessments and plans for return to schooling for all are included as Annexes and include one primary and two secondary schools (rural and urban). This specific information from the English context is included to illustrate the complexity of school planning.

In England, from which we had reports of a vacuum of national leadership, a group of educators drawn from different parts of the country, teaching in different phases and with different responsibilities came together in June/July 2020 to develop advice on the reopening of schools. This group of headteachers, teachers, researchers and academics drew together their experiences across regions of the country, alongside analysis of government briefings and ministers' policies, to produce a report on the reopening of schools in England in the autumn of 2020; the group was called the EAGLE Research Group (Emergency Advisory Group for Learning and Education). (The full report is included in the Annexes for those needing an exemplar, with a clearly crafted set of recommendations to which we contributed.)

The EAGLE Report (2020) summarises the challenges for reopening schools under the headings:

1 Scientific advice on transmission involving students
2 The impact of school closure on students: well-being; school achievement, poverty and disadvantage
3 Government policy and media emphasis
4 Conditions and challenges for reopening: preventing the spread of infections; the urgency of catching up

5 Curriculum
6 Assessment and accountability
7 Primary schools
8 Secondary schools
9 Distance/remote/home learning
10 Well-being: the challenges of a return to school
11 Taking care of teachers
12 The school in the community

The report is worth reading in full. Table 10.1 has recommendations from the EAGLE report specifically for the English context, other countries will have learned different lessons which need to be recorded and used to revise existing plans. The list in Table 10.1 may provide a useful starting point.

Table 10.1 Case Study England – recommendations for reopening from educators

The EAGLE Report (July 2020) generated specific recommendations: the following list provides a summary of key proposals and principles.

1 'Although different human needs have to be balanced, public health cannot be sacrificed to unrealistic educational demands.
2 Rapid improvement is needed in communicating medical information to local authorities and school governors, in order to facilitate sound decision making.
3 While infection levels remain serious, arrange for smaller classes in primary schools; and new forms of curriculum organisation in secondary schools in a combination of on-site and distance learning.
4 Recognise young people's experiences during recent months, and adopt a sensitive approach to re-engaging them, rather than threatening parents with fines.
5 Support parents and teachers in monitoring and caring for students' mental wellbeing, providing specialist support where needed.
6 Schools should prioritise children's wellbeing, thinking in terms of a 'recovery curriculum'. Young people should be re-engaged by a curriculum which is not only broad and challenging, but which engages their interests and concerns and develops independence and initiative.
7 Improve the quality of distance learning resources, and ensure that all disadvantaged students have access to computers and internet.
8 Increase the funding of tutorial support for students who have encountered the greater barriers to learning, and route this through schools.

9 Reduce the pressures of public examinations and primary school tests, including reduced content for GCSEs, greater use of coursework and portfolios, and cancelling universal testing in primary schools for the coming year.

10 Provide a supportive environment for teachers and other staff, by increasing trust, cooperation, and professional development, whilst removing sources of threat such as inspections which could serve as a distraction from students' needs.

11 Encourage stronger links between schools and communities, particularly in more disadvantaged areas.'

Specific challenge 10.2 Managing teacher and pupil absences

In preparation for school to start on Tuesday 1st September, the English ministry of education issued guidance on reopening schools at 5.30pm Friday 29th August 2020.[3] Monday 31st August was a public holiday. Secondary school headteachers were faced with usually more than 1000 children arriving on the Tuesday and with a government that suggested all plans were changed after schools closed on the Friday. This is the worst case of a ministry of education not showing leadership or forward planning and indeed making teachers' work impossible that we came across in the research for this book and we spoke to teachers from at least 30 countries.

In England following the September return to school for all, an attempt was made to keep schools open but this meant the sending home of whole year groups as staff and children tested positive and everyone who had been near these individuals was required to self-isolate for two weeks. Such a system was clearly unsustainable as the learners or teachers could be back at school for a couple of days and have to isolate again. Class sizes rocketed.

There seemed no obvious solution to ensuring continuity of education apart from remote learning. Teachers found they were covering for absent colleagues as well as doing their regular teaching as well as providing lessons for those sent home: making an impossible workload. With this approach of groups of children being sent home and then coming back perhaps there was more opportunity for children to miss schooling than if a remote schooling approach had been continued with.

In Scotland, Watson (2020) reported five lessons in mid-August following reopening in August.

1 Infections rose, but there was not a surge
2 Cautious parents put a strain on testing
3 Pupil absences (85% pupils were present)

4   Guidance needed to evolve

5   Hand sanitiser strained tight budgets.

Citing Jim Thewliss, from School Leaders Scotland, which represents senior school staff, Watson (2020) observed, 'Parents are taking a fail-safe approach.[4] They're thinking my child is not well, we're going to get a test and keep them off in the meantime . . . [Absenteeism] is an emerging issue' and as a result he believes 'schools will have to find better ways of supporting learning for children who are being kept home'.

In the first few days of September, there were the first cases of transmission within schools located at two schools in Glasgow. Schools reopened across England in September and the UK soon had a shortage of testing kits. By October, virus transmission was out of control nationally (with similar spread happening across Europe). In Northern Ireland, schools were closed again in October for two weeks to slow spread of the virus.[5]

Specific challenge 10.3 Anxieties among parents and teachers and absenteeism

Anxieties among parents and teachers about the safety of children returning to school is well documented. A major risk in schools being open was that teachers and schools provide a hub, a meeting point in communities. This means schools link nearly all community members so the potential for cross-infection and the risks for teachers, children and communities can be expected to be higher than for most employment sectors apart from some areas of health, hospitality and public transport.

However, other factors in absenteeism of children that were found during the Ebola epidemics in Africa were identified as needing to earn money, inability to pay school fees and teenage pregnancy (Selbervik 2020). In Liberia, Selbervik cites World Bank survey data as suggesting about 25% children did not return to school after Ebola.

Table 10.2 provides early examples of outbreaks from different countries as schools reopened after extensive periods of lockdown. Outbreaks with pupils and teachers were regularly reported from mid-2020 as schools reopened through to the end of the year which is the point at which the recording of data for this book ceased. An internet search provides further examples. Some countries were more cautious than others for example due to the rate of spread of the virus, in Mexico the decision was taken to close schools until 2021 and the government invested in TV and radio educational programmes. In Northern Ireland schools were closed in mid-October for an indeterminate period.

Table 10.2 Outbreaks as schools resume make the headlines

Scotland: 'Seventeen members of staff and two pupils have tested positive for coronavirus at a school in Dundee less than two weeks after Scottish schools returned' (Culbertson 24 August 2020). Numbers rose steadily over subsequent days.

Australia: 'Cherrybrook's Tangara School for Girls has been linked to 17 cases among staff and students in just two days' (Moore 12 August 2020)

England: 'English schools suffered 30 outbreaks of coronavirus after reopening in June, an analysis of official figures has found. A Public Health England (PHE) report released on Sunday said that there were 198 confirmed Covid-19 cases associated with schools reopening following the easing of national lockdown. Some 128 of those were among staff and 70 were in children. A total of 121 cases were linked to the outbreaks, 30 in children and 91 in staff, the analysis said' (www.standard.co.uk/news/uk/30-coronvavirus-outbreaks-schools-reopened-june-a4531326.html).

USA: 'Florida confirmed almost 9,000 new Covid-19 cases among children within 15 days in August as schools reopen, according to state data released Tuesday' (Coleman 24 August 2020). (Interestingly, the cases in Florida were reported on the early BBC news on 28 August 2020, but by mid-morning the story no longer appeared in the newsfeed. This leads to speculation as to why.)

Lessons learned: about reopening schools

10.1 Recurring closures: Outbreaks are to be expected with subsequent whole school closures or sending home of groups of learners and individual teachers in an ad hoc way.

10.2 Learning is more disrupted: Learning is disrupted more perhaps than if remote teaching had continued, as learners and teachers are in and out of school as outbreaks occur but teachers are busy with teaching those still in school and are unable to fit in remote teaching in the same way as before.

10.3 Schools need support with extra costs: Additional funds have to be found from somewhere to cover extra staffing and learning costs.

Planning toolkit: for reopening schools

For reopening of schools as every school and every country is different, we suggest two strategies.

At the national level, we suggest reopening plans consider the advice of the EAGLE Report (2020) which, as mentioned, directs the planner to the key questions to consider about how to safely reopen schools under the following headings.

1 Scientific advice on transmission involving students
2 The impact of school closure on students: well-being; school achievement, poverty and disadvantage
3 Government policy and media emphasis
4 Conditions and challenges for reopening: preventing the spread of infections; the urgency of catching up
5 Curriculum
6 Assessment and accountability
7 Primary schools
8 Secondary schools
9 Distance/remote/home learning
10 Well-being: the challenges of a return to school
11 Taking care of teachers
12 The school in the community.

At the school level, we suggest those responsible for reopening plans consider Annexes 2–6, which at the school level, direct the planner to the key questions to consider about how to safely reopen schools.

Futurecasting: about reopening of schools

What is certain is that there will be other pandemics, epidemics, human crises of conflict and natural disasters which are likely to disrupt young people's schooling. Concern has been expressed by the educators from many countries, who took part in the discussions which informed this book, that national politicians and their advisors making decisions about reopening schools do not have the specialist depth of knowledge to understand how their policies and planning will be operationalised and what the unintended consequences will be.[6] The detailed school plans referenced in this chapter are included so that non-educators making policy decisions can be better informed about the far reaching and nuanced complexities in making schools as safe as possible and can benchmark their decisions against those of informed colleagues.

At the time of writing, December 2020, some, not all, countries that locked down early on and minimised viral transfer experienced significant fresh outbreaks as they eased lockdowns, so the futurecasting scenarios need to include school openings, closings, re-openings, re-closings.

As is reported in the previous chapters, the learners who experienced minimal disruption were either in schools with students and teachers who all had personal and anytime access to the latest internet connected devices, or they were already in either the Schools of the Air in Australia or the Telephone School in Canada or they were in areas, such as islands, which the virus had not yet reached. Futurecasting scenarios for other areas should be based on complete closure of schools – the value of a national online/radio online school seems to be the only solution in such cases – if continuity of learning and assessment is to be provided. Telephone/personal visits by teachers or email contact in addition need to be used by teachers to keep in touch with students.

Notes

1 Chinese build a new hospital within weeks www.bbc.co.uk/newsround/51285450
2 Trump's super spreader events www.independent.co.uk/news/world/americas/us-election-2020/trump-white-house-election-night-party-covid-super-spreader-b1721492.html; www.independent.co.uk/news/world/americas/us-election-2020/trump-coronavirus-superspreader-polls-covid-19-amy-coney-barrett-b1186362.html; https://chicago.suntimes.com/columnists/2020/10/28/21539209/trump-maga-rally-super-spreaders-typhoid-mary-gene-lyons
3 Re-opening risks www.bbc.co.uk/news/education-53960265
4 Absenteeism on reopening of schools www.bbc.co.uk/news/uk-scotland-54013125
5 NI schools to close for two weeks www.bbc.co.uk/news/uk-northern-ireland-54593770
6 The complementary text by the authors, on *Education System Design: foundations, policy options and consequences* (Hudson et al. 2021) outlines policy options and their consequences for policymakers who have extremely limited or no background in education.

Post Covid-19

Opportunities and international will

Introduction and context

The quotations that follow highlight the potential for the education of young people to change the world and outline an opportunity for international leadership to support the education of young people.

> *Education is the most powerful weapon which you can use to change the world*
> (Nelson Mandela[1])

> *Never before have we witnessed educational disruption on such a scale. Partnership is the only way forward. This Coalition [The Global Education Coalition] is a call for coordinated and innovative action to unlock solutions that will not only support learners and teachers now, but through the recovery process, with a principal focus on inclusion and equity.*
> (UNESCO Director-General Audrey Azoulay, August 2020c).

The lessons learned from the Covid-19 pandemic coupled with the rapid worldwide mass adoption of affordable personal digital technologies supporting remote education alongside radio, TV, telephone and desk-top computers, solar power and low-flying satellites show that we could have a world where every young person could access high-quality education.

The technologists have made remote learning for all possible, and the Covid crisis has raised awareness worldwide not only about how remote learning can be achieved but of the serious damage to individuals and communities of the digital divide. Too many young people have been left behind in their learning, marginalised and denied the chance to be the best they can be for themselves, their communities and their countries.

DOI: 10.4324/9781003155591-16

In reflecting on the experience of learners during the Covid pandemic, we ask: could there be the same level of international will and determination to provide high-quality education for all as there is in solving the Covid-19 pandemic, or the commitment driving the eradication of polio, and as there was for the eradication of smallpox?

There is hope for the longer term. It seems that the Covid crisis has precipitated actions which could support achieving the aim of the United Nations Sustainable Development Goal 4c: high-quality education for all by 2030 – if money and the will to act can be found.

A 'Global Education Coalition' has been created by UNESCO in response to the loss of young people's learning due to Covid. UNESCO's Coalition brings together business and educational organisations 'to support countries in scaling up their best distance learning practices and reaching children and youth who are most at risk'.

Is it possible that an unexpected outcome of the pandemic is an acceleration of actions to make online educational resources, remote learning up to school leaving levels and further lifelong learning accessible to all including the most marginalised?

Might an outcome be not only secondary and primary school online services but open and distance learning at vocational and further education levels, funded like the Open University (OU) system which is found in many countries? An OU model for secondary and vocational education could be publicly funded and made freely available to all learners or privately funded through a fee-paying system. Alternatively, a hybrid model of partly public and private might be the answer, with countries deciding what content would be a national priority for learners, thereby making that aspect free. The Government of New South Wales in Australia has an Open University type institute for remote learning of vocational subjects – TAFE Digital[2] (TAFE colleges are Technical and further education colleges). Might something like this be replicated, adapted for particular cultures, countries and needs and open to learners everywhere?

Might teacher leaders be fully engaged and consulted?

Politicians have the unenviable job of leading when there may be no consensus about the direction of travel.

However, to protect the education of young people, should those taking decisions at least be expected to reach agreement with teacher leaders so that the teachers having to implement plans can trust that the plans are built on the reality of educational practices and not just created, as seems to have happened in countries with populist governments, to appeal to the voter base? (See newspaper reports on Trump [USA] and Johnson [UK] where they call for schools to be reopened even when infection rates were rising.)

Teachers know that best practice for marginalised learners benefits all learners. Imagine, if, in this pandemic, national politicians had focused on how to keep continuity of learning for the most marginalised as perhaps could be realised by the UNESCO Global Coalition for Education plans.

Those opportunities, however, are for the future. In the concluding chapter of this book, we look to the present and at lessons about remote learning and the inclusion of marginalised learners from the Covid-19 period.

Overall challenge: political will to seize opportunities to provide access for all to high-quality education

Might UNESCO and UNESCO's supporters taken advantage of the opportunities which opened up by teachers having to adapt through the Covid crisis to make, as a minimum, remote schooling available to all.

Four forms of remote schooling seem to have had the most success in providing continuity of learning and assessment to learners in a wide range of settings during the Covid-19 period.

1   Australia's School of the Air model[3](a tried and tested and quality-assured model for remote schooling using satellite technology to connect remote learners to their teachers which combines the next three forms).
2   Telephone School – Canada has a working model in Manitoba – the teacher mediated option for schooling (TMO) or Telephone School[4]
3   Television and radio programmes were provided by many national governments
4   Internet accessible resources for use online or offline coupled with teacher input were provided by many national governments.

If funds were available, the preceding approaches – applied consistently with teacher support – seem to have the potential of supporting all learners, including the most marginalised, anywhere, particularly, as VSO research shows,[5] if coupled with community-based or volunteer teachers where there are teacher shortages. Surveys undertaken by VSO (2020a, b) during Covid-19 indicate the challenges teachers and communities face with no telephone connection for schools in some remote areas. Looking to the future, couldn't the 4G internet aerial balloon or low-flying satellites that support connectivity in other parts of the world bring connectivity to these areas? In any case there are well-established technologies for sharing offline, internet-originated materials. See, for example, E-Granary. All that is needed is Blue-tooth technology, a couple of devices and a memory stick, and materials can be transferred phone to phone or to a computer. Solar cells for power are another tech-nology that is well established.

Opportunity 1: school as usual during crises: an example from Australia's School of the Air

Australia's School of the Air model is a 'virtual school' delivering schooling in remote areas, which uses a tried, tested and quality-assured model for remote schooling using whatever technologies are available to connect teachers and learners who are not in the same place. It was established in 1951 with pedal-operated short-wave radio before moving to telephone and internet technologies. The School of the Air goal is 'Inspiring isolated students to recognise and realise their potential'. Kerrie Russell, Principal of the Alice Springs School of the Air in Australia's Northern Territory, reported to us in August 2020 that her learners – who live in isolated homesteads across inland Australia, perhaps hundreds of kilometres from a town – have experienced 'business as usual' during the Covid pandemic period:

> We have been very fortunate in that during the pandemic there have been very few changes to the education experience for our students. Their day to day learning has not been interrupted at all.

> What has been affected is:

> 1 Last term we could not hold our termly in-school/residential (the Department of Education guidelines at that time would not allow it; however, we are holding the one scheduled for this term, in three weeks' time)

> 2 We had to delay our Home Visit schedule (each primary teacher visits each student (usually an overnight trip) in their home – we did not do those last term but are doing them now and into next term

> 3 We have a few families living across the state border and due to departmental guidelines at the moment, the interstate students are not getting a teacher visiting them.

> On the whole though it has been business as usual – we feel very grateful for that.

Opportunity 2: teacher training and improvements in pedagogies

> *In many countries, education is still far from being a knowledge industry in the sense that its own practices are not yet being transformed by knowledge about the efficacy of those practices.*
>
> (OECD Teaching and learning International Survey 2009 p. 3)

Given the challenges outlined in this book, there is clearly a need for the training of teachers, now and in the future, to include relevant and appropriate skills, knowledge and understanding in order to be prepared for:

* teaching within a world that is subject to the sudden disruption to formal education due to emergencies such as pandemics, epidemics and natural disasters which includes being able to mix online/remote learning with both face-to-face teaching and intergenerational learning at home;
* a different approach to evaluation, assessment and validation of achievement in online/distance learning environments and informal settings as well as more traditional formal learning environments.

Therefore, teacher training programmes now need to include study of pedagogical models and approaches that are suitable for online/distance learning, formal and informal learning and intergenerational learning to an equal level and standard as their specialist subject knowledge.

Teacher training will need to equip teachers with the ability to devise models for semi-independent learning drawing on learners' own interests and motivations, and maximising input from parents, siblings and other family members while providing support in the form of the specialist knowledge and support that schools and outside professional agencies can provide as and when necessary.

The special edition of the *Journal for Technology, Pedagogy and Education* (to be published in 2021, www.tandfonline.com/toc/rtpe20/current) provides detailed records and analysis of practices which emerged across the education sector in different countries at this time. Countries might do well to look to Finland's approach to teacher training, with the study of pedagogies included to an equivalent level and standard as subject specialisms (Halinen 2016). Teacher training needs to also include how teachers can build learning through valuing and understanding how the social and cultural capital in the local community can support learning.

Opportunity 3: knowledge mobilisation: improved health and hygiene through health education

Improved knowledge about health and hygiene resulting from Covid-19 may have long-term positive impact on the health of communities. The impact of the opportunities offered through the UNESCO Coalition could be far reaching if they adopt well-tested knowledge mobilisation strategies. For example, an expert research institute on infectious diseases at De Montfort University worked with teachers to translate research findings into appropriate curricula materials. These were tested in a number of countries to evaluate their impact on children's understanding and behaviour and were found to significantly increase effective hand hygiene. These were turned into a MESHGuide for early years educators which can be seen here[6] and for free learning resources in multiple languages for use across the world, see the Germs Journey website (www.germs.journey.com). The MESHGuides site provides a building set of resources in early years education, education of deaf children and, forthcoming, key aspects of primary education.[7]

Opportunity 4: lifelong catch-up opportunities

> *[W]e need a new focus on the quality of education and the relevance of learning, on what children, youth and adults are actually learning . . . We need an ever stronger focus on teachers and teacher educators as change agents across the board.*
>
> (Irina Bokova Director General of UNESCO 2015, p. 4)

The Covid-19 pandemic has had worldwide impact on schooling, and much concern has been expressed in the press worldwide about the loss of education for young people.

Some children are born to marginalisation through poverty, disability or location. However, marginalisation and the accompanying loss-of-life chances can come to all through the sudden disruption of young people's schooling which is happening year on year somewhere in the world because of wars, emigration, epidemics and natural disasters.

Missed schooling dashes young people's hopes of what they might do in the world. It robs their communities and countries of the benefits they might have brought if they had been able to go on to study to become medical staff, teachers, inventors, entrepreneurs, farmers using the latest techniques to improve harvests, engineers, designers, builders and so on.

Do we, as members of a global community have to accept this loss of opportunity? Earlier we mention the possibility of secondary and vocational education being available on the model of Open Universities (OU) which have been successful around the world. Imagine the opportunities for communities and individuals which might result.

Opportunity 5: digital systems to deal with complex knowledge

> *The 20thC has given us a volume of knowledge and skills that is beyond what any individual can simply hold in their head, can know how to deliver on and simply do it on their own. The volume of knowledge and skills has*

exceeded our individual capabilities . . . We need systems to help us deal with complex knowledge.

(Gawande 2015)

Why doesn't every country have an open, public, knowledge-base for schooling supporting improving of teaching and learning regardless of whether there is a crisis or not? Earlier we mention the online teacher resource banks available in Australia, China, Ghana, the Netherlands, Singapore, South Korea, Scotland. However, the World Bank (2017) reports highlight the vulnerability of these if they are under the direct control of one government – when the government changes, the resource can disappear overnight. Table 11.1 provides, however, a cautionary tale.

Table 11.1 Case Study: England – lost opportunities and lessons learned

Up to 2010, teachers in England were supported with online advice through several specialist government agencies: on the use of technology in teaching and on technology infrastructure by BECTA, on curriculum and assessment by the QCDA, on teacher training and professional development by the TDA, through Teachers' TV and through the DFE TeacherNet.[8]

All of these resources, costing taxpayers tens of millions of pounds, were removed in 2010 by the incoming government with the Secretary of State Michael Gove and his advisor Dominic Cummings telling civil servants they were sending a bushfire through the education system, reducing the collective online knowledge-base of the English education system to ashes.

At the time of the Covid-19 pandemic these resources could have supported parents, teachers and pupils as they moved to remote learning. The lack of central leadership and vision meant that teachers in the English education system experienced patchy support. This removal of government-funded online resources when priorities change has been mirrored in India, Australia, Sweden and no doubt in other places. If the resources had been books, there would have been a publicly outcry with a noticeable burning of books, no doubt. A lesson from this tale is that educators would be wise to protect any resources developed with government money from destruction should any future government be careless or malevolent. The UK's 2010 Secretary of State for education Michael Gove called teacher educators 'the blob' and teachers 'enemies of promise'. Part of his brushfire incinerated the online resources for schools on pandemic planning;[9] the lack of resources for English teachers and learners during Covid has potentially dulled the promise of many a young learner and meant teachers were replicating what Gove and his cronies destroyed.

Opportunity 6: a marginal gains knowledge mobilisation strategy – for sustainability

The education sector has within it the knowledge needed to improve the education of all children but this knowledge is held in isolated pockets and is not yet accessible to all teachers in developing or developed countries, in large and small nation states. To improve this situation a knowledge mobilisation (KMb) strategy is proposed led by an international body of educators, mobilised to use low cost digital tools to:

- *collect, codify, summarise and index existing knowledge to create an accessible 'Edupedia'*
- *collaborate internationally to identify knowledge gaps; and to share and build knowledge across the school-based education sector, through an online network of educators.'*

(Education Futures Collaboration Charity/MESHGuides
Global Knowledge Mobilisation Summit Report 2017)

The pandemic may provide an opportunity to do education differently. It is possible that UNESCO's Coalition has some chance of providing a low-cost, sustainable remote-learning portal, open to all and thus supporting the achievement of UNESCOs sustainable development goals for high-, medium- and low-income countries of high-quality learning for all children.

But it could fail if it does not engage teachers from the outset and if it does not use systems which support sustainability. The European SchoolNet model – established in 1995 and still operating today, supported by 34 ministries of education – is a model to follow for sustainability: shared endeavour, shared risk, focused on teachers' needs. As the references to the World Bank (2017) review of digital educational resources in individual countries shows, individual ministries of education in many countries lost interest in knowledge banks for teachers and closed them down regardless of how they were used and what needs were being met.

This loss of resources has been a concern for teachers and teacher educators worldwide.

In the light of the loss of these resources and in response to UNESCO Director General Irina Bokova's call to teachers and teacher educators to be 'change agents' to achieve with SDG 4, five international education professional associations came together to hold knowledge mobilisation conferences/webinars over the period 2016/2017/2020 to consider what educators could do.

People from ten countries attended the first Global Teacher Education Knowledge Mobilisation Summit for SDG 4c, and Table 11.2 sets out the strategy that was proposed following the Summit. Teacher research briefing/research summary prototypes were subsequently developed and tested with people from over 200 countries which are now using these. (See www.MESHGuides.org.)

The 2016 Summit report summary is included in Table 11.2 (Education Futures Collaboration Charity/MESHGuides 2016). The proposed knowledge mobilisation strategy for making the latest knowledge available to teachers takes a 'marginal gains' approach showing what could be achieved from resources already in the system.

Table 11.2 Summary report: A low cost 'marginal gains strategy' to support SDG4 – engaging educators and aid agencies as 'change agents' to bring a step change in teacher quality.

A 'marginal gains' strategy for SDG 4 – key features from the 1st Global Teacher Education Knowledge Mobilisation Summit 2016

The Knowledge Mobilisation (KMb) strategy outlined here draws on existing processes, relationships, and resources already in the education system to bring a step change in teacher quality within three years.

The strategy is based on providing teachers (parents and policymakers) wherever they are, with access via a mobile phone to a dynamic evidence base for practice which summarises the best evidence available in pedagogy and subject content knowledge.

The proposition is that

* the education sector has within it the knowledge needed to improve, but knowledge is held in isolated pockets and is inaccessible to all stakeholders. Much knowledge of potential benefit to teachers and communities is held in university databases, research institutes, academic articles or doctorates, and by individual aid agencies;
* 'marginal gains' achieved through minor changes in processes and practices at all levels and by all players could ensure the effective use of existing assets, to provide, cumulatively, a self-sustaining system for keeping teachers' knowledge up to date.

The strategy proposes the following actions

1   **Adopting low cost ways of working** including online networking and new forms of digital publishing to

  * publish in a usable form summaries of research as teacher research briefings;
  * index and localize existing research-based knowledge for teaching every concept for every subject for every age group (Wikipedia

---

demonstrates the simplicity of this concept and the complexity of what can be achieved);

* fill in the knowledge gaps by scaling up promising research, harnessing the energies of educators who are active in research.

2   **Governance and structures:** an international network of educators (e.g. deans of education) benchmarking standards and sharing knowledge, handbooks and resources, supporting initial and lifelong learning for teachers. Such professional development could include developing teachers' skills to generate, access and apply new knowledge and so become 'bottom-up' agents for context-relevant change and innovation.

3   **Educators as change agents.**Professional/subject associations/networks have a wide range of minimal cost, practical levers for change, such as

* personal contact with student teachers/teachers through initial/continuing professional learning programmes;
* programme design which typically includes values, skills, knowledge and attitudes;
* publications: textbooks, training materials, web-based materials;
* teaching content and style, including professional attitudes;
* research publications: reports, articles, summaries;
* idea-sharing through networking, professional associations, national and international conferences and networks.

4   **Maximizing the value of existing capital assets** including existing published research through:

* accounting for existing intellectual capital assets through an Intellectual capital register to limit the devaluing and disregarding of existing assets.

5   **Repurposing/localising existing intellectual capital assets** also proposed to UNESCO by Udnaes et al. (2014), Hennessy (2016), Payler (2016).[10]

6   **Modernizing research commissioning processes**and bringing together research funders (governments, charities, aid agencies, corporate sponsors, and philanthropists) and journal editors/publishers to support this KMb strategy. For example, research commissioners could

* require new forms of publication, which make knowledge easily available;
* prioritise synthesis and gap analysis so as to avoid unnecessary replication;
* consider value for money of localizing and repurposing existing materials;
* register outputs on the 'Edupedia'.

7 **Reframing research and publishing expectations of academic staff**to include

- new accountability/promotion standards and requirements;
- new journal publishing/research processes to support cumulative research rather than proliferation of small studies;
- syntheses to build an accumulating evidence base;
- new university processes to provide access to the latest research summarised for teachers/policy makers to support lifelong learning for teachers and research-informed policy making;
- leveraging the MESHGuides approach which has been built on 30 years' research and development to provide an international standard.

8 **Reframing teachers' roles**

- to become a bridge between experts and those in their communities whose lives could be transformed by such knowledge (e.g. on water purity, health issues, energy, agriculture, entrepreneurship etc.);
- to use and contribute to the evidence for practice.

9 **UNESCO support is central** to achieving the commitment of government and aid agency stakeholders.

Source: Extract from EFC/MESHGuides (2016, 2017)[11]

Subsequently, members of the MESHGuides network developed different models for knowledge mobilisation relevant to different knowledge holders. See Table 11.3.

Opportunity 7: lifelong teacher learning: using resources already in the system

Following the first global summit, work commenced with members of the professional associations and other education stakeholders to test out and implement ideas which have resulted in the MESHGuides teacher research briefings/research summaries/(www.MESHGuides.org) and with models for knowledge mobilisation for the education sector involving different stake holders. Seven models for mobilising existing research knowledge and translating it for use in teachers practice have been developed and tested. The models mobilise research-based knowledge relevant to teachers from the 'generators of new knowledge' listed in Table 11.3.

Table 11.3 Mobilising expert knowledge to underpin teaching using resources already in the system

The following seven sources hold research-based knowledge relevant to teachers which has already been paid for by charities, universities, governments as well as through the voluntary contributions of teachers and teacher educators:

* professional education associations
* NGOs, working in education contexts
* regional and local networks
* university PhD education supervisors and students
* specialist research units
* teacher researcher networks
* individual researchers.

Given that smartphones are widely available across the world, including in LMICs (low- and middle-income countries), then a digital solution using cheap mobile technology to provide continuity for learning – life long – is possible. For each country, one way to ensure continuity of learning is investment (finances and training) in an effective education technology strategy. A collaboration, such as that with the European SchoolNet which is supported by 34 ministries, may be beneficial and cost effective for some countries, and we argue any such strategy should consider the following five elements (with thanks to Carl Smith):

1   An effective combination of rewards and controls to track and **enforce engagement** with learning by all students (engagement cannot be left to choice or chance).
2   The removal or limitation of **access** issues, so that access to digital online learning is a universal right for all children and adults who missed out on education the first time.
3   Development and widespread dissemination of **effective automated assessment systems** for all subjects linked to subject-specific resources covering key curriculum content.
4   **Investment in delivery systems** that enable effective asynchronous teaching and learning, including training CPD for teachers in online learning and creative pedagogies for distant/remote learning.
5   **Definitions of effective remote-learning** pedagogies made **an expectation** that all schools and teachers can deliver by providing the tools and systems discussed previously.

Points 2–5 could be covered by an effective national digital technology strategy – covering infrastructure/access for all schools/learners, curriculum assessment opportunities available through technology and online pedagogies.

All students will benefit from these, not only in the further event of a general or localised lockdown but as part of a national digital education strategy designed to raise standards in all schools, for all learners and at all times.

However, certain questions remain, namely:

- How much money can be devoted to setting up these systems? How might resources existing in education systems already be harnessed and deployed for the good of all of a society's children?
- Should they be nationally funded systems or are they better coordinated by the government but provided by commercial organisations?
- What are the expected outcomes and how can their effectiveness be monitored?
- Who needs to do what and when to ensure the futurecasting process is kept up to date?

Futurecasting: opportunities arising from the Covid-19 period

What if UNESCO's Global Education Coalition meant there were a coordinated national and international effort, applied with a sense of ambition and urgency, so an international digital education strategy could be set up quickly?

How would the Coalition engage with a wide range of educationalists, including teachers on the ground, professional associations and educational technology experts as well as access to whatever resources it takes to get the process started.

The economic and educational benefits could be both profound and game changing, but the process could also easily become embroiled in ideological battles, vested interests and appeasing political prejudices.

However, the resources are already in the system and with a vision for a research-informed knowledge-base for education following the marginal gain strategy, as outlined in Opportunity 6 and Tables 11.2 and 11.3, remote learning could be supported for young people and other community members everywhere.

> Unfortunately, as always in education, the consequence of a failure to act decisively will be borne by others long after the main decision makers have deserted the political stage. National and international leaders have the opportunity in their hands to minimise marginalisation of learners.
>
> Will they grasp it?

(Carl Smith Headteacher October 2020)

Notes

1 Mandela quotation https://blog.usaid.gov/2013/04/education-the-most-powerful-weapon/
2 TAFE Digital www.tafensw.edu.au/digital
3 A day in the life of an Australian child receiving remote teaching www.australian-children. com/school-of-the-air; Alice Springs School of the Air www.assoa.nt.edu.au
4 The teacher mediated option for schooling (TMO) or Telephone School www.edu.gov. mb.ca/k12/dl/index.html
5 VSO information www.vsointernational.org/news/blog/closing-the-education-gap-for-generation-covid
6 MESHGuide Early Years www.meshguides.org/guides/node/1343
7 For a list of MESHGuuides http://meshagain.meshguides.org/articles/
8 BECTA: https://libguides.ioe.ac.uk/c.php?g=482245andp=3299063; Teacher Training Resource Bank https://webarchive.nationalarchives.gov.uk/20110214161120/www.ttrb. ac.uk/; Qualifications and Curriculum Authority https://webarchive.nationalarchives.gov. uk/20110813032310/www.qcda.gov.uk/
9 Here is the UK School pandemic advice 2006 published originally on www.teacher-net.gov.uk/humanflupandemic and taken off line by government in 2010. We found an archived copy here: https://schools.oxfordshire.gov.uk/cms/sites/schools/files/folders/folders/documents/healthandsafety/main_schools_guide.pdf
10 See the summary and full reports on http://new.meshguides.org/wp-content/uploads/ 2019/07/Summary-of-Marginal-Gains-strategy.pdf and http://new.meshguides.org/wp-content/uploads/2019/07/TeacherEdKMBsummit2016report.pdf
11 See the summary and full reports on http://new.meshguides.org/wp-content/uploads/ 2019/07/Summary-of-Marginal-Gains-strategy.pdf and http://new.meshguides.org/wp-content/uploads/2019/07/TeacherEdKMBsummit2016report.pdf

References

Aljazeera (2020, August 17) *Which Countries Have Made Wearing Face Masks Compulsory*. www.aljazeera.com/news/2020/04/countries-wearing-face-masks-compulsory-200423094510867.html. Accessed 3 November 2020.

Angus Reid Institute (2020) *Kids and COVID-19: Canadian Children Are Done with School from Home, Fear Falling Behind, and Miss Their Friends*. http://angusreid.org/covid19-kids-opening-schools/. Accessed 3 November 2020.

ASCL (2020, March) *Coronavirus (Covid-19) Guidance for School and College Leaders*. https://docs.google.com/document/d/10PLqdGi2LX5KqqaZjMBdhru24-ZVwbFqbvjkNvNpO48/edit?usp=sharing. Accessed 3 November 2020.

Askew, M., Bishop, S., Christie, C., Eaton, S., Griffin, P., and Morgan, D. (2020) *Teaching for Mastery: Questions, Tasks and Activities to Support Assessment – Year 3*. Oxford: Oxford University Press and NCTEM. www.ncetm.org.uk/media/oaqfcvjq/mastery_assessment_y3.pdf. Accessed 3 November 2020.

Baska, M. (2020, June 4) *What Has Coronavirus Taught us about Leadership and Where Do We Go from Here?* www.peoplemanagement.co.uk/long-reads/articles/coronavirus-taught-leadership-where-go-from-here. Accessed 3 November 2020.

BBC (2020a) *Coronavirus Has Revealed the Scale of the Digital Divide*. www.bbc.co.uk/news/education-52399589. Accessed 3rd November 2020.

BBC (2020b, August 22) *Coronavirus Pandemic Could Be Over Within Two Years – WHO Head*. www.bbc.co.uk/news/world-53870798. Accessed 3 November 2020.

BECTA (2004) *What the Research Says about Virtual Learning Environments in Teaching and Learning*. http://archive.teachfind.com/becta/research.becta.org.uk/upload-dir/downloads/page_documents/research/wtrs_vles.pdf. Accessed 3 November 2020.

BECTA (2009) *Home Access Programme: One Year on – Summary December 2009*. https://dera.ioe.ac.uk/1541/1/becta_2009_ha1yearonsummary_report.pdf. Accessed 1 November 2020.

Blamires, M. (2015) 'Building Portals for Evidence-informed Education: Lessons from the Dead. A Case Study of the Development of a National Portal Intended to Enhance Evidence Informed Professionalism in Education'. *Journal of Education for Teaching: International Research and Pedagogy*, 41(5) [Special Issue], 597–607.

Bodycote, B. (2019, October) *Understanding School Refusal: Parental Perspectives.* Doctoral Research Seminar, De Montfort University, Leicester.

Bokova, I. (2015) *The Right to Education for All Children.* Paris: UNESCO. https://resourcecentre.savethechildren.net/library/right-education-all-children. Accessed 4 June 2021.

Capel, S., Leask, M., and Younie, S. (2019) *Learning to Teach in the Secondary School: A Companion to School Experience*, 8th ed. Abingdon: Routledge.

CBI (2010a) *Fulfilling Potential: The Business Role in Education.* London: Confederation of British Industry.

CBI (2010b) *Ready to Grow: Business Priorities for Education and Skills. Education and Skills Survey 2010.* London: Confederation of British Industry.

CBI (2012) *First Steps: A New Approach for Our Schools.* London: Confederation of British Industry.

CDC (Centre for Disease Control and Prevention, USA) (2020, August 11) *Cloth Face Masks in Schools.* www.cdc.gov/coronavirus/2019-ncov/community/schools-childcare/cloth-face-cover.html. Accessed 3 November 2020.

Center on Education Policy (2016, May) *Listen to Us: Teacher Views and Voices.* https://files.eric.ed.gov/fulltext/ED568172.pdf. Accessed 3 November 2020.

Children's Society Report (2020) Good Childhood. *London: Children's Society.* www.childrenssociety.org.uk/sites/default/files/2020-09/PRE022a_Good%20 Childhood%202020_V6_LR.pdf. Accessed 1 November 2020.

Click2Houston (2020, April) *Texas School District Supplied Over 100 School Buses Equipped with Wifi for Students Without Internet Access.* www.google.co.uk/amp/s/www.click2houston.com/news/local/2020/04/15/texas-school-district-deployed-over-100-school-buses-equipped-with-wifi-for-students-without-internet-access/%3foutputType=amp. Accessed 3 November 2020.

Coleman, J. (2020, August 24) *Florida Confirmed Almost 9,000 New COVID-19 Cases Among Children Within 15 Days in August as Schools Reopen, According to State Data Released Tuesday.* https://news.sky.com/story/coronavirus-outbreak-at-dundee-school-17-staff-members-and-two-pupils-test-positive-12055594. Accessed 3 November 2020.

Connell, A. (2020a) *We Must Create an Independent Teacher Resource Bank Group.* SecEd Blog, 13th May 2020. www.sec-ed.co.uk/blog/teacher-resource-bank-group-subject-teaching-coronavirus-home-learning/. Accessed 3 November 2020.

Connell, A. (2020b) *Correspondence between Department for Education and UK Council for Subject Associations.* www.subjectassociations.org.uk. Accessed 28 June 2021.

Crawford, A. (2020) *Our Plans for New Specialist Lessons.* www.thenational.academy/blog/our-plans-for-new-specialist-lessons. Accessed 3 November 2020.

Culbertson, A. (2020, August 24) *Seventeen Members of Staff and Two Pupils Have Tested Positive for Coronavirus at a School in Dundee Less than Two Weeks After Scottish Schools Returned.* https://news.sky.com/story/coronavirus-outbreak-at-dundee-school-17-staff-members-and-two-pupils-test-positive-12055594. Accessed 1 November 2020.

DCSF (Department for Children, Schools and Families) (2008, December) *Supporting Learning If Schools Close for Extended Periods during a Flu Pandemic.* www.wokingham.gov.uk/EasysiteWeb/getresource.axd?AssetID=192722&type=full&servicetype=Attachment. Accessed 3 November 2020.

Devitt, R. (2018) *What Is Home Schooling?* https://howdoihomeschool.com/2018/07/30/what-homeschooling-definition/. Accessed 3 November 2020.

DfE (2011) *Evaluation of the Home Access Programme – Final Report (Research Report DFE-RR132).* https://assets.publishing.service.gov.uk/government/uploads/system/uploads/attachment_data/file/181525/DFE-RR132.pdf. Accessed 3 November 2020.

DfE (2020) *Devices and 4G Wireless Routers Data as of 27 August Ad-hoc Notice – Laptops, Tablets and 4G Wireless Routers for Disadvantaged and Vulnerable Children: By Academy Trust, and Local Authority.* https://assets.publishing.service.gov.uk/government/uploads/system/uploads/attachment_data/file/912888/Devices_and_4G_wireless_routers_progress_data_as_of_27_August_2020.pdf. Accessed 3 November 2020.

DfES (Department for Education and Skills) (2006) *Planning for a Human Influenza Pandemic Guidance to Schools Every Child Matters.* https://schools.oxfordshire.gov.uk/cms/sites/schools/files/folders/folders/documents/healthandsafety/main_schools_guide.pdf. Accessed 3 November 2020.

DHS (Department of Health and Social Care) and the Cabinet Office (2020, August 21) *Face Coverings: When to Wear One and How to Make Your Own.* www.gov.uk/government/publications/face-coverings-when-to-wear-one-and-how-to-make-your-own/face-coverings-when-to-wear-one-and-how-to-make-your-own#when-you-do-not-need-to-wear-a-face-covering. Accessed August 2020.

Dickens, J. (2020) *DfE Fails to Meet Target of Delivering 230k Laptops by End of June.* https://schoolsweek.co.uk/dfe-fails-to-meet-target-of-delivering-230k-laptops-by-end-of-june/. Accessed 3 November 2020.

Dierking, L. (2005) 'Lessons Without Limit: How Free-choice Learning Is Transforming Science and Technology Education'. *História, ciências, saúde – Manguinhos*, 12, 145–160. https://doi.org/10.1590/S0104-59702005000400008. Accessed 3 November 2020.

Doucet, A., Netolicky, D., Timmers, K., and Tuscano, F. J. (2020, March 29) *Thinking about Pedagogy in an Unfolding Pandemic: An Independent Report on*

Approaches to Distance Learning During COVID19 School Closures. Independent Report written to inform the work of Education International and UNESCO. Version 2.0. https://teachertaskforce.org/sites/default/files/202004/Thinking%20 about%20Pedagogy%20in%20an%20Unfolding%20Pandemic.pdf. Accessed 3 November 2020.

Duffield, S., and O'Hare, D. (2020) *Teacher Resilience During Coronavirus School Closures*. British Psychological Society: Leicester. www.bps.org.uk/sites/www. bps.org.uk/files/Member%20Networks/Divisions/DECP/. Accessed 3 November 2020.

EAGLE Report (2020, July) *Schools in England: A Safe Return in September?* Emergency Advisory Group for Learning and Education (England). https://eagleresearchgroup.org/can-schools-open-safely-in-september/Editor:ProfessorTerryWri gleyonbehalfoftheEAGLEGroup.

EC (European Commission) (2009a) *Why Is Pandemic Preparedness Planning Important?* www.ecdc.europa.eu/en/seasonal-influenza/preparedness/why-pandemic-preparedness. Accessed 3 November 2020.

EC (European Commission) (2009b) *Guide to Public Health Measures to Reduce the Impact of Influenza Pandemics in Europe – 'The ECDC Menu'*. www.ecdc. europa.eu/en/publications-data/guide-public-health-measures-reduce-impact-influenza-pandemics-europe-ecdc-menu. Accessed 3 November 2020.

EC (European Commission) (2016) *Competence Frameworks: The European Approach to Teach and Learn 21st Century Skills*. https://ec.europa.eu/jrc/en/ news/competence-frameworks-european-approach-teach-and-learn-21st-century-skills. Accessed 3 November 2020.

ECDC (European Centre for Disease Prevention and Control) in collaboration with the European Commission and the World Health Organisation Regional Office for Europe (2006, September) *Assessment Tool for Influenza Preparedness in European Countries – With a Main Focus on Pandemic Preparedness*. www. ecdc.europa.eu/sites/default/files/media/en/healthtopics/seasonal_influenza/ Documents/Tool/0609_Pandemic_Influenza_Assessment_Tool.pdf. Accessed 3 November 2020.

Education Futures Collaboration Charity/MESHGuides (2016) *A Low Cost 'Marginal Gains Strategy' to Support SDG4 – Engaging Educators and Aid Agencies as 'Change Agents' to Bring a Step Change in Teacher Quality*. http://new.mesh-guides.org/wp-content/uploads/2019/07/Summary-of-Marginal-Gains-strategy. pdf. Accessed 3 November 2020.

Education Futures Collaboration Charity/MESHGuides (2017) *Making a Difference to Teacher Quality – To Ensure Inclusive and Quality Education for All by 2020 a Knowledge Mobilisation Strategy Enabling Teachers and Teacher Educators to Become 'Change Agents' for UNESCO SDG4. This Report Is the Outcome of the First Global Teacher Education Knowledge Mobilisation Summit for SDG 4c*, April

2016. http://new.meshguides.org/wp-content/uploads/2019/07/TeacherEdKMB summit2016report.pdf. Accessed 3 November 2020.

Education International (2020) *International Summit on the Teaching Profession 2020: Teachers Recognised as the Heroes of the Covid-19 Crisis in Education.* www.ei-ie.org/en/detail/16814/international-summit-on-the-teaching-profession-2020-teachers-recognised-as-the-heroes-of-the-covid-19-crisis-in-education. Accessed 3 November 2020.

EEF (2020a) *Rapid Evidence Assessment: Distance Learning.* https://educationen-dowmentfoundation.org.uk/public/files/Publications/Covid-19_Resources/Remote_learning_evidence_review/Rapid_Evidence_Assessment_summary.pdf. Accessed 3 November 2020.

EEF (2020b) *Covid-19 Resources on What Good Online Teaching Is About.* https://educationendowmentfoundation.org.uk/covid-19-resources/best-evidence-on-supporting-students-to-learn-remotely/. Accessed 3 November 2020.

Falk, J., and Dierking, L. (2002) *Lessons Without Limit: How Free-choice Learning Is Transforming Education.* Lanham: Rowman Altamira.

Friedman, S. L. (2014) '"There Are Decades Where Nothing Happens; and There Are Weeks Where Decades Happen" – Vladimir Ilyich Lenin'. *Journal of Hepatology*, 60(3), 471–472. Accessed 22 April 2020.

Gallagher, J. (2020, August 11) 'Coronavirus: Is the World Winning the Pandemic Fight?' *BBC News*. www.bbc.co.uk. Accessed 11 August 2020.

Gash, T., Magee, I., Ritter, J., and Smith, N. (2012) *Read Before Burning: Arm's Length Government for a New Administration.* Institute for Government. www.institute-forgovernment.org.uk/publications/read-burning. Accessed 29 July 2020.

Gawande, A. (2015) *The Century of the System.* BBC Reith Lecture. www.bbc.co.uk/programmes/b04sv1s5. Accessed 3 November 2020.

Georgiou, N., Delfabbro, P., and Balzan, R. (2020) 'COVID-19-related Conspiracy Beliefs and Their Relationship with Perceived Stress and Pre-existing Conspiracy Beliefs'. *Personality and Individual Differences*, 166, 110201. https://doi.org/10.1016/j.paid.2020.110201. Accessed 3 November 2020.

Gillett-Swan, J. (2017) 'The Challenges of Online Learning Supporting and Engaging the Isolated Learner'. *Journal of Learning Design*, 10(1), 20–30. www.jld.edu.au/article/download/293/293-749-1-PB.pdf. Accessed 3 November 2020.

Giroux, H. A. (1988) *Teachers as Intellectuals: A Critical Pedagogy for Practical Learning.* South Hadley, MA: Bergin and Garvey Publishers, Inc.

Great Schools Partnership (2018) *Glossary of Education Reform.* http://edglossary.org/21st-century-skills/. Accessed 3 November 2020.

Guardian (2020, May 12) *Unions Tell Staff 'Not to Engage' with Plan for 1 June School Openings.* www.theguardian.com/education/2020/may/12/plans-to-reopen-schools-on-1-june-in-jeopardy-as-education-unions-tell-staff-not-to-engage-with-prepartions-1. Accessed 3 November 2020.

Guardian (2020, June 9) *Reopening Schools: What Is Happening in England?* www.theguardian.com/education/2020/jun/09/reopening-schools-what-is-happening-in-england). Accessed 3 November 2020.

Guardian (2020, July 2) *'I'm Worried': Parents React to England's School Reopening Plans.* www.theguardian.com/education/2020/jul/02/im-worried-parents-react-to-englands-school-reopening-plans. Accessed 3 November 2020.

Halinen, I. (2016) *Collaborating to Create a Relevant Curriculum Based on Well-being for All.* Keynote address to Learning Teacher Network Conference, Tallinn, Estonia.

Hall, S. (2021) *Doing Education Differently: A New Vision For Education post-Covid 19.* Fabians Blog, 7th April 2020. https://fabians4education.edublogs.org/2020/04/07/doing-education-differently/. Accessed 3 November 2020.

Halstead, J. M., and Taylor, M. J. (2000) 'Learning and Teaching about Values: A Review of Recent Research'. *Cambridge Journal of Education*, 30(2), 169–202.

Haskell-Dowland, P., and Vasileiou, I. (2020) *Cyber Threats at Home: How to Keep Kids Safe While They're Learning Online*, 24 April 2020, 6.00am. https://theconversation.com/cyber-threats-at-home-how-to-keep-kids-safe-while-theyre-learning-online-136264. Accessed 26 August 2020.

Hatami, H., Sjatil, P. E., and Sneader, K. (2020) *The Toughest Leadership Test.* McKinsey Report, 28 May 2020. www.mckinsey.com/featured-insights/leadership/the-toughest-leadership-test. Accessed 11 August 2020.

Hazell, W. (2020a, June 5) *Worryingly High Number of Schools Unable to Offer Teacher Training Placements Next Year Due to Coronavirus.* www.google.co.uk/amp/s/inews.co.uk/news/education/schools-unable-offer-teacher-training-coronavirus-434330/amp. Accessed 3 November 2020.

Hazell, W. (2020b, July 13) *Coronavirus Latest: Academy School Chain Tells Heads They Will Not Be 'Liable for Prosecution' If Covid-19 Caught in School.* https://inews.co.uk/news/coronavirus-academy-school-chain-tells-heads-not-liable-prosecution-school-429002. Accessed 3 November 2020.

Hennessy, S. (2016) *School-based Programmes & OER Support Lifelong Learning: Research Into Teacher Development in Sub-Saharan Africa.* Cambridge, UK: University of Cambridge.

Hodges, C., Moore, S., Lockee, B., et al. (2020) 'The Difference Between Emergency Remote Teaching and Online Learning'. *Educause Review.* https://er.educause.edu/articles/2020/3/the-difference-between-emergency-remote-teaching-and-online-learning. Accessed 26 August 2020.

Hood, M. (2020) *Tweet 20:58–21.04.2020.* https://twitter.com/matthewhood/status/1252688056349593607?s=21. Accessed 25 August 2020.

Hudson, B., Leask, M., and Younie, S. (2021) *Education System Design: Foundations, Policy Options and Consequences.* London: Routledge.

ICET/MESHGuides. (2020, October) *Teacher Experiences and Practices during Covid-19 Interim Report*, eds. C. Hordatt Gentles and M. Leask. www.icet4u. org and www.MESHGuides.org. Accessed 1 November 2020.

Institute for Government (2012) *Bonfire of the Quangos*. London. www.institutefor-government.org.uk/news/latest/bonfire-quangos. Accessed 22 April 2020.

Inter-Agency Standing Committee-UNICEF, WHO and IFRC (2020, March) *Interim Guidance for Covid-19 Prevention and Control in Schools*. https://www.wfp. org/publications/interim-guidance-covid-19-prevention-and-control-schools. Accessed 4 June 2021.

International Labour Organisation (2020) *ILO Sectoral Brief: COVID-19 and the Education Sector*. www.ilo.org/wcmsp5/groups/public/-ed_dialogue/-sector/docu ments/briefingnote/wcms_742025.pdf. Accessed 22 April 2020.

Jayaram, S. (2012) *Skills for Employability: The Need for 21st Century Skills*. Washington, DC: Results for Development Institute.

Jeffs, T. and Smith, M. K. (2011) *'What Is Informal Education?' The Encyclopedia of Pedagogy and Informal Education*. https://infed.org/mobi/what-is-informal-education/. Accessed 26 April 2020.

Leask, M. (2020) *Did the Government Take Its Eye Off the Ball on Pandemic Planning?* https://schoolsweek.co.uk/did-the-government-take-its-eye-off-the-ball-on-pandemic-planning/. Accessed 3 November 2020.

Leask, M., Lee, C., Milner, T., Norton, M., and Rathod, D. (2008) *Knowledge Management Tools and Techniques: Helping You Access the Right Knowledge at the Right Time*. Improvement and Development Agency for Local Government, Now Merged with the Local Government Association. www.managingforimpact.org/ search/apachesolr_search/leask. Accessed 31 July 2020.

Leask, M., and Pachler, N. (2013) *Learning to Teach Using ICT in the Secondary School a Companion to School Experience*. Abingdon: Routledge.

Leask, M., and Younie, S. (2001a) 'The European SchoolNet. An Online European Community for Teachers? A Valuable Professional Resource?'. *Teacher Development*, 5(2), 157–175.

Leask, M., and Younie, S. (2001b) 'Communal Constructivist Theory: Pedagogy of Information and Communications Technology and Internationalisation of the Curriculum'. *Journal of Information Technology for Teacher Education*, 10(1 and 2), 117–134.

Leask, M., and Younie, S. (2013) 'National Models for Continuing Professional Development: The Challenges of Twenty-First-Century Knowledge Management'. *Journal of Professional Development in Education*, 39(2), 273–287.

Matthews, B. (2021) 'Aims and Values: Direction with Purpose'. In Chapter 2 (pp. 20–30) Hudson et al. (op. cit.).

McLaren, P. (2014) *Life in Schools: An Introduction to Critical Pedagogy in the Foundations of Education*, 6th ed. Boulder, CO: Paradigm Publishers.

McLeod, S. A. (2007) *Maslow's Hierarchy of Needs*. www.simplypsychology.org/maslow.html. Accessed 26 April 2020.

MESHGuides (2020a, April) *COVID-19 SUPPORT: MESH International Advisory Council Reports and Meetings*. www.meshguides.org/covid-19-support-mesh-international-advisory-council-reports-and-meetings/. Accessed 22 April 2020.

MESHGuides (2020b) *Classroom Dialogue and Learning*. www.meshguides.org/guides/node/1148 with acknowledgments to Dr Victoria Cook, Dr Louis Major, Dr Sara Hennessy with Farah Ahmed, Elisa Calcagni and other colleagues from the Cambridge Educational Dialogue Research Group (CEDiR) Accessed 22 November 2020.

MESHGuides (2020c) *Numeracy for All MESHGuide*. www.meshguides.org/guides/node/1588 and Numeracy for all MESHGuide videos www.youtube.com/playlist?list=PLa35dKvXL0xL3WzGOWctNuctQEOkhcl84. Accessed 1 November 2020.

Moore, H. (2020, August 12) *NSW Australia Tangara Outbreak Leads to Senior School Masks Call*. www.dailytelegraph.com.au/subscribe/news/1/?sourceCode=DTWEB_WRE170_a_GGL&dest=https%3A%2F%2Fwww.dailytelegraph.com.au%2Fnewslocal%2Fhornsby-advocate%2Fcoronavirus-cherrybrook-cluster-spike-in-cases-linked-to-tangara-school%2Fnews-story%2Fdcfa7436857cb05ab31d63266801068f&memtype=anonymous&mode=premium. Accessed 1 November 2020.

Morton, R. (2010, October) 'Home Education: Constructions of Choice'. *International Electronic Journal of Elementary Education*, 3(1).

Müller, L.-M., and Goldenberg, G. (2020) *Education in Times of Crisis: The Potential Implications of School Closures for Teachers and Students. A Review of Research Evidence on School Closures and International Approaches to Education During the COVID-19 Pandemic*. https://my.chartered.college/wp-content/uploads/2020/05/CCTReport150520_FINAL.pdf. Accessed 3 July 2020.

New Zealand Government (2011, August) *Influenza Pandemic Planning Guide for Early Childhood Education Services, Schools and Tertiary Organisations*. www.education.govt.nz/assets/Documents/Ministry/Initiatives/Health-and-safety/PandemicPlanningGuideForEdSectorAug2011.doc. Accessed 23 April 2020.

New Zealand Government (2020, March 30) *Planning for an Epidemic/Pandemic Event* (quick guide). www.education.govt.nz/school/health-safety-and-wellbeing/emergencies-and-traumatic-incidents/pandemic-planning-guide/. Accessed 23 April 2020.

NFER (2020) *Schools' Responses to Covid-19: Pupil Engagement in Remote Learning*. National Foundation for Educational Research. www.nfer.ac.uk/schools-responses-to-covid-19-pupil-engagement-in-remote-learning/. Accessed 1 November 2020.

Nuki, P. (2020, June 12) *Face Shields Recommend for Teachers and Shop Keepers to Help Britain Open Up Again Global Health Security Editor*. Telegraph, London. www.google.co.uk/amp/s/www.telegraph.co.uk/global-health/science-and-disease/

face-shields-recommend-teachers-shop-keepers-help-britain-open/amp/. Accessed 3 November 2020.

O'Meara, J. (2020) *Contribution to ICET/MESHGuide Webinar: Teachers' Experiences at the Time of Covid-19*. International Council on Education for Teaching. www.icet4u.org. Accessed 28 June 2021.

O'Reilly, L. (2020) *Teenagers Less Anxious During Lockdown*. Evening Standard, 24 August 2020. www.standard.co.uk/news/uk/teenager-anxiety-coronavirus-lockdown-improves-a4531646.html. Accessed 5 September 2020.

O'Sullivan, E. (1999) *Transformative Learning: Educational Vision for the 21st Century*. London: Zed Books.

Parkin, T. (2017) *Is It Time to Bring Back the EdTech Quango Becta?* SchoolsWeek. https://schoolsweek.co.uk/is-it-time-to-bring-back-the-edtech-quango-becta/. Accessed 29 July 2020.

Payler, J. (2016) *The Open University International Teacher Education Programmes*. Milton Keynes: Open University.

Pellegrino, J. W., and Hilton, M. (2012) *Education for Life and Work: Developing Transferable Knowledge and Skills in the 21st Century*. Washington, DC: National Academies Press.

Ramos, G., and Schleicher, A. (2016) *Global Competency for an Inclusive World*. www.oecd.org/education/Global-competency-for-an-inclusive-world.pdf. Accessed 3 November 2020.

SAM Learning (2020) www.samlearning.com/targeted-intervention/=. Accessed 3 November 2020.

Selbervik, H. (2020) *Impacts of School Closures on Children in Developing Countries: Can We Learn Something From the Past?* Bergen: Charis Michelsen Institute. https://www.cmi.no/publications/7214-impacts-of-school-closures-on-children-in-developing-countries-can-we-learn-something-from-the-past. Accessed 18 May 2021.

Shermer, M. (2005) *Rumsfeld's Wisdom – Where the Known Meets the Unknown Is Where Science Begins*. www.scientificamerican.com/article/rumsfelds-wisdom/ Accessed 12 August 2020.

Sherwood, H. (2020, July 11) *Global 'Catastrophe' Looms as Covid-19 Fuels Inequality*. www.theguardian.com/world/2020/jul/11/global-catastrophe-looms-as-covid-19-fuels-inequality. Accessed 3 November 2020.

Shrestha, P., and Lal, J. (2020) *When School Stops, Learning Must Not. Teaching the Most Marginalised*. www.vsointernational.org/news/blog/when-school-stops-learning-must-not.VSO. Accessed 1 November 2020.

Smith, M. K. (2020) *Dealing with the 'New Normal'. Offering Sanctuary, Community and Hope to Children and Young People in Schools and Local Organizations. The Encyclopedia of Pedagogy and Informal Education*. https://infed.org/mobi/dealing-with-the-new-normalcreating-places-of-sanctuary-community-and-hope-for-children-and-young-people/. Accessed 4 August 2020.

Spec, D. (2020, April 30) *A Third of Teachers Have Covid-19 Mental Health Fears*. London: Times Educational Supplement. www.tes.com/news/third-teachers-have-covid-19-mental-health-fears. Accessed 22 April 2020.

Thatcher, M. (1987) *In There Is Such a Thing as Society: Has Boris Johnson Repudiated Thatcherism?* Interview with New Statesman, 31 March 2020. www.newstatesman.com/politics/uk/2020/03/boris-johnson-thatcher-society-no-such-thing-policies. Accessed 11 August 2020.

Thomas, D. (2020, April 19) *What's Wrong with Oak National Academy*. http://davidthomasblog.com/2020/04/whats-wrong-with-oak-national-academy/. Accessed 25 August 2020.

Tokuhama-Espinosa, T. (2020) *Decision Tree for Going on Line: The Virtual Classroom*. https://thelearningsciences.com/site/portfolio-items/virtual-class-organization/?lang=en. Accessed 22 April 2020.

Udnaes, M., Titlestad, G., and Johannessen, Ø. (2014) *Policy Brief – Open Educational Resources in Your Own Language, in Your Way*. LangOER consortium. http://langoer.eun.org/, https://iite.unesco.org/pics/publications/en/files/3214739.pdf. Accessed 4 June 2021.

UNESCO (2020a) *Half of World's Student Population Not Attending School: UNESCO Launches Global Coalition to Accelerate Deployment of Remote Learning Solutions*. https://en.unesco.org/news/half-worlds-student-population-not-attending-school-unesco-launches-global-coalition-accelerate. Accessed 23 April 2020.

UNESCO (2020b, June) *Framework for Re-opening Schools*. Paris: UNESCO. https://unesdoc.unesco.org/ark:/48223/pf0000373348. Accessed 3 November 2020

UNESCO (2020c, August) *Policy Brief: Education During COVID-19 and Beyond*. www.un.org/development/desa/dspd/wp-content/uploads/sites/22/2020/08/sg_policy_brief_covid-19_and_education_august_2020.pdf. Accessed 3 November 2020.

UNESCO International Teacher Task Force (2020d) *Response to the COVID-19 Outbreak – Call for Action on Teachers*. https://teachertaskforce.org/knowledge-hub/response-covid-19-outbreak-call-action-teachers-0. Accessed 3 November 2020.

UNESCO International Teacher Task Force (2020e, April) *Policy Note – Guidance for School Leaders and Teachers for Schools Re-opening*. Paris: UNESCO.

UNESCO, UNICEF, World Bank (2020, April) *Framework for Reopening Schools*. https://en.unesco.org/news/back-school-preparing-and-managing-reopening-schools. Accessed 22 April 2020.

United Nations Development Programme (UNDP). (2020) *COVID-19 and Human Development: Assessing the Crisis, Envisioning the Recovery*. 2020 Human Development Perspectives, New York: UNDP. http://hdr.undp.org/en/hdp-covid. Accessed 3 November 2020.

Uscher-Pines, L., Schwartz, H. L., Ahmed, F., et al. (2018) 'School Practices to Promote Social Distancing in K-12 Schools: Review of Influenza Pandemic Policies and Practices'. *BMC Public Health*, 18(406). https://doi.org/10.1186/s12889-018-5302-3. Accessed 23 April 2020.

van der Rheede, C. (2010, October 20) 'It Takes a Village to Raise a Child'. *NGO Pulse*. http://www.ngopulse.org/article/it-takes-village-raise-child. Accessed 18 May 2021.

Voogt, J., and Roblin, N. P. (2013) *21st Century Skills*. Enschede, Netherlands: University of Twente.

VSO (MNEC) (2020a) *Myanmar and Mon National Education Committee: Rapid Assessment Survey: Education and Covid-19 in Myanmar*. London: VSO.

VSO (2020b) *Nigeria Survey on Marginalised Children's Access to Distance Education During COVID 19 Pandemic in Nigeria*. London: VSO.

VSO (2020c) *Uganda: Early Childhood Care and Education – COVID 19 Response*. London: VSO.

Wang, C., Horby, P. W., Hayden, F. G., and Gao, G. F. (2020) 'A Novel Coronavirus Outbreak of Global Health Concern'. *The Lancet*, 395(10223), 470–473. https://doi.org/10.1016/S0140-6736(20)30185-9. Accessed 23 April 2020.

Watson, C. (2020) *Coronavirus: What Lessons Can Rest of UK Learn from Scotland's School Return?* BBC Scotland News website, 5 September 2020. www.bbc.co.uk/news/uk-scotland-54013125. Accessed 5 September 2020.

Weale, S. (2020, August) 'Headteachers Launch Stinging Criticism of Education Secretary'. *The Guardian*. www.theguardian.com/politics/2020/aug/24/headteachers-launch-stinging-criticism-of-education-secretary. Accessed 1 November 2020.

Wespieser, K. (2020) *What's Wrong with Oak Academy's Specialist Curriculum?* 4 May 2020. Special Needs Jungle. www.specialneedsjungle.com/whats-wrong-oak-academy-specialist-curriculum/. Accessed 25 August 2020.

West, D. M. (2015) *Digital Divide: Improving Internet Access in the Developing World Through Affordable Services and Diverse Content*. Brookings Center for Technology Innovation. www.brookings.edu/wp-content/uploads/2016/06/West_Internet-Access.pdf. Accessed 23 April 2020.

Whalley, C., and Greenway, H. (2021) 'Politics Aside: From Fragmentation to Coherence'. In Chapter 5 Hudson et al. (op. cit.).

White, G., and Parker, L. (2016) *Building and Sustaining National ICT/education Agencies: Lessons from Australia (EdNA) World Bank Education, Technology and Innovation: SABER-ICT Technical Paper Series (#16)*. http://documents1.worldbank.org/curated/en/270521488907905829/text/113215-NWP-PUBLIC-ADD-SERIESVAgencies-Australia-EdNA-SABER-ICTno16.txt. Accessed 3 November 2020.

White, G., and Parker, L. (2017) 'Lessons from Australia (EdNA)'. In Trucano, M. & Dykes, G. (Eds.) *Building and Sustaining National Educational Agencies: Lessons, Models and Case Studies from Around The World*. Washington, DC: The World Bank. https://www.worldbank.org/en/topic/edutech/publication/

building-and-sustaining-national-educational-technology-agencies-lessons-models-and-case-studies-from-around-the-world. Accessed 18 May 2021.

Wink, J. (2010) *Critical Pedagogy: Notes from the Real world*, 4th ed. London: Pearson.

World Bank (2017) *Building and sustaining national educational agencies: Lessons, models and case studies from around the world* (M. Trucano and G. Dykes, Eds.). Washington, DC: The World Bank. www.worldbank.org/en/topic/edutech/publication/building-and-sustaining-national-educational-technology-agencies-lessons-models-and-case-studies-from-around-the-world. Accessed 3 November 2020.

World Economic Forum (2020) *3 Ways the Coronavirus Pandemic Could Reshape Education*. www.weforum.org/agenda/2020/03/3-ways-coronavirus-is-reshaping-education-and-what-changes-might-be-here-to-stay. Accessed 23 April 2020.

World Health Organisation (2005) *Checklist for Influenza Pandemic Preparedness Planning*. www.who.int/csr/resources/publications/influenza/FluCheck6web.pdf. Accessed October 2020.

World Health Organisation (2009) *Reducing Transmission of Pandemic (H1N1) 2009 in School Settings*. www.who.int/csr/resources/publications/reducing_transmission_h1n1_2009.pdf. Accessed 22 April 2020.

World Health Organization (2020) *Covid-19 Strategy Update*. www.who.int/publications/i/item/covid-19-strategy-update-14-april-2020. Accessed 22 July 2020.

Younie, S. (2020) *Covid-19 MESHGuide*. www.MESHGuides.org and http://www.meshguides.org/guides/node/1667. Accessed 4 June 2021.

Younie, S., and Leask, M. (2013) *Teaching with Technologies*. Buckingham: Open University Press.

Younie, S., and Leask, M. (2019) *Lessons from the Bonfire of the Quangos: The Case for Legislation to Provide Checks and Balances to the Powers of the Secretary of State for Education*. SES (Society for Education Studies) Colloquium on Education reform legislation.

Younie, S., Leask, M., Audain, J., Preston, C., and Procter, R. (2021c) 'CPD, Knowledge Services and Research: 21st Century Solutions'. In Chapter 19 (p. 235) in Hudson et al. (op. cit.).

Younie, S., Leask, M., and Hall, S. (2021a) 'Education in Emergencies: Pandemic/disaster Planning for Education Sector Continuity'. In Chapter 21 in Hudson et al. (op. cit.).

Younie, S., Leask, M., and Hudson, B. (2021b) 'Policy Options and Consequences: What Has to Be Done, When and With Whom'. In Chapter 20 in Hudson et al. (op. cit.).

Annexes

Annex 1

EAGLE research group report – advice on reopening schools

Schools in England: a safe return in September?
Emergency Advisory Group for Learning and Education (England)
(https://eagleresearchgroup.org/can-schools-open-safely-in-september/)

The Emergency Advisory Group for Learning and Education (EAGLE) Group is a of teachers, teacher educators and researchers led by Professors Helen Gunter, University of Manchester; Pam Jarvis, Leeds Trinity University; Liz Todd, University of Newcastle; Terry Wrigley, Northumbria University.

Context and purpose

Independent SAGE, a body of scientists with substantial expertise, undertook in May 2020 to assess the situation of prolonged school closures and the prospects for reopening. Their report *When Should a School Reopen?*[1] concluded that the government's insistence on 1 June was premature because the number of infections and the reproduction rate were still high and test, track and isolate programmes were not running effectively. A small group of experienced education researchers produced a note that informed this report.[2] The education group has since had further meetings, involving a larger number of researchers as well as experienced educational professionals (teachers, headteachers, local authority officers). This note attempts to summarise the issues arising from these discussions, in the context of empirical data, available medical knowledge, educational research and standard school practices in England. It has some relevance to other parts of the UK, but it is useful to consider England separately, given different infection patterns and school characteristics.

The aim of this report is to consider how the interests of children and young people can best be served. It was begun before the 2 July *Guidance for full opening – schools*[3] but includes specific comments on that document. Whilst we believe that schools should open to all students[4] as fully as possible in September, we do not believe the government's position is realistic, and aim to present some more practical alternatives.

Our argument is that schools will need flexibility in order to welcome all their students back in September, including funding for smaller classes (particularly in primary schools) and a combination of on-site and distance learning in many secondary schools. This report outlines some ways in which this could happen, whilst emphasising that decisions can only be taken locally because of the particular characteristics of each school's student population, curriculum and buildings. *Our aim is to make a return to school healthy and sustainable.*

We ask for a resounding national gratitude for the extremely hard work of everyone working in schools over the last few months. It has not just been about teaching and learning, important though this is. COVID-19 has made clear once more the crucial role of schools in terms of the whole community. Schools became a key focus for many crucial issues such as families having enough to eat, safeguarding concerns, planning summer activities and much more.

The report argues that wellbeing and learning are interrelated. A lack of attention to children's social, emotional and mental health will undermine effective education. We also believe that active and engaged forms of learning can have a significant impact on children and young people's enjoyment and wellbeing. This will not be helped by returning to the pressures of formal assessment and inspection. A narrow emphasis on 'catching up' is likely to be counterproductive. Rather than a return to 'normal', this situation provides opportunities to take stock and build a more satisfying and engaging education for children and young people.[5]

Scientific advice on transmission involving students

Serious concerns were raised by the medical scientists in Independent SAGE (28 May 2020)[6] because infections were still high and test-track-and-trace had scarcely begun. It was also not known whether children, including those not/not yet showing symptoms, could transmit the virus to adults or other children.

Although the pandemic is no longer as intense, there are ongoing problems with test-and-trace and data sharing. This is well illustrated by the recent outbreak in Leicester: local officials were only informed of the 71 'Pillar 1' cases (tests at hospitals) but not the 873 'Pillar 2' cases[7] (i.e. commercial laboratories that process at-home and drive-through tests).[8] The Director of Education complained that he had not been told the age of the infected children, so was unable to intervene appropriately.[9]

This demonstrates the systemic undermining of public health in England, a service which has been made even more incoherent in recent months by outsourcing testing to private companies lacking relevant experience. As medical researchers explain, this has resulted in serious inadequacies in the analysis and transfer of data to doctors and local authorities.[10]

Although local authorities are now being supplied with Pillar 2 data online, local authorities are still not receiving adequate details of new outbreaks. The Local Government Association (3 July)[11] have pointed out that confidential communication of details of postcodes, home addresses and workplaces/schools is essential if local government officers and medical professionals are to prevent local outbreaks escalating.

Whether children can spread the virus is still uncertain, with conflicting medical research. Indeed, health secretary Matt Hancock has justified the decision to close Leicester schools by asserting that they do.[12] This justifies the caution of Independent SAGE, the National Education Union, many local authorities, governing bodies and parents towards the government's earlier decision that schools had to open from 1 June.

Government advice is currently incoherent. The Department of Education's key document of 2 July[13] contains very strong warnings from Public Health England followed by pragmatic guidelines on how to organise schools with full-time attendance of all students. Many schools will find it impossible to follow the organisational guidance without breaching the health warnings. The contradictions are particularly strong for secondary schools, as we explain below.

We welcome the thorough and detailed explanation on preventing infections contained in Section 1, derived from Public Health England, but do not believe many of them can be achieved given the limited physical and human resources of most state schools whilst attempting to provide for full-time attendance for all students.

Recommendations

1   Government, and decision-making bodies such as school governors, local authorities and academy trusts, should make it clear that health and safety is paramount over the desire to provide for full-time school attendance for all students.

2   Further exploration is needed of forms of blended learning in the school context, involving a suitable mix of on-site and home learning, for those schools which are unable to provide for full-time attendance safely. There is a need to learn from what schools have been doing over the last few months and publicise case studies of best practice.

3   A reliable test-track-trace system with full involvement of public health departments is essential for schools to operate safely. The system for data sharing about local outbreaks to schools must be clarified, as well as the channels for schools to obtain help from public health bodies.

The impact of school closure on students: a summary

Wellbeing

Studies of earlier pandemics provide evidence of the psychological impact of quarantine,[14] including the need for extra support for people with pre-existing poor mental health.[15] Indications quickly emerged that the Covid-19 outbreak and lockdown was impacting on mental health of students and families in various ways[16] though for some there was a sense of relief at escaping problematic situations at school.[17]

While adults can be persuaded of the mutual and altruistic benefits of physical distancing and other measures, it is possible that children and adolescents will feel more acutely disempowered due to the way the instructions about lock-down were received. Many schools closed down very rapidly, before young people had an adequate chance to say good-bye to friends, which was particularly significant for those in transition to secondary, further or higher education. Moreover, adults tend to set the agendas in homes and where there is poor communication, children and adolescents may experience a lack of control.

Schools and families need to be supported to put the social, emotional and health needs of students first, as a moral imperative and as a foundation for progression with learning. We know from teacher's experience with more students returned to school that students of all ages will need time to get back into learning dispositions and behaviours, such as coping with sitting in a classroom and the pattern of a school day. Where individual and collective healing needs to happen, the starting point is to meet students where they are, as they return to school, helping them to take proper account of these experiences: it will not be 'back to normal' for many of them, or for their teachers and families.

School achievement, poverty and disadvantage

Covid-19 related death rates reveal place-based (inner-city urban, rural) patterns relating to poverty. Those living in overcrowded housing, in multi-generational households or care homes have been more at risk of infection. The death rate among BAME groups is over twice that of white British groups[18] and most of these deaths occur in major conurbations such as inner London, Birmingham and Liverpool. It has been poverty and population density, rather than NHS capacity, which has resulted in high death rates. Some of this has been related to government austerity cuts. Students from these environments are more likely to return to school in September having suffered bereavement, as well as anxiety about the risks to their friends and families. This is in addition to the increased mental health risk for students growing up in poverty.[19]

Many students will have fallen behind in their learning during this extended period of school closures, although home learning has worked well for some. Research has consistently shown that the most economically disadvantaged students tend to have the poorest educational outcomes, even without schools being closed.[20] Despite frequent government claims to be 'closing the gap', research has shown that, at the current rate of progress, this would take 50 years[21] even without schools being closed.[22]

It is a matter of great concern, therefore, that the poorest students have encountered additional barriers to learning in recent months. However, we believe the problems cannot be solved by a 'business as usual' response, and require acknowledgment of structural roots of disadvantage, and actions to prevent child poverty and reduce its educational impact such as through poverty proofing of the school day[23] (See the section 'Conditions and challenges for reopening' below.)

Teachers and heads (and other school-based professionals) are in an excellent position to analyse needs, provide schools with direct access to funding and resources, for example to ensure equitable access to appropriate technology for home learning. Students themselves are also in an excellent position to inform others of their needs and greater opportunity needs to be found for the voice of the student without reliance on questionnaire surveys that are not accessible to all.

Recommendations

1   Schools should be encouraged to prioritise the mental and physical health and wellbeing of children, and consider the full implications of providing a 'recovery curriculum'.[24]
2   Policy makers, school professionals and workers, and students should work with education researchers to make a thorough assessment of the differential effects of school closures, and the complex impact on students who were already indicated as disadvantaged.
3   Because teachers and heads are in a better position to analyse needs, schools should be given direct access to funding and resources, for example to ensure equitable access to appropriate technology for home learning.

Government policy and media emphasis

The major emphasis from government and the media has been on the losses to academic learning, accompanied by pressure to resume full time schooling. Part of the motivation is the economic pressure for parents to return to work.[25] Many teachers have shown greater insight into the experiences of children, the need to re-engage them, and the futility of a race to 'catch up' what has been missed.[26]

Gradually the media have become more aware of these broader issues, and they are reflected to some extent in the DfE advice of 2 July.[27]

Considerable blame has been directed at teacher organisations, particularly the National Education Union, for resisting the 1 June target, yet schools could have been in a better position to receive students earlier if public health arrangements had been better. The Leicester outbreak is an indication that the flow of information needs considerable improvement, especially communications with schools.

What has been absent and is of great importance is the need for public recognition of the dedication, professionalism and service to society that all those working in schools since the outbreak of COVID-19. There has been too little gratitude expressed, and too little emphasis on building trust and cooperation between decision-makers, professionals and parents during this crisis. These are essential if a wider reopening of schools is to work. There is also a need to learn from the best examples from how both individual teachers and whole schools have operated since COVID-19 and this is essential if we are to prepare for further possible lockdowns in the future.

Recommendations

1   A campaign of national and public recognition for those in schools since COVID-19.
2   There is an urgent need to improve the flow of information on new infections to schools to aid local decision making.
3   Better planning is needed to build a more resilient society and environment if new outbreaks of Covid-19 or other infections occur, including safe physical spaces and social activities for families in overcrowded conditions or without gardens.[28]

 # Conditions and challenges for reopening

This section considers in more detail steps which should be considered to improve readiness for a wider reopening of schools.

Preventing the spread of infections

Medical scientists and education unions have pointed to the high level of infections and the inadequacies of test-and-trace as creating dangers for staff, students and their families. The government's initial response, inspired by countries such as Denmark[29] which had reopened earlier, was to propose distancing and 'bubbles', with fewer than 15 in each room. This failed to recognise the difficulties arising from much larger classes in English primary schools, for example, or the fact that children start school here earlier and many of the youngest children would be unable to comply with distancing. Moreover, the separation of students into 'bubbles' within school is negated if they travel together to and from school by bus or even mingle outside the school gates.

That position has largely been abandoned, and the Secretary of State for Education is currently insisting on full classes, and suggesting that 'bubbles' in secondary schools can consist of the entire year group (often 180 or 240 students). This is clearly a dangerous proposal; it allows far too many opportunities for infection to spread and would make tracing the course of infections almost impossible. Worse, the real 'bubble' is likely to be the whole school, given siblings in others' years, bus travel to and from school, lunches and toilet visits.[30] Some alternatives are considered below.

The urgency of 'catching up'

Various attempts have been made to forecast the learning loss of students, but this is highly problematic. The US Brookings Institute, for example, based its forecasts on summer vacation 'learning loss', which does not recognise that home learning has taken place during lockdown.[31] There may also have been some gains: one survey showed that, although many learners miss the interaction and social environment of school, some also appreciated a more flexible work pattern and high-quality online resources.[32]

It seems likely, however, that relative advantage and disadvantage will have been exacerbated. In other words, the learning loss will have been minimal among students with good internet access, distance learning resources from school, and support from well-educated parents. Students growing up in poverty are likely to have fallen even further behind than if they had been at school.

A study by Professor Francis Green (UCL Institute of Education) showed that home learning had diminished, during the lockdown, to an average of 2.5 hours a day, with a fifth of students doing less than an hour a day.[33] It should not be assumed, however, that these differences in study time map automatically onto socioeconomic differences: only 11 per cent of students on free school meals were spending more than four hours a day on schoolwork but also only 19 per cent of other students.

As argued elsewhere in this document, there has to be a broad understanding of what students will need as they return to school but clearly support for studying the academic curriculum must be taken very seriously. Although we have reservations about the notion of 'catch up' (catch up with what or who? in pursuing which aim? in which area of learning?), it is clear that many students will have missed out on some important learning in recent months. What steps need to be taken?

Firstly the fund for tutorial support is valuable, though the promised budget is limited even if only spread among students with the greatest needs. It will provide far less tuition, for example, than many better off parents buy to prepare children for 11 plus tests or GCSEs.[34] Moreover, a third of the funding will not be distributed directly to schools but to national organisations favoured by the government. There is a danger that large providers will not meet local needs. There are also dangers that the tutors they hire may not be of sufficiently high quality; they will not know the students they are supporting or the curriculum in their schools.

The need for individual tuition must also be set against the larger class sizes in England compared with elsewhere: an average of 27 in English primary schools compared with the European average of 20. Independent schools in England have half as many students per teacher as state schools.[35]

There is potential for employing more teachers to ensure smaller classes and enabling some physical distancing. There are at present more than 250,000 people under 60 with a teaching qualification who are not working in schools. However, many have left because classes are too large, the curriculum is not engaging young people, or because they found top-down surveillance in the English school system unacceptable; many might return if conditions were more favourable. As the Independent SAGE report suggested, schools can also facilitate safe distancing by hiring spaces in community centres, church halls and so on.

Curriculum

Initially advice from ministers was to concentrate on literacy and numeracy (English and Maths) at the expense of other subjects. This advice contradicted a widespread concern about curriculum narrowing, including from Ofsted, and has now changed. The document of 2 July 'Guidance for full opening – schools'[36] quite rightly emphasises a 'broad and ambitious curriculum'. It says students should be able to study the full range of subjects at KS3 and all their expected KS4 or post-16 subjects. It also recognises that an additional emphasis on reading, for example, across different curriculum subjects will help students recover lost ground.

At the same time, the advice assumes that curriculum is simply defined by official lists of knowledge. In our view, a 'recovery curriculum' should not only involve time for social and emotional care but also ensure re-engagement of students' interests and their concerns for the world they are growing up in. This is an essential part of developing knowledge in a deeper sense than the memorisation of inert facts. Students need to be re-engaged through active and creative learning in art, drama or sport, for example.[37] Some of those currently unable to work in the creative arts and performance industries might be able to support learning temporarily, to facilitate smaller classes and social distancing.[38]

It is arguable that switching to home learning in March was more challenging because recent curriculum policy in England has emphasised direct instruction and passive learning. Many students couldn't cope when suddenly expected to learn more independently.[39] A greater emphasis in the future on sustained individual and small group work would have many advantages, including less need to sit in crowded classrooms and the development of initiative and commitment. It would also make any sudden closures more manageable.

One important way of developing students' engagement in learning, common in other European countries, is through well organised investigative projects.[40] This kind of learning is relevant for students of all ages, and rewarded in the International Baccalaureate and other qualifications such as the A-level Extended Project Qualification. Projects should not be seen as isolated individual activity: a well-planned project begins with teachers discovering and stimulating children's interests, finding what they know already, and agreeing with individuals or small groups a plan for more specific investigation in coming weeks. The final stage involves individuals and groups presenting their findings to the class and receiving feedback to correct misunderstandings. Research shows positive outcomes for children's learning and development of 'skills for the future', including responsibility, independence, discipline and motivation as well as improved academic results.[41]

This form of work is valuable in itself, as a way of learning, but would also give the curriculum resilience in case of lockdown and could be pursued in situations of part-time attendance. Projects can spread across a group of subjects, if the theme is well chosen, with many opportunities for out of school learning.

Assessment and accountability

The document of 2 July[42] places an important emphasis on planning on the basis of the educational needs of students, informed by 'an assessment of students' starting points and addressing the gaps in their knowledge and skills'. It suggests use of informal observation and questioning, and issues a salutary warning against 'unnecessary tracking systems'.

However, it does not tackle with sufficient urgency the difficulties for current Year 10 students of preparing for GCSEs which place a lot of emphasis on covering all the material, memorisation and second-guessing possible exam questions. Problems arose for current Year 11 students when the exams were abandoned and they had to be assessed on the basis of their work during the year: there wasn't a ready stock of evidence because coursework had been virtually eliminated from GCSEs. Government policy in recent years has led to a virtual elimination of coursework from GCSEs. The education system will be more balanced and resilient when the value of coursework is accepted once more; in the event of future school closures, teachers will have a body of evidence on which to base professional judgements. There is an urgent need for a decision for 2021 GCSEs.

The same is true for primary school KS2 tests. The government has a chance to change direction and to remedy a situation which has caused widespread dissatisfaction. Better forms of assessment are available. For example, a portfolio, selected by the student with guidance from teachers, would provide richer and more reliable information for parents and future secondary school teachers than a score or grade in a test does at present. Unfortunately, although it has delayed the Baseline test for the start of Reception, the document of 2 July[43] insists on the full battery of primary school tests (phonics, KS1, Y4 multiplication tables, and KS2 tests and teacher assessment). This will continue to distort primary education and undermine recovery. For both primary and secondary education, the focus on accountability in core subjects undermines the 2 July guidance advocating a 'broad and ambitious' curriculum cited earlier: with a sense of 'lost' time, schools will be compelled to focus on what is measured. Whatever one's views on primary school testing in general, it would be wise to cancel the tests for 2020–21.

One unforeseen benefit of school closures has been the halt to Ofsted inspections. Ironically, Ofsted appear to have stopped operations altogether, and despite the importance of monitoring safeguarding, the organisation's inspectors appear not to be investigating, even on a sample basis, issues such as whether schools are losing contact with more vulnerable students. The Chief Inspector has not commented, for example, on the non-delivery of promised laptops, the impact of lack of access to the internet, or the quality of the distance learning resources available. If Ofsted has any future, it must be based on 'thematic reviews' to evaluate and offer guidance on national provision based on a research sample rather than 'hit-and-run' visits to schools. A first step has been taken by focusing, for the autumn, on a thematic review of distance learning and the return to school across the country, based on sample visits, rather than grading individual schools. There is enormous potential for sharing effective practices for the benefit of all schools through detailed independent investigations.

Primary schools

Classes in England's primary schools are larger than almost anywhere in Europe. The average class size here is 27, compared with a European average of 20. When schools in Denmark reopened, in a situation with less infection than England now, children were taught in classes of 10–15.[44] With suitable government investment, that could happen here, and would help create a world-class education system. In the short term, there are circumstances in which a class could be shared between a teacher and experienced teaching assistant in adjacent rooms, but efforts should be made to encourage qualified teachers back into schools, with suitable budgetary increases.

There are good educational and safety reasons why students should remain with their class, rather than being redistributed into different classes for literacy or numeracy – a recent practice which is almost unknown in other countries.

Younger children will have missed out on exploratory and play-based learning in nurseries. Primary schools will need to adjust by sustaining an early years approach rather than rushing into more formal teaching. Finally, there are considerable educational and health benefits in children spending more time learning outdoors.

We are starting to know what students and parents have valued over lockdown.[45] We know that communication with school and with individual teachers has been highly appreciated, that in some cases this has been easier that schools expected with families they thought might not engage. Children have loved videos of their teachers reading books. Not enough is known about best practice of individual teachers or of the strategies of schools that has worked well. Research is needed to gather this evidence and this is crucial to best prepare for further lockdowns in the future.

Secondary schools

The particular difficulties of opening secondary schools during a pandemic was raised in the Independent SAGE report[46] at the end of May:

> There are also particular features of English secondary schools which will make a return to school more difficult. Pupils are frequently allocated to different sets (ability groups) for specific subjects, and between different subject options in

Years 10 and 11 (often starting in Year 9). By contrast, a common core curriculum is the norm in many European countries, with less subject choice.

It is the failure to think beyond this pattern that has now led the Secretary of State for Education to propose 'bubbles' consisting of the entire year group.

The Independent SAGE report[47] included, as an initial suggestion, that:

> New arrangements will need to be carefully planned, so that pupils remain together with one teacher in a class of 15 or fewer. They might have to be taught by a single subject teacher for several days, supplemented by distance learning with other subject specialists.

This is only one of a number of possibilities, and was written at a time when the virus was much more prevalent. Such a dramatic change in organisational norms may still be necessary in areas where there are serious outbreaks, as an alternative to avoid complete closure. More open-minded discussion of alternative ways of conducting secondary education is urgently needed given the government's drive to have all students in school in September. Without pretending to offer a specific model, which would depend on the physical layout of the school and many other factors, the following points give some indicators and possibilities.

Firstly however, it is important to recognise the tension between the infection control advice in the 2 July document[48] (particularly Section 1), derived from Public Health England, and the DfE's advice for organising schools and the curriculum (especially Sections 2 and 3). The groups of headteachers we have heard from are already reaching the conclusion that they can either follow the former or the latter, but cannot reconcile both.

Secondly, it is apparent that the document's proposals for reorganising schools and curriculum are undermined by the physical problems of movement between lessons, for lunch time, access to toilets and handwashing facilities, and walking or transport to and from school. In many schools, one or more of these factors presents a serious obstacle to safe opening with full attendance.

In the light of these factors, it seems likely that most secondary schools will *need some combination of on-site and distance learning*. Few schools will be able to accommodate all their students full-time whilst complying with Public Health England advice as contained in the DfE document of 2 July.

The following points are intended to suggest some ways of organising the curriculum which might enable secondary schools to operate safely.

1 'Bubbles' of 180 or 240 have a high risk of infections spreading and would make tracing the source almost impossible. This can be reduced somewhat by dividing year groups into two or three parts.

2   The layout of many schools means that students in different 'bubbles' would have to pass close to each other through narrow corridors or stairs on the way to specialist accommodation (science, arts, PE etc). This problem could be avoided by timetabling subjects in half-day sessions rather than 40 or 60 minutes.

3   Pressure could be relieved by agreeing to home-based distance learning for some half-days each week. Those students needing additional learning support, including many with SEND or students who have been unable to study at home, could be provided with tutorials or small group learning support at school during these half days.

4   Many schools will not be able to accommodate students safely at lunch time, with cleansing as recommended in the DfE statement of 2 July. A longer break between morning and afternoon sessions would allow those living nearby to eat at home, if that is a possibility, especially those required to be at school for only the morning or afternoon session.

5   Many schools have a carousel arrangement for some subjects in KS3, for example in creative arts each class is taught music, art and drama in different school terms. This has certain educational advantages and would make schools safer by reducing movement.

6   Redistributing classes into ability sets for different subjects adds to the amount of movement. Where this cannot be avoided, these subjects should be taught in blocks on particular half days, as suggested earlier.

7   The DfE document recommends that KS4 and KS5 students should generally study the normal range of GCSE or A-level subjects. Movement between subject options creates particular difficulties, but these can also be avoided by using half-day blocks in conjunction with distance learning.

We are aware that other solutions will emerge, and that their viability is dependent on the physical layout and human resources of each individual school. We also recognise that major curricular reorganisations take time to plan. However, this level of reorganisation may be the only way in which all secondary school students can enjoy a full curriculum while Covid remains a risk.

Distance learning

Better use of distance learning to support revision and homework when schools are open would be of benefit in itself, but would also help establish habits of independent learning in case of closure.

The recommendation in the DfE document of 2 July[49] that schools should continue to prepare for distance learning is sound though very demanding of teachers working full time. The sudden switch to distance learning in mid-March was exceptionally difficult, and teachers had to identify at great speed a range of available resources. It is to the credit of thousands of teachers that they were able to rise to the challenge and achieve this. They were helped in this by subject associations, for example. Although many commercial organisations offered free use of their online resources, much of this material was narrowly focused on practice exercises in English and Maths, for example arithmetic calculations and spellings. Although this has value, it should not be allowed to exacerbate the imbalance already existing in the English primary curriculum.

Notwithstanding the achievements of most teacher and schools, there are some schools where the quality of communication with students and the provision of on-line learning opportunities for students has been poor. It is essential to begin a broad consultation about expectations, best practice, skill requirements etc in terms of what counts as good practice.

The lack of a computer has been a major difficulty for many children, with deliv-eries of promised machines coming very late if at all. New figures show that of the 230,000 laptops promised ten weeks earlier (mid-April), only 202,212 had been delivered or dispatched by 30 June, and nearly a quarter were sent out only in the last week.[50] Many of these have not yet got beyond delivery to local authorities or academy trusts to reach schools and students. These delays might have been avoided if funding had gone directly to schools. It should be noted that the scheme does not cover the cost of internet access, and apart from care leavers and families with a social worker, only reaches disadvantaged students if they are in Year 10. The Prime Minister has refused to commit to free laptops for all students on free school meals.[51]

A survey conducted in June by Professor Francis Green (UCL Institute of Educa-tion)[52] showed that 20 per cent of students on free school meals had no computer access at home. It also revealed that private schools were able to use their superior resources to advantage.

This leaves a very poor basis for any future lockdown, or for schools which do not have the space for all students to attend full time and therefore need some mix of attendance and home learning.

Other ways of supporting education through distance learning have remained rudimentary. For example, BBC broadcasts were based largely on short video clips produced nearly 20 years ago. More interesting material including the TedEd col-lection[53] with many thought-provoking videos and tasks did not align well with the narrower view of education of the English National Curriculum.

Recommendations

1 Reduce as far as possible the mixing of students beyond a small 'bubble', including smaller classes in primary schools and a different timetabling model in secondary schools.

2   Increase funding for individual and small group tuition for students with additional needs.

3   Improve the quality of resources for distance learning, both when schools are open to all students and in case of any future restrictions, and with particular attention to students with underlying health conditions.

4   Ensure a 'broad and challenging' curriculum, as advised by the DfE, paying attention to the need to engage young people's interests and concerns and develop more independence and initiative.

5   Reduce the size of classes in primary school to around 15, by encouraging qualified teachers back into schools.

6   Devise alternative forms of curricular organisation for secondary schools which reduce movement whilst providing a high quality of education, including a mixture between on-site and home learning where necessary.

7   Work with employers and further and higher education to ensure this year's school leavers are not disadvantaged in relation to entry requirements and communicate this clearly into schools to reduce anxiety.

8   Reduce the pressures created by public examinations and primary school tests, including reduced content for GCSEs, greater use of coursework and portfolios, and cancelling universal national testing in primary schools.

9   Ensure that all disadvantaged students, not only those in examination years, and those vulnerable through health conditions, have access to computers and internet at home.

10 Encourage headteachers to share their knowledge and experience to develop guidance for different levels of alert in the future, including the health and education needs of vulnerable students.

Wellbeing: the challenges of a return to school

The complexity and variability of students' responses to the sudden closure of schools cannot be underestimated.[54] A study by Barry Carpenter (Professor of Mental Health in Education at Oxford Brookes University) and Matthew Carpenter (Principal, Baxter College Kidderminster) points to the loss of self-esteem and self-image when the peer group is taken away, and in some cases this could trigger a bereavement response. Anxiety could arise from listening to daily reports of the spread of the pandemic and the death toll[55] and many have had direct experience of bereavement or trauma in their families.

Mary Myatt (education consultant) emphasises the importance of 'recovery conversations' both among staff and with students – conversations in which personal narratives are expressed and shared, acknowledging a common experience.[56] We should remember, of course, that not all students have had a negative experience or reactions since many have enjoyed time with family and may have been released from school-based anxieties.

A report by Childline[57] as early as mid-April identified the following range of issues for the students most seriously affected by school closures and lockdown:

> *Mental health issues:* depression, anxiety, increase of panic attacks, sleeping problems and feeling isolated, lonely and trapped; for some, dark thoughts and self-harm are connected with coronavirus; for some, mental health support has reduced or stopped which has worsened their mental health, or they are in hospital without visitors;
>
> *Family relationships:* more stressful home environment, arguments, removal of refuge with grandparents or friends, anxiety about vulnerable family members;
>
> *Schoolwork:* many aspects of the lockdown have made learning harder – family arguments about schoolwork, difficulty of accessing learning support leading to confusion and stress, difficulty of finding a quiet place to study and the challenge of self-motivating; students are worried about their future;
>
> *Bullying:* in the early days of the pandemic, students were bullied about race or ethnicity and blamed for the virus spreading and although this has died down, it may have a legacy;
>
> *Abuse:* where confined to home, students have no access to usual means of support, including school, clubs and relatives, and report physical, emotional and sexual abuse and neglect.

We should not make too casual use of terms such as trauma or Adverse Childhood Experiences, which can result in a negative categorisation of children. However, we should not underestimate the suffering of different children in recent months. Some will have lost relatives or dealt with relatives being seriously ill. Others will have been locked down in dysfunctional families. Both of those definitely rank as trauma.

On the other hand, some students will have experienced a release of stress, due to being able to learn in nurturing homes with parents on furlough who are maybe better able to support their needs than schools, due to adult-child relationships and ratios. Other students will have been reasonably happy at home but will have been with adults who are too busy trying to keep their careers ticking over through online working and don't have much time to pay much attention to what the children are doing. Some will be generally happy at home but missing their friends. These different experiences and stories need to be heard and acknowledged by trusted teachers. The value of creativity in addressing and alleviating some of these concerns is well established.[58]

The danger that some students will not return to school in September is recognised by DfE. There are various possible reasons for this. Some families with medically vulnerable members will fear infection. Some students may have become completely disconnected from their schools and some schools may not have monitored or remedied this well enough. Others may be afraid they have fallen too far behind. Some students with Special Educational Needs may not have had suitable support and may experience additional difficulties in returning to school. These different situations need to be handled sensitively. The threat of fines and prosecution is unhelpful.

Recommendations

1   Support parents and guardians in looking after students' mental wellbeing, including recognising and responding to stress/trauma and building resilience.
2   Provide guidance and training to school staff on how to support students who have suffered bereavement, stress or challenging situations at home.[59]
3   Fund creative programmes and projects inside and out of school that address wellbeing and build relationships in positive and enjoyable ways (Children's Society Report, 2020).
4   Remove the threat of fines and prosecution.

Taking care of teachers

Teachers, heads and other school staff have experienced extraordinary pressures in recent months, regardless of whether they have been keeping schools open for vulnerable students, partially reopening them, or supporting distance learning from home. Uncertainty itself has been incredibly stressful. Thought needs to be given to the kind of support they will need in preparing for a more extensive reopening in September.

Firstly they need to be congratulated for their work and supported to recognise the stress of their own time in lockdown and the difficulties of working online and remotely, while preparing to support students. Covid has created challenges for teachers and teacher assistants as they try to negotiate the different phases of the emergence from lockdown and the different educational and health and wellbeing needs of the students. For example, under stressful conditions, teachers undergo something akin to an identity passage[60] where many cherished aspects of the teacher's self become dislocated. Earlier research into teachers retiring has identified a sense of disorientation, what Nias[61] described as grieving for their lost selves before they gradually relocate and modify their teacher identity. As they return to classroom teaching many will have gained insights into students' distress through online interactions delivering resources to homes and seeing the home conditions of families living in poverty. Some of this may feel overbearing and undermine a sense of professional competence. The importance of mutual support needs to be recognised, and some staff will need professional counselling.

Headteachers have been placed under considerable strain when facing government demands for schools to reopen quickly which at the same time placed the burden of responsibility on the headteacher and governors for ensuring this is safe. In many areas, local authorities have been run down so seriously that they have received little support. Headteachers and governors have experienced the frustration of not having the money to provide what they know is needed, while acute concerns for care and safeguarding as well as learning of their students have never gone away. These issues are exacerbated in disadvantaged catchments and run through holidays as well as term time.

This tension will be repeated in preparing for a wider reopening in September, and responding to the multiple demands of the DfE statement of 2 July.[62] Headteachers need to be trusted, listened to and allowed to do their job, in consultation with staff and governors. They know what is needed for their schools, staff and students and they have a great deal of wisdom to draw upon. Decisions should not be made independently of them and there should be enough scope for them to tailor policy to local circumstances and needs. Attention should be given to ensuring headteachers can get advice and support for leadership, in a manner which supports wellbeing and leadership through reflexivity.[63]

Many staff are expressing concern about returning to work in terms of their own underlying health issues, and are anxious that conditions outlined in the DfE report of 2 July[64] do not provide adequate protection. These include staff with medical conditions, those with vulnerable people in their households (including elderly relatives), and many members of BAME communities. They will need to be risk assessed before return and provided with sound advice. Some will need to be offered the opportunity to work from home.

The DfE document of 2 July[65] rightly recommends that schools continue to improve resources for distance learning in case of future lockdowns. The difficulties are not recognised of simultaneously teaching classes face-to-face full time and preparing quality online resources. Teachers need to be consulted on ways of overcoming this problem. The value of resources provided by professional bodies such as subject associations should be recognised and funding provided to extend this.

It should also be recognised that teachers have been placed under excessive pressure of top-down surveillance and control in recent years, which has been a major cause of people leaving the profession. This cannot continue in the current challenging circumstances. School staff need to be able to concentrate on children's academic and wellbeing needs without being placed under excessive pressure to satisfy other demands.

Recommendations

The following aspects would help teachers to plan for September:

1 *Safe working environment:* teachers should not be asked to work in unsafe conditions, should be given clear health and safety advice for self, colleagues and classes, and should be involved in action planning for a second wave or a local lockdown.
2 *Clear focus:* fund improved support for social, emotional, mental and physical health, particularly in disadvantaged communities, so that teachers can concentrate on curriculum and pedagogy.
3 *Appropriate resourcing:* in order to address current inequalities, ensure that every child and young person has online access to learning not only in preparation for another spike or local lockdown, but also to support their ongoing in-school learning.
4 *Professional trust*: remove judgmental monitoring and performance management; use Ofsted to gather evidence to monitor national patterns and support progress and to develop best practice case studies; encourage school-based responsibility and accountability; involve teachers in decision making.
5 *Training and development:* convene a national panel for teachers to contribute ideas on what professional learning would be most useful to them in the short, medium and long term, and to discuss how this might best be provided given financial constraints.
6 *Targeted support*: provide individual support and respite for teachers who have individual needs as a legacy of the pandemic (bereavement, mental health struggles, anxiety about safety of the workplace, extra caring responsibilities).
7 *A proper holiday*: teachers need time to recharge, refresh and re-engage before preparing for a period of further uncertainty.

The school in the community

The recent situation has shown how much the education and development of children and young people requires diverse individuals and agencies. There is a need to rebuild external services that interact with schools, including libraries, youth services, children's centres, leisure centres, sports clubs, youth theatres and music groups.

Given the concerns about students' mental health needs, Child and Adolescent Mental Health Services (CAMHS) and counselling services need to be given high priority, while SureStart centres and local youth services can provide connections and support that reach out into families and communities. All of these have suffered from reductions in funding so a process of rebuilding is needed.

COVID has also made clear once more that schools have a crucial role for the whole community. This is by no means limited to enabling parents to go to work. In particular, schools in areas of deprivation should be funded and encouraged to develop as centres of education and activity for the whole community.

A closer partnership between schools and communities would bring multiple benefits for children and their families. Schools should be encouraged to work with resources in their community, including voluntary groups such as the scout movement, creative artists, sports clubs to provide a richer curriculum than the school operating in isolation. The school curriculum should, in part, engage with issues of local concern as well as the concerns of young people.

Covid has also highlighted the extent to which school learning depends on families being able to afford equipment, books and other resources. The work of organisations such as Children North East and the project of 'poverty proofing' schools is essential and needs funding. Children North East's new programme Local Matters trains teachers to become community researchers in order to stand alongside the community and identify and respond to local issues. Research projects led by various universities, such as the Teachers Attitudes Towards Poverty survey, has identified that a significant minority of school staff hold deficit views of families in poverty. It has also identified a low awareness level of benefit rates and the benefit process in schools. There are training needs for staff in these issues.[66]

Recommendations

1   Encourage stronger links between schools and communities, particularly in disadvantaged areas.
2   Support staff development which improves understanding of families and neighbourhoods under the stress of poverty.
3   Fund community/university /school partnerships for investigating and responding to local issues and leading change.

Conclusion

The crisis we have experienced this year poses serious challenges to policy makers and professionals. It exposes fault lines in society and reveals problems which had previously only been noticed by a minority. It can also highlight the distance between policy makers and practitioners and the gap between their understandings of how schools work.

At the same time, such a crisis presents opportunities to address serious problems and make lives better. This requires more than short-term technical fixes, it requires vision.

We hope that this document, drawn up through cooperation between researchers and teaching professionals, will both point to solutions for specific problems and offer a route towards a better education system and a better society.

Each section in the report has generated specific recommendations. The following provides a summary of key proposals and principles.

1 Although different human needs have to be balanced, public health cannot be sacrificed to unrealistic educational demands.
2 Rapid improvement is needed in communicating medical information to local authorities and school governors, in order to facilitate sound decision making.
3 While infection levels remain serious, arrange for smaller classes in primary schools; and new forms of curriculum organisation in secondary schools in a combination of on-site and distance learning.
4 Recognise young people's experiences during recent months, and adopt a sensitive approach to re-engaging them, rather than threatening parents with fines.
5 Support parents and teachers in monitoring and caring for students' mental well-being, providing specialist support where needed.
6 Schools should prioritise children's wellbeing, thinking in terms of a 'recovery curriculum'. Young people should be re-engaged by a curriculum which is not only broad and challenging, but which engages their interests and concerns and develops independence and initiative.
7 Improve the quality of distance learning resources, and ensure that all disadvantaged students have access to computers and internet.
8 Increase the funding of tutorial support for students who have encountered the greater barriers to learning, and route this through schools.
9 Reduce the pressures of public examinations and primary school tests, including reduced content for GCSEs, greater use of coursework and portfolios, and cancelling universal testing in primary schools for the coming year.
10 Provide a supportive environment for teachers and other staff, by increasing trust, cooperation, and professional development, whilst removing sources of threat such as inspections which could serve as a distraction from students' needs.
11 Encourage stronger links between schools and communities, particularly in more disadvantaged areas.

Notes

1 www.independentsage.org/wp-content/uploads/2020/06/Independent-Sage-Brief-Report-on-Schools.pdf
2 Annexe, pages 34–40 of note (1)

3 www.gov.uk/government/publications/actions-for-schools-during-the-coronavirus-outbreak/guidance-for-full-opening-schools

4 The term 'student' is used for convenience throughout the document to refer to children and young people of all ages.

5 see for example www.theguardian.com/commentisfree/2020/jul/05/our-school-systems-are-broken-lets-grab-this-chance-to-remake-them

6 as (1)

7 www.gov.uk/government/publications/coronavirus-covid-19-testing-data-methodology/covid-19-testing-data-methodology-note

8 John Burn-Murdoch and colleagues: Lack of local Covid-19 testing data hinders UK's outbreak response (Financial Times, 30 June 2020) www.ft.com/content/301c847c-a317-4950-a75b-8e66933d423a and Public Health England: Preliminary investigation into Covid-19 exceedances in Leicester (29 June 2020) https://assets.publishing.service.gov.uk/government/uploads/system/uploads/attachment_data/file/897128/COVID-19_activity_Leicester_Final-report_010720_v3.pdf

9 https://schoolsweek.co.uk/leicesters-covid-19-response-thwarted-by-poor-data/?mc_cid=f8510837d9&mc_eid=7ecb3b7756

10 Peter Roderick, Alison Macfarlane and Allyson Pollock: Getting back on track – control of covid-19 outbreaks in the community (BMJ 26 June 2020) www.bmj.com/content/bmj/369/bmj.m2484.full.pdf

11 LGA: Coronavirus – LGA responds to publication of Pillar 2 testing data (3 July 2020) www.local.gov.uk/coronavirus-lga-responds-publication-pillar-2-testing-data

12 www.bbc.co.uk/news/uk-england-leicestershire-53261339

13 see note (3)

14 Alvarez, J., and Hunt, M. (2005). 'Risk and resilience in canine search and rescue handlers after 9/11'. *Journal of Traumatic Stress: Official Publication of the International Society for Traumatic Stress Studies*, 18(5), 497–505; Cukor, J., Wyka, K., Jayasinghe, N., Weathers, F., Giosan, C., Leck, P., . . . Difede, J. (2011). 'Prevalence and Predictors of Posttraumatic Stress Symptoms in Utility Workers Deployed to the World Trade Center Following The Attacks of September 11, 2001'. *Depression and Anxiety*, 28(3), 210–217.

15 Brooks, S. K., Webster, R. K., Smith, L. E., Woodland, L., Wessely, S., Greenberg, N., and Rubin, G. J. (2020). 'The psychological impact of quarantine and how to reduce it: Rapid review of the evidence'. *The Lancet*, 395(10227), 12–20.

16 https://learning.nspcc.org.uk/media/2195/what-children-are-saying-to-childline-about-coronavirus.pdf

17 www.leedstrinity.ac.uk/blog/blog-posts/exam-factory-spring-a-lockdown-reflection.php

18 https://assets.publishing.service.gov.uk/government/uploads/system/uploads/attachment_data/file/892085/disparities_review.pdf

19 E. Fitzsimons, A. Goodman, E. Kelly, and J. Smith (2017) 'Poverty Dynamics and Parental Mental Health: Determinants of Childhood Mental Health in the UK'. *Social Science and Medicine*, 175, 43–51. https://pubmed.ncbi.nlm.nih.gov/28056382/

20 for example, C. Raffo, et al. (2009) *Education and Poverty: Mapping the Terrain and Making the Links to Educational Policy*. www.researchgate.net/publication/255661769_Education_and_poverty_Mapping_the_terrain_and_making_the_links_to_educational_policy; J. Smyth and T. Wrigley (2013) *Living on the Edge: Rethinking Poverty, Class and Schooling*. New York: Peter Lang; I. Thompson (2017) *Tackling Social Disadvantage Through Teacher Education*. Northwich: Critical Publishing.

21 J. Andrews, D. Robinson, and J. Hutchinson (2017) *Closing the Gap? Trends in Educational Attainment and Disadvantage*. https://epi.org.uk/publications-and-research/closing-gap-trends-educational-attainmentdisadvantage/

22 for example, C. Raffo, et al. (2009) *Education and Poverty: Mapping the Terrain and Making the Links to Educational Policy*. www.researchgate.net/publication/255661769_Education_and_poverty_Mapping_the_terrain_and_making_the_links_to_educational_policy; J. Smyth and T. Wrigley (2013) *Living on the Edge: Rethinking Poverty, Class and Schooling*. New York: Peter Lang; I. Thompson (2017) *Tackling Social Disadvantage Through Teacher Education*. Northwich: Critical Publishing; J. Andrews, D. Robinson, and J. Hutchinson (2017) Closing the Gap? Trends in Educational Attainment and Disadvantage. https://epi.org.uk/publications-and-research/closing-gap-trends-educational-attainmentdisadvantage/

23 https://cpag.org.uk/projects/cost-school-day and www.children-ne.org.uk/poverty-proofing-the-school-day

24 www.evidenceforlearning.net/recoverycurriculum/

25 See for example the 19 June press briefing from the Secretary of State for Education.

26 See for example Matthew Evans https://educontrarianblog.com/2020/06/04/knee-jerk-ill-informed-catch-up-plans/ and Aidan Severs www.thatboycanteach.co.uk/2020/06/back-to-school-recovery-or-catch-up.html

27 see note 3

28 www.ncl.ac.uk/press/articles/latest/2020/03/playingout/ https://blogs.ncl.ac.uk/alisonstenning/

29 www.bbc.co.uk/news/education-52550470

30 See the warning from the Education Policy Institute that there is "no credible solution" to the problem of year group bubbles mixing with others while travelling to and from school. https://schoolsweek.co.uk/significant-number-of-pupils-will-likely-mix-on-school-transport-warns-epi/?mc_cid=f8510837d9&mc_eid=7ecb3b7756

31 https://edworkingpapers.com/ai20-226

32 https://bigeducation.org/lfl-content/learning-from-the-students-in-lockdown/

33 www.ucl.ac.uk/news/2020/jun/children-doing-25-hours-schoolwork-day-average

34 www.suttontrust.com/wp-content/uploads/2017/09/Extra-time-report_FINAL.pdf

35 https://assets.publishing.service.gov.uk/government/uploads/system/uploads/ attachment_data/file/826252/Schools_Pupils_and_their_Characteristics_ 2019_Accompanying_Tables.xlsx table 7a and https://stats.oecd.org/Index.aspx? DataSetCode=EAG_PERS_RATIO

36 www.gov.uk/government/publications/actions-for-schools-during-the-coronavi- rus-outbreak/guidance-for-full-opening-schools

37 https://bigeducation.org/lfl-content/metamorphosis-using-re-entry-as-a-spring- board-for-helping-vulnerable-primary-school-pupils-fly/

38 see Creative Partnerships www.creativitycultureeducation.org/programme/creat ive-partnerships/

39 See Chartered College of Teaching report https://my.chartered.college/wp-con tent/uploads/2020/05/CCTReport150520_FINAL.pdf

40 D. Leat, ed. *Enquiry and Project Based Learning: Students, School and Society.* Abingdon: Taylor & Francis, 2017.

41 see Bell 2010. www.tandfonline.com/doi/full/10.1080/00098650903505415

42 see note (3)

43 see note (3)

44 www.bbc.co.uk/news/education-52550470

45 https://cpag.org.uk/policy-and-campaigns/report/cost-learning-lock down-family-experiences-school-closures

46 see note (1)

47 see note (1)

48 see note (3)

49 see note (3)

50 https://schoolsweek.co.uk/dfe-fails-to-meet-target-of-delivering-230k-laptops- by-end-of-june/

51 www.tes.com/news/pm-refuses-commit-free-laptops-all-fsm-pupils

52 www.ucl.ac.uk/news/2020/jun/children-doing-25-hours-schoolwork-day- average

53 ed.ted.com

54 see for example www.thelancet.com/journals/lancet/article/PIIS0140-6736(20)3 1481-1/fulltext?utm_campaign=tlchildhealth20_infocus20&utm_content= 133772107&utm_medium=social&utm_source=twitter&hss_channel= tw-27013292

55 www.evidenceforlearning.net/recoverycurriculum/

56 https://schoolsweek.co.uk/a-recovery-curriculum-or-recovery-conversations/

57 https://learning.nspcc.org.uk/media/2195/what-children-are-saying-to-childline-about-coronavirus.pdf

58 www.tes.com/news/podcast-could-creativity-save-students-mental-health

59 see Chartered College of Teaching report https://my.chartered.college/wp-content/uploads/2020/05/CCTReport150520_FINAL.pdf

60 P. Woods and D. Carlyle (2002) 'Teacher Identities Under Stress: The Emotions of Separation and Renewal'. *International Studies in Sociology of Education*, 12(2), 169–189.

61 J. Nias (1989) *Primary Teachers Talking: A Study of Teaching as Work*. London: Routledge.

62 see note (3)

63 A. Bainbridge, H. Reid, and G. Del Negro (2019) *Towards a Virtuosity of School Leadership: Clinical Support and Supervision as Professional Learning*. Professional Development in Education. www.tandfonline.com/doi/abs/10.1080/1941 5257.2019.1700152

64 see note (3)

65 see note (3)

66 See for example C. Emery and L. Dawes (2020) *Local Matters: Educating with a Sense of Place*. www.research.manchester.ac.uk/portal/en/publications/local-matters-educating-with-a-sense-of-place(3e6fc351-325d-4c33-8ecf-56e2380 56b39).html also work with early years by Donald Simpson (Teesside University)

Annex 2

Association of School and College Leaders: coronavirus (Covid-19) guidance for school and college leaders

CORONAVIRUS (COVID-19)
GUIDANCE FOR SCHOOL AND COLLEGE LEADERS

Contents

Introduction

The situation with regard to Coronavirus (Covid-19) is fast-moving and hard to predict. The most up-to-date guidance from the Department for Education and Public Health England for educational settings can be accessed here, and further information about the government response here.

This document is intended to supplement that official guidance. It is designed to help school and college leaders to prepare for a widespread outbreak of the virus, and the major implications for their pupils and staff.

Leaders with specific questions are advised to contact the DfE's Coronavirus helpline on coronavirushelpline@education.gov.uk or 0800 046 8687. ASCL's member support hotline is available on 0116 2991122. Please be advised that both helplines will be extremely busy at the moment, and it may take a while to get through. See Section 2 of this document for further sources of information and support.

Section 1 | Ten steps to plan and prepare

These ten steps aim to assist school and college to plan and prepare for a widespread outbreak of the virus. Most will already have done or considered everything here, but they provide a useful checklist to refer back to as the situation evolves.

1   Check emergency plan details, reminding families and staff to update their details, in case a closure is required during school opening hours. **Consider asking families if they have members working in vital services, such as emergency services and food distribution.**

2   Revise or draft a risk assessment (see Section 3), ensuring clear delegation of responsibilities and decision making. It should take into consideration how vulnerable pupils' needs will be met (including alternative ways to raise safeguarding concerns in the event of a partial or full closure) and identify staff or pupils who are at higher risk, i.e. those who have underlying health conditions.

3   Communication is key to dispelling rumours and myths. Consider designating a liaison and communications role for keeping up to date with information and fielding inquiries within the school.

4   For school trips, obtain a clear understanding of the cancellation policy put in place by the travel company, venue and transport provider. Check to see if any changes have been made in the light of the current situation. Pursue a full refund as a priority. **We recommend keeping a record and evidence of all additional costs and losses incurred due to coronavirus.**

5   Ensure regular health and safety processes and procedures are being followed robustly, check medical equipment and plans such as inhalers, asthma plans and medication. Consider ways to reduce the risk of spread in and around school, i.e. additional handwashing on entering school and/or classes, waste handling and disposal.

6   Consider ways to reduce person-to-person close contact and potential pinch points, such as assemblies, sporting activities, and group cookery/tasting activities. There are various measures schools could consider, but they need to decide what is workable in their specific circumstances. These could include individual snack plates for nursery children; children keeping water bottles with them rather than in communal trays; additional cleaning between dinner sittings; reducing self-service options from food service; and providing protective equipment for those preparing and serving food.

7   Check consumable stocks and supplies are in place, i.e. food, hand wash, tissues, hand sanitisers, cleaning materials and equipment. Consider alternatives if some supplies are unavailable, such as changing school meal menus or a reciprocal arrangement with other local schools to support each other.

8   Check that cleaning and site maintenance staff and contractors have appropriate and necessary supplies to undertake cleaning.

9   If a site is multi-use, consider measures that could collectively be taken with the other organisations, such as asking all visitors to clean their hands before entering any of the buildings on site.

10 In the event of a partial or full closure, provide clear expectations to families and staff of what work will be carried out. For staff, consider any additional infrastructure, equipment and advice needed for those adjusting to homeworking, i.e. appropriate working hours and use of equipment, login details and remote access. For pupils, check what equipment they have access to at home and consider how to support those who are unable to access digital resources.

Section 2 | Sources of information and support

Downloadable posters

COVID-19 guidance for educational settings

COVID-19 travel guidance for the education sector

NGA information for governing boards

DfE helpline | coronavirushelpline@education.gov.uk or call 0800 046 8687

ASCL member support hotline | 0116 299 1122

For NHS advice call 111

Section 3 | Risk assessment template

The following is an exemplar risk assessment template to help schools, trusts and colleges to consider risks, trigger points and measures to implement. Inevitably, this can't anticipate specific risks in every institution, but it could form a starting point, or serve as a checklist against organisations' existing risk assessments.

School/trust/college name
Risk assessment template

Government Response Stage	Trigger Points	Measures to consider	Responsibility
Phase 1 – 'containment' This involves trying to catch cases early and capture contacts to avoid the spread of disease	None; follow generally accepted guidance and practice.	Whole school/trust/college reminders for hygiene measures via posters, assemblies and classes. Handwashing facilities and soap available. Follow school policy for sickness. Check code for recording absences.	
Phase 2 - 'delay' If phase 1 does not work, the government will increase their response to delay the spread of illness	Increased absence rates of pupils or staff. Local increases in sickness. Public Health England alerts. Specific guidance from the Department for Education. Government COBRA committee announcements. Suspected cases of specific illness in school or within the community.	Increase hygiene procedures and reminders. Communicate vital information to all users and visitors to the school. Hygiene lessons for all pupils in a way they can understand, e.g. visual prompts. Increased enforced use of handwashing before eating of food and snacks. Robustly enforce the 48-hour exclusion from school after all symptoms have stopped. Consider the viability of trips and events. Review the situation daily. Check code for recording absences.	
Phase 3 - 'research' If delaying the spread fails, the government will focus on finding out how the virus spreads and how people can be effectively treated	Direct case or increased likelihood of cases. Public Health England alerts on restrictions. Specific guidance from the Department for Education. Government COBRA committee announcements.	Reduction of person-to-person close contact (where possible), for example, whole school assemblies and school events. Screening options, i.e. taking temperature where there is concern. Increasing the period of exclusion (above 48 hours) from school where specific symptoms are present. Sending pupils home showing any of the symptoms in school. Additional cleaning measures. Restrictions or exclusions placed on visitors to school site. Check code for recording absences.	
Phase 4 - 'mitigate' If infections are considered widespread, expect NHS services to focused on the most severe cases and restrictions to be put in place	High levels of sickness. High rates of absence. Significance of danger of disease or illness. Specific guidance from the Department for Education. Government COBRA committee announcements.	Partial or full closure of classes/school/site. Additional cleaning measures. Reduction or exclusion of visitors. Check code for recording absences.	

Section 4 | Suggested actions in response to specific issues

Specific issue	Actions	Responsibility
Pupil or staff member displaying or reporting possible symptoms	Individual plus all other members of their household to self-isolate for 14 days and follow guidance from the NHS and Public Health England (if required call 111 for advice). Inform headteacher/line manager as soon as possible. Consider distancing measures for those they have come into recent close contact with. Cleaning measures, waste disposal and checks on hot water. Inform staff. Reminder staff, parents and pupils of the school/trust/college's hygiene and sickness procedures. Contact relevant stakeholders and agencies, where advice is required, for example, the local authority, trust CEO/COO, Public Health England.	
Teacher shortage	Consider options to cover classes or groups, for example, supply cover, splitting classes, senior leaders, partial closure for certain classes or year groups, part-time timetables.	
Support staff shortage	Consider options to cover key roles, for examples, supply covers, prioritising highest need children and/or classes with capacity available.	
Protection for most vulnerable children	Identify the most vulnerable children, particularly those with underlying health conditions. Discuss with parents/carers the initial steps and agree key actions and measures, e.g. isolation.	
Staff with known underlying health issues, including pregnant staff	Ask them to contact their medical advisor/consultant to seek advice on their condition. Consider options for flexible working, e.g. working from home.	
Kitchen and catering (including potential partial closure or shut down)	Consider if parents/carers are able to provide packed lunches, whether other schools or catering providers could provide alternatives, provision of food vouchers, reduced menus. Check cleaning and hygiene measures. Consider reducing self-service options and providing protective equipment for those preparing and serving food, for example, face masks and disposable gloves.	
Site team shortage	Discuss with cleaning team and/or contractor potential cover arrangements. Consider coverage of key tasks, for example, site unlocking and locking, checking water temps	
Leadership team shortage	Consider options for covering, e.g. utilising middle leaders. Consider options for ensuring that staff and suppliers continue to be paid. Consider options to fulfil completion of statutory duties (where they are still expected), e.g. financial returns.	
Admin shortage	Consider options for covering essential tasks, e.g. other members of support staff and/or senior leaders. Inform parents of alternative arrangements, e.g. not to phone unless it is an emergency, leave answer phone messages, email a generic email address. Consider coverage of key tasks and potential revisions to processes and procedures, e.g. first aid provision.	
Other school users	Inform visitors and other users of the school site of control measures, including the possibility of additional hand washing and suspension of access or usage.	

Long period shut down	Consider options for continuation of learning and communication with pupils and families, e.g. possible use of technology to deliver assemblies, project work, tasks, reading, software/apps.	
Safeguarding	Continue to proactively check on any unexplained absences as you ordinarily would, for example, if a pupil is off but parents/carers don't call in. Consider alternative arrangements for raising safeguarding concerns, e.g. hotline number. Should all designated safeguarding leads be absent, consider alternative arrangements. Schools may have limited communication methods with pupils but remind staff not to share their personal phone numbers or contact details. With online learning, remind staff and pupils/students of vital principles such as avoiding one-to-one tutoring or messaging unless this is pre-approved and auditable. (There are useful safeguarding considerations here about online learning and what is and isn't appropriate www.lgfl.net/about/coronavirus) Reduce worry and talk to young people about what is happening. (This Coronavirus video series from CBBC Newsround is reassuring, and explains what is happening in a child-friendly way. You may also find these Top Ten Tips for 'Talking to Your Children About Scary World News' from the Mental Health Foundation helpful.) Check that other emergency plans can still run effectively and safely, e.g. should the fire alarm sound, are key roles covered?	
Pupils with SEND	Where medical needs are acute, school visitors and multi-agency visits between classes should be kept to a minimum. Home visits, therapy visits should be conducted virtually wherever possible. Supporting SEND pupils in the case of closure: Pupils with SEND will be better served with home learning that consolidates knowledge rather than introducing new learning. When making decisions about how and if schools will be able to deliver education to students during the period of closure, schools must take into consideration any reasonable adjustments it could make to enable students with disabilities to access those arrangements. Special settings may want to consider the loan of equipment that can support physical health, for example, postural management should continue during school closures and parents may not have access to equipment such as standing frames.	

Vulnerable pupils, staff and families	Maintain regular contact with alternative provision providers to check absences of pupils and any potential safeguarding issues arising. In the event of school closures, check if/what work the AP has set too. Some special schools and those with vulnerable youngsters have taken the decision to stay open at the moment but are excluding visitors, unless urgent, to the school. This means for the school, no visitors or visits except urgent ones. There may be vulnerable family members connected to pupils or staff who require consideration, for example, where a lone parent is immunodeficient or immunocompromised. **Supporting vulnerable pupils in the case of closure** Consider how families experiencing extreme financial hardship will access the hardship fund at your school or local authority. Some schools are considering a central base for food distribution for those who won't have access to food bank vouchers. Work packs for pupils who don't have access to technology. Hotline numbers shared with most vulnerable families where they can get support. A phoneline for school support.	
Financial risks	Consider additional costs and losses that maybe incurred, for example: • Staff sickness absence insurance may not cover illness related to a pandemic. • Contracted services may continue to incur costs, e.g. fixed catering contract charges. • Cancellation of trips, events and lettings. • Additional supply cover and cleaning costs. • Rising prices of essential supplies. We recommend keeping a record and evidence of all additional costs and losses incurred due to coronavirus.	
Communication	Communicate necessary information and guidance to pupils, staff, parents and governors. Share where and how official notices will appear (and will not), for example, school/trust website, telephone answer phone message, social media. Update emergency key contacts list i.e. site staff, senior leadership team, transport providers, catering, cleaning, IT, local authority/trust. **Consider asking families if they have members working in vital services, such as emergency services and food distribution.**	
Governors and trustees	Refer to guidance from the National Governors Association (NGA) and the information sheet they have produced. We recommend that schools and colleges review their governance documents, e.g. instrument, articles and standing orders, to check what flexibilities exist around the convening of meetings to transact business. Some schools and trusts have taken the decision to hold governance meetings via teleconference as an interim measure, to reduce the number of visitors into school. Restricting meetings may also be necessary to protect governors themselves, who may be in high risk groups or self-isolating.	
School travel and transport	Consider advice and additional precautions required for children travelling with escorts, via taxi, rail and private/public bus routes.	
Examinations and statutory assessments	Refer to announcements from the Department for Education and the regulator Ofqual. www.gov.uk/government/news/updated-statement-on-coronavirus	

Flexible/home working	Communicate expectations for staff and pupils around, for example, working hours (including that staff will not be expected to be available 24 hours a day or to respond immediately).
	
	Consider if additional safeguarding advice or reminders are required.
	
	Develop guidelines for teachers to support continued learning in the event of a lengthy school closure, for example:
	• Staff to communicate to pupils via XXXX
	• Children to have XXXX activity per day based on current topics (where possible)
	• Online access is available to XXXX via XXXX (provide separate instructions and access information where required)
	• IT support is available by contacting XXXX
	• Consider whether is appropriate to introduce new topics
	• Set project work and longer tasks where appropriate
	• Other activities could include:
	   • Online learning
	   • Outstanding homework activities
	   • Daily reading
	   • Daily challenges
	   • Creative/mindfulness/wellbeing activities
	• Children to submit work via XXXX
	• School-based message to parents explaining the expectations from parents to support their child/children
	Make staff aware that there are ongoing cyber security phishing scams around the Coronavirus. Scammers are starting to distribute fake emails pretending to be an employer, with an option to sign up to get the latest updates on coronavirus, whereas it is really a scam to harvest personal details.	

Ofsted	An announcement was made on 16 March 2020 that all routine inspections of schools, social care, early years and further education providers will be put on hold, though Ofsted may still inspect settings where there are safeguarding concerns. It is not clear at the time of writing (17 March 2020) what the longer-term view will be and when inspections will re-start.	

Section 5 | Control measures

Control Measure	Control Stage	Actions	Person responsible
Tissues	1	Provide adequate stock levels of tissues and replenish stocks where possible.	
Handwashing and gel cleansing dispensers	1	Ensure hand wash/gel dispensers are full and regularly re-filled. All children to use available hand washing/cleansing facilities before eating. Replenish stocks where possible. Consider options for external hand washing, e.g. outside taps. Supervise young children to ensure they wash their hands for 20 seconds.	
Other users of the building	2/3	Contact users and visitors to inform them of usage expectations. Use clear signage.	
Monitoring absences	2	Daily report to the senior leadership teams of pupil and staff absences. Regular analysis of individual classes and year groups.	
Communicating travel arrangements	3	Ask parents/carers to inform school of any close family member who has returned from abroad within the last month. Staff to inform headteacher of any travel arrangements to high-risk areas including those of any close friends or family they have been in contact with.	
Reducing close person-to-person contact activities	2	Ensure extremely high hygiene for any food consumption and making activities. Avoid activities passing items around a class, for example, circle time objects, artefact sharing, and touching activities, e.g. contact games in PE, gymnastics. Cease handshaking and hugging of children and visitors. Use disposable cups for drinks. Ask parents to ensure children have a water bottle in school and to keep these in their own bag/drawer/locker.	
Personal hygiene	2	Provide regular communication to parents/carers of hygiene expectations and ask them to discuss them with their children, e.g. washing hands immediately after arriving home. Supervise all children washing their hands if necessary. Classes to teach and regularly remind children about hand washing techniques. Hand washing before snacks and before eating dinner. Distribute information posters.	
Review cleaning	2/3	Meet with cleaning supervisor/contractors to review cleaning arrangements and make any necessary amendments. Increase focus cleaning on touch points, e.g. handles, rails and tables, redirecting from other tasks or increase hours where possible to accommodate measures. Daily cleaning routines. Deep clean if required.	
School visitors and site users	2/3	Consider and communicate additional safety measures before entering school. Request that they inform school of any suspected or confirmed cases connected to them.	
Absence policy	2/3	Review the time period of exclusion for children or staff who are ill with other conditions and increase if necessary, at least to the minimum 48 hours clear of symptoms.	

Control Measure	Control Stage	Actions	Person responsible
Support for families affected (wellbeing checks)	2/3	Communicate to parents/carers and staff ways to contact school and who to contact if they need advice and support. Keep regular contact with affected families and staff.	
Taking temperature of anyone in school who may begin to feel unwell	2/3	Consider purchasing a non-contact thermometer.	

ASCL Policy Team
March 2020

0116 2991122

info@ascl.org.uk

ascl.org.uk

Annex 3

Primary school (England) – full reopening school August 2020

Activities Covered by this Assessment	Full Reopening of schools during COVID 19 (August 2020)	
Site Address/Location	<School name>	Department/Service/Team

Note: A person specific assessment must be carried out for young persons, disabled staff and new and expectant mothers conducting this activity

Every setting should carry out a risk assessment before opening. The assessment should directly address risks associated with coronavirus (COVID-19), so that sensible measures can be put in place to control those risks for children and staff. All employers have a duty to consult employees on health and safety, and they are best placed to understand the risks in individual settings.

Person becomes unwell during the day. Please refer to: www.gov.uk/government/publications/actions-for-schools-during-the-coronavirus-outbreak/guidance-for-full-opening-schools What happens if someone becomes unwell at an educational or childcare setting?

Attendance: No one with symptoms should attend a setting for any reason. *All children are expected to attend their education setting*, unless they are presenting Covid symptoms, self-isolating, or they are clinically extremely vulnerable (in which case they should follow medical advice). Where the child, young person or staff member tests positive, the rest of their class or group within their childcare or education setting should be sent home and advised to self-isolate for 14 days.

It is advised that schools carry out an inspection of the premises before opening and record the findings.

Hazard (Something with a potential to cause harm)	Who might be Harmed & How?	Existing Controls (Consider Hierarchy of Control)	Initial Risk Rating (S x L)			Further Controls Required (Consider Hierarchy of Control)	Final Risk Rating (S x L)			Action Required		
			Severity	Likeli-hood	Risk Rating		Severity	Likelihood	Risk Rating	Who (Initial)	Date By: (--/--/--)	Done?
Staff exiting cars in staff car park	Staff, visitors and contractors. Reduced infection control which may result in spread of COVID19	◦ Staff are encouraged to cycle or walk to work. ◦ Courtesy when alighting cars to maintain 2m distance. ◦ Staff to use different entrances to enter the building to avoid congestion, maintaining social distancing wherever possible.										
Entry to site	Staff, pupils, parents/ guardian, visitors and contractors. Reduced infection control which may result in spread of COVID19	◦ Social distance of 2m in queue outside. ◦ Temperatures taken before entry to site. Staff taking temperature to wear clinical mask and hold thermometer at arm's length. ◦ Visitors to site are restricted. ◦ Only visitors with prearranged appointments are allowed on site, except in emergency. ◦ All visitors must sign in and provide contact details. ◦ Guidance given on arrival to all visitors.										

		• Visitors are asked if they have any symptoms of COVID19 or have had contact with anyone who has symptoms of COVID19, before they arrive on site. Signage at door. • Keep windows in entrance closed • Operate a one in one out system into entrance area, with signage.									
Poor hygiene practice	Staff, student and visitors may become infected.	• Posters are displayed throughout the school in handwash areas advising all pupils and staff to wash their hands after using the toilet, before and after handling food, after touching any animals and any other actions which may increase the risk of infectious disease, such as coughing or sneezing. • Any face coverings to be removed on entrance to site. Disposable masks to be put in the bin, and non-disposable to be put in a plastic bag and kept securely in school bag until the end of the day				• SLT to review the Government guidance daily (Coronavirus outbreak) and take relevant action when required.					

(Continued)

(Cont).

Hazard (Something with a potential to cause harm)	Who might be Harmed & How?	Existing Controls (Consider Hierarchy of Control)	Initial Risk Rating (S x L)			Further Controls Required (Consider Hierarchy of Control)	Final Risk Rating (S x L)			Action Required		
			Severity	Likeli-hood	Risk Rating		Severity	Likelihood	Risk Rating	Who (Initial)	Date By: (--/--/--)	Done?
		⦾ Sufficient amounts of soap and washing liquids, warm water and paper towels are supplied in toilets and kitchen areas. ⦾ Alcohol-based hand gel and wipes to be supplied *around school* ⦾ Water supply checked to all toilet areas and remedial action taken if necessary ⦾ Pupils and staff are encouraged to wipe their mouths and noses with tissues after sneezing or coughing, and to dispose of these using the lidded bins provided around the school. ⦾ *Tissues available in all classrooms* ⦾ Pupils educated through class time on best practice for personal care & protecting others *in order to build handwashing into school culture.*										

		* *Young children or those with additional needs who struggle to wash hands effectively can use skin friendly wipes.* * Cleaners are employed by the school to carry out *regular*, thorough cleaning that follows national guidance, is compliant with the control of substances hazardous to health (COSHH), and the school's Health and Safety Policy. *Increased cleaning times throughout the day.*										
Social distancing not being carried out at drop off time	Staff, pupils, parents/ guardian, visitors and contractors. Reduced infection control which may result in spread of COVID19	* Drop off times are staggered. * Arrangements for drop off are communicated to staff, pupils and parents/guardian in advance. * Only one parent/guardian attends the school. * Access to site and pupils' classrooms are communicated to pupils, parent and guardian before arrival to the site.			* Children at infants to join allocated teacher in playground. * Children at Juniors to come straight to fire door into classrooms.						

(Continued)

(Cont).

Hazard (Something with a potential to cause harm)	Who might be Harmed & How?	Existing Controls (Consider Hierarchy of Control)	Initial Risk Rating (S x L)			Further Controls Required (Consider Hierarchy of Control)	Final Risk Rating (S x L)			Action Required		
			Severity	Likeli-hood	Risk Rating		Severity	Likelihood	Risk Rating	Who (Initial)	Date By: (--/--/--)	Done?
		* Direct access to the pupils allocated classroom if available. i.e. final emergency exits. * One-way systems are used around the playground for parent drop off * Signage is installed i.e.										
Use of cloakroom/ toilet areas	Staff and pupils Reduced infection control which may result in spread of COVID19	* Pupils remain in their outdoor clothing until they are in their allocated classroom. * Limit items brought to school * Teacher or member of staff to supervise toilet usage and inform cleaning staff of any issues. (See cleaning hazard and controls). * One in one out for toilets at difficult times of the day. * Each bubble to be allocated their own toilet or cubicle.										

Social distancing not being carried out within the classroom	Staff, pupils, visitors and contractors. Reduced infection control which may result in spread of COVID19	* Arrangements for the day are communicated to staff, pupils and parents/guardian. * Staff and pupils remain in *class size bubbles.* * *All teaching to take place as far as possible within classrooms or outside.* * Teachers (and other staff) are allocated to a group and remain with their allocated group, as far as possible, during the day and on subsequent days. * *Staff working across bubbles limited as far as possible, and work with small groups. Socially distancing where possible.* * The bubble distance themselves from other groups. * *Juniors – Desks are placed as far apart as possible and facing forwards.*				* Anyone showing symptoms or in contact with someone with symptoms not to be in school until negative test or self-isolation. * Regular handwashing. * Children and staff allowed to wear masks if wish.						

(Continued)

(Cont).

Hazard (Something with a potential to cause harm)	Who might be Harmed & How?	Existing Controls (Consider Hierarchy of Control)	Initial Risk Rating (S x L)			Further Controls Required (Consider Hierarchy of Control)	Final Risk Rating (S x L)			Action Required		
			Severity	Likeli-hood	Risk Rating		Severity	Likelihood	Risk Rating	Who (Initial)	Date By: (--/--/--)	Done?
		• *Infants – Small groups of 4. Chairs facing one another to be at least 2m apart.* • Pupils are allocated a desk and are seated at the same desk each day. • Pupils remain in the same classroom throughout the day. • Any equipment used is cleaned after use. • Staff not in bubble socially distance from all members of bubble at all times (2m).										
Sharing Classrooms	*Staff, pupils. Reduced infection control which may result in spread of COVID19*	• *Limit occasions when classrooms are shared across groups.* • *Where rooms are shared, cleaning of desks, door handles, and other resources between groups.*				• Limit the numbers of children working in these groups. Only use in very limited circumstances.						

Sharing equipment	Staff, pupils, visitors and contractors. Reduced infection control which may result in spread of COVID19	<ul><li>Pupils do not bring in equipment from home/share equipment</li><li>*Teaching resources kept within the bubble, and regularly cleaned. Any equipment used across bubbles cleaned meticulously and left for 72 hrs before use by another bubble.*</li><li>*Any outdoor equipment cleaned between bubble use.*</li><li>Soft toys and furnishings that are difficult to clean are removed from the classroom before reopening.</li><li>Small, intricate items that are difficult to clean are removed from the classroom before the school reopens.</li></ul>				<ul><li>Yr 6 children or staff to wipe desks and equipment regularly with wipes.</li><li>Yr6 children instructed not to share resources.</li></ul>						
Social distancing not being carried out at break times	Staff, pupils, visitors and contractors Reduced infection control which may result in spread of COVID19	<ul><li>Breaks are staggered, and timings identified and communicated.</li><li>Pupils to wash hands before and after eating/drinking.</li><li>*Class bubbles* maintained and not mixed.</li><li>Movement around school *limited*</li><li>Allocation of dedicated areas outside for *class bubbles*.</li><li>Levels of supervision considered, and additional information needed for supervisors.</li><li>Procedures identified when First Aid is required.</li><li>Activities considered, and the range of equipment reduced to minimise risk.</li><li>At wet breaks stay in classrooms.</li></ul>										

(Continued)

(Cont).

Hazard (Something with a potential to cause harm)	Who might be Harmed & How?	Existing Controls (Consider Hierarchy of Control)	Initial Risk Rating (S x L)			Further Controls Required (Consider Hierarchy of Control)	Final Risk Rating (S x L)			Action Required		
			Severity	Likeli-hood	Risk Rating		Severity	Likelihood	Risk Rating	Who (Initial)	Date By: (--/--/--)	Done?
		◦ Use of toilets to ensure that social distancing is maintained as far as practicable, consider how numbers using the facilities will be monitored. ◦ Hand washing arrangements/use of sanitiser provision. ◦ Flexibility on length of breaks ◦ How these periods are monitored for effectiveness and how issues are reported.										
Social distancing not being carried out at lunch time	Staff, pupils, visitors and contractors Reduced infection control which may result in spread of COVID19	◦ All the potential control measures suggested for break times. ◦ Pupils to wash their hands before and after eating and encouraged not to touch their mouth, eyes and nose. ◦ All food preparation and eating areas are thoroughly cleaned and disinfected before and after use. ◦ Food preparation limited to packed lunches in the first instance										

		* Any cutlery or cups brought from home and kept in child's packed lunch box. No cutlery or cups used as part of school prepared packed lunch * Communication with Catering provider (External or LTS Catering). * Cleaning regimes to be established for after eating packed lunches.									
Social distancing not being carried out at pick up	Staff, pupils, parents/ guardian, visitors and contractors. Reduced infection control which may result in spread of COVID19	* Pick up times are staggered. * Arrangements for pick up are communicated to staff, pupils and parents/guardian in advance. * Only one parent attends the school (Infants) * Parents to stay 2m apart. * Egress to schools and classrooms are communicated to pupils/ parent before arrival to the site. * One-way systems are used around the site (Infants)									
		* Classes use 3 different routes out. * Signage is installed i.e.									

(Continued)

(Cont).

Hazard (Something with a potential to cause harm)	Who might be Harmed & How?	Existing Controls (Consider Hierarchy of Control)	Initial Risk Rating (S x L)			Further Controls Required (Consider Hierarchy of Control)	Final Risk Rating (S x L)			Action Required		
			Severity	Likeli-hood	Risk Rating		Severity	Likelihood	Risk Rating	Who (Initial)	Date By: (--/--/--)	Done?
Outdoor play/ PE	Staff and pupils Reduced infection control which may result in spread of COVID19	※ Play equipment is cleaned and disinfected between each group of users ※ Teacher ensuring social distancing is in place. ※ Classes allocated an area to use outdoors and stay there.										
Carrying out 1st aid	First Aider Person being treated. This activity requires the 2mtr social distancing rule to be broken. This could lead to either	*Ensure parents know not to send children if they or anyone at home is presenting Covid Symptoms.* *Temperatures of everyone to be taken before entering the site. Staff taking temperatures to wear clinical mask and stay at arm's length.* ※ A first aider will NOT be treating a person who has the symptoms of COVID-19				※ Ensure a stock of surgical face masks that conform to **BS EN 14683:2019 Type IIR** are procured. These should be procured through the school's normal supply chain, should this fail they may be able to be procured from the local resilience forum (LRF).						

person involved in becoming infected with COVID-19 through close contact with an asymptomatic carrier, transmitting the virus through bodily fluids or respiratory droplets entering the person's eyes, nose or mouth. The First aider may have an allergic reaction to latex gloves.	as specified by the NHS and Government unless life threatening condition use St John's ambulance guidance (link at end of document). If need for resuscitation, only use compressions not rescue breaths. * If a child presents symptoms of COVID-19 they will be isolated 2m away from people, in a spacious room identified for this purpose and parents called to collect them. * Persons who have symptoms will isolate for 7 days and will not be in school. * The first aider will wash their hands for at least 20 seconds with soap and water. * Nitrile Gloves conforming to BSEN455 will be worn. * Latex gloves will be avoided to remove the risk of allergic reaction.				(Please see PPE suppliers list P21 * Ensure aprons, nitrile/latex disposable gloves and splash resistant goggles are procured. These should be procured through the school's normal supply chain, should this fail they may be able to be procured from the local resilience forum (LRF)						

(Continued)

(Cont).

Hazard (Something with a potential to cause harm)	Who might be Harmed & How?	Existing Controls (Consider Hierarchy of Control)	Initial Risk Rating (S x L)			Further Controls Required (Consider Hierarchy of Control)	Final Risk Rating (S x L)			Action Required		
			Severity	Likeli-hood	Risk Rating		Severity	Likelihood	Risk Rating	Who (Initial)	Date By: (--/--/--)	Done?
		• The first aider will cover any cuts on their hands with waterproof plasters. • The first aider will wear a fluid resistant surgical mask and avoid putting their fingers in their mouth and touching their face. • The first aider will avoid touching any part of a dressing that will come into contact with a wound. • The first aider will wear goggles or visor to prevent bodily fluids being splashed into the eyes. • After each first aid treatment is given all equipment and surfaces, including goggles used will be cleaned down using either a combined detergent disinfectant solution at a dilution of 1000 parts per million (ppm) available chlorine (av.cl.) or a neutral purpose detergent followed by disinfection (1000 ppm av.cl.) the google and visor will be rinsed with clean water after being disinfected.										

		• After using the face masks, aprons and gloves they will be correctly doffed and placed straight into a clinical waste bag and the bag tied. The bags will then be stored in a locked room for 72 hours before putting them into the external waste skip/bin. • Face masks and gloves will only be used for 1 treatment of first aid they will not be used to treat a second person requiring first aid. • First aiders have been given information on how to correctly don and doff their PPE. • No food will be stored or eaten in the first aid room. • After first aid treatment is given and cleaning has been completed the first aider will wash their hands with soap and water for at least 20 seconds before commencing any further work. • There is a dedicated room for first aid that will be used solely for first aid treatment to help prevent										
		bodily fluids contaminating other parts of the building.										

(Continued)

(Cont).

Hazard (Something with a potential to cause harm)	Who might be Harmed & How?	Existing Controls (Consider Hierarchy of Control)	Initial Risk Rating (S x L)			Further Controls Required (Consider Hierarchy of Control)	Final Risk Rating (S x L)			Action Required		
			Severity	Likeli-hood	Risk Rating		Severity	Likelihood	Risk Rating	Who (Initial)	Date By: (--/--/--)	Done?
School not engaging with Track and Trace requirements	Staff, pupils, parents/ guardian, visitors and contractors. Wider Community. Unable to facilitate information for Track and Trace puts all at risk.	⁎ Make staff and parents aware of responsibility not to attend if symptomatic and how to book tests. ⁎ Request test results immediately ⁎ All visitors need to sign in. Records kept ⁎ Rigorous records of all groupings and any close contact across bubble groupings. ⁎ Use LA flow diagram and follow advice from Public Health following positive cases.				⁎ Ensure all actions are timely and provide any requested information immediately.						
Intimate care		⁎ The staff member providing the intimate care will wash hands thoroughly before and after providing intimate care, using soap and water for at least 20 seconds. Use alcohol-based hand sanitiser if soap and water is not available.				⁎ Ensure a stock of surgical face masks that conform to **BS EN 14683:2019 Type IIR** are procured. These should be procured through the school's normal supply chain, should						

		* NHS hand washing posters have been installed above sinks to give information on good hand washing techniques. * Face coverings will not be worn during this activity by those who may not be able to handle them as directed (for example, young children, or those with special educational needs or disabilities) as it may inadvertently increase the risk of transmission. * Children whose care routinely already involves the use of PPE due to their intimate care needs will continue to receive their care in the same way, using the same PPE as they have always done for this task. * If a child becomes unwell with symptoms of coronavirus while in their setting and needs direct personal care until they can return home. A fluid-resistant surgical face mask should be worn by the supervising adult if			this fail they may be able to be procured from the local resilience forum (LRF). (Please see PPE suppliers list P21) * Ensure aprons, nitrile/latex disposable gloves and splash resistant goggles are procured. These should be procured through the school's normal supply chain, should this fail they may be able to be procured from the local resilience forum (LRF)						

(Continued)

(Cont).

Hazard (Something with a potential to cause harm)	Who might be Harmed & How?	Existing Controls (Consider Hierarchy of Control)	Initial Risk Rating (S x L)			Further Controls Required (Consider Hierarchy of Control)	Final Risk Rating (S x L)			Action Required		
			Severity	Likeli-hood	Risk Rating		Severity	Likelihood	Risk Rating	Who (Initial)	Date By: (--/--/--)	Done?
		2 meters social distancing cannot be maintained. The surgical masks used conform to **BS EN 14683:2019 Type IIR**. ◦ After using the face masks, aprons and gloves they will be correctly doffed and placed straight into a clinical waste bag and the bag tied. The bags will then be stored in a locked room for 72 hours before putting them into the external waste skip/bin. ◦ If contact with the unwell child is necessary, then nitrile/latex disposable gloves, a disposable apron and a fluid-resistant surgical face mask should be worn by the supervising adult. If a there is a risk of splashing to the eyes, for example from coughing, spitting, or vomiting, then eye protection should also be worn.										

Child's behaviour causes a risk.	Children and staff may be hurt, or their safety compromised by behaviour of child. Positive handling not possible.	* If child is known to spit, staff may choose to wear gloves, goggles or visor. * Purchase waterproof overalls for staff to wear should they choose to when working with pupils known to spit or who have positive handling plans. * *Behaviour Policy reviewed to assess additional risk and to update to Covid arrangements.*				* Take early advice from Inclusion Team, and implement * If child already has a positive handling plan, before they return to school, risk assessment needs to be updated					
Social distancing not being carried out during the use of Staff facilities	Staff, pupils, visitors and contractors Reduced infection control which may result in spread of COVID19	* Staff to observe social distancing from each other. * Consider the number of staff that can be accommodated in the area to achieve social distancing and rearrange the furniture where possible * Consider the use of another room in addition to usual one * Staggering of break times to reduce numbers * Use of signs to inform of hand washing prior to entering/using facilities.				* Limit office staff in at any one time. * Identify rooms that must be one in one out. * All staff meetings to be done via zoom with opportunities to stay at home.					

(Continued)

(Cont).

Hazard (Something with a potential to cause harm)	Who might be Harmed & How?	Existing Controls (Consider Hierarchy of Control)	Initial Risk Rating (S x L)			Further Controls Required (Consider Hierarchy of Control)	Final Risk Rating (S x L)			Action Required		
			Severity	Likeli-hood	Risk Rating		Severity	Likelihood	Risk Rating	Who (Initial)	Date By: (--/--/--)	Done?
		• Staff are to have their own crockery and cutlery and not to use shared items from the staff room. • Reusable sponges are removed • Cleaning of room between use • Operation of dishwasher/water dispensers' procedures										
Assembly	Staff and pupils Reduced infection control which may result in spread of COVID19	• Assemblies/Collective Worship (CW) are only to take place remotely, in classrooms.										
Cleaning	Reduced infection control which may result in spread of COVID19	• A detailed cleaning schedule will be implemented throughout the site, ensuring that contact points, e.g. worksurfaces, door handles, taps etc. are all thoroughly cleaned and disinfected regularly.										

		<ul><li>Hard surfaces to be cleaned with soap and water prior to disinfecting.</li><li>Disinfecting should be performed using either a combined detergent disinfectant solution at a dilution of 1000 parts per million (ppm) available chlorine (av.cl.) or a neutral purpose detergent followed by disinfection (1000 ppm av.cl.) the google and visor will be rinsed with clean water after being disinfected.</li><li>Extra attention is to be given to frequently touched areas and surfaces, e.g. doors, toilets, door handles, phones, light switches and door fobs, etc.</li><li>Hand towels and hand wash are to be checked and replaced as needed by the Premises Officer and cleaning staff.</li><li>Enhance the cleaning regimes for toilet facilities, particularly door handles, locks and the toilet flush, etc.</li></ul>										

(Continued)

(Cont).

Hazard (Something with a potential to cause harm)	Who might be Harmed & How?	Existing Controls (Consider Hierarchy of Control)	Initial Risk Rating (S x L)			Further Controls Required (Consider Hierarchy of Control)	Final Risk Rating (S x L)			Action Required		
			Severity	Likeli-hood	Risk Rating		Severity	Likelihood	Risk Rating	Who (Initial)	Date By: (--/--/--)	Done?
		* Only cleaning products supplied by the school are to be used. * Please refer to the school's COSHH risk assessments for further control measures in relation to cleaning chemicals used. * PPE required for cleaning will be noted in the outcome of the COSHH risk assessments conducted for cleaning chemicals used. * Bin liners should be used in all bins and waste bins should be emptied into the external waste bin/skip.										
Carrying out daily building maintenance	Staff and pupils. Reduced infection control which may result in spread of COVID19	* General maintenance is carried out when the school is closed to staff and pupils. (See lone working risk assessment). * Only essential maintenance is carried out during school opening hours. * Staff are informed of any maintenance being carried out in communal areas, toilets, etc., and the area is cordoned off.										
		* Social distancing is maintained throughout working procedures.										

Contractors working on site	Staff, pupils, parents/ guardian, visitors and contractors. Reduced infection control which may result in spread of COVID19	* Wherever possible, contracted work is carried out when the school is closed to staff and pupils. * If it needs to be carried out in the day, it must be away from any staff/ pupils and the area cordoned off. * Any documentation required is sent/received prior to the contractor arriving on site. * Safe systems of work/Risk assessment, which include COVID19 control measures, are received and agreed by the school before work commences.										
Emergency procedures	Staff, pupils, parents/ guardian, visitors and contractors. Reduced infection	* Changes to emergency evacuation procedures are communicated to all persons on site i.e. changes of egress from building. * Emergency evacuations take place following social distancing										
	control which may result in spread of COVID19	principles as far as is reasonably practicable. (In an emergency risk to life takes precedence). * Staff, pupils, visitors and contractors' social distance at assembly areas (2m separation) as far as is reasonably practicable.										

(Continued)

(Cont).

Hazard (Something with a potential to cause harm)	Who might be Harmed & How?	Existing Controls (Consider Hierarchy of Control)	Initial Risk Rating (S x L)			Further Controls Required (Consider Hierarchy of Control)	Final Risk Rating (S x L)			Action Required		
			Severity	Likeli-hood	Risk Rating		Severity	Likelihood	Risk Rating	Who (Initial)	Date By: (--/--/--)	Done?
Curriculum Considerations	Staff, pupils, parents/ guardian, visitors and contractors. Reduced infection control which may result in spread of COVID19	⁕ No residential trips to be undertaken. Day trips can be but coach travel needs to follow guidance. ⁕ MUSIC – groups limited to 15. Seated in a single line facing front with teacher socially distanced at 2m. Wind instruments not shared. No mass singing of larger than these groups. ⁕ PE – Outdoors wherever possible. All equipment cleaned between groups. No contact sports.										

⁕ Source: www.gov.uk/government/publications/actions-for-schools-during-the-coronavirus-outbreak/guidance-for-full-opening-schools

⁕ **Source:** www.gov.uk/government/publications/actions-for-educational-and-childcare-settings-to-prepare-for-wider-opening-from-1-june-2020/ actions-for-education-and-childcare-settings-to-prepare-for-wider-opening-from-1-june-2020

⁕ **Hand wash video** www.gov.uk/guidance/coronavirus-covid-19-information-for-the-public

⁕ **Guidance for education and childcare settings on how to implement social distancing** www.gov.uk/government/publications/ coronavirus-covid-19-implementing-social-distancing-in-education-and-childcare-settings/coronavirus-covid-19-implementing-social-distancing-in-education-and-childcare-settings

⁕ **Guidance on infection prevention and control for COVID-19** www.gov.uk/government/publications/wuhan-novel-coronavirus-infection-prevention-and-control

* **Managing premises** www.gov.uk/government/publications/managing-school-premises-during-the-coronavirus-outbreak/managing-school-premises-which-are-partially-open-during-the-coronavirus-outbreak#other-points-to-consider

* **Source NHS:** www.nhs.uk/conditions/coronavirus-covid-19/check-if-you-have-coronavirus-symptoms/

* **Coronavirus (COVID-19): implementing protective measures in education and childcare settings:** www.gov.uk/government/publications/coronavirus-covid-19-implementing-protective-measures-in-education-and-childcare-settings/coronavirus-covid-19-implementing-protective-measures-in-education-and-childcare-settings

* **COVID-19: cleaning in non-healthcare settings**: www.gov.uk/government/publications/covid-19-decontamination-in-non-healthcare-settings/covid-19-decontamination-in-non-healthcare-settings

* **St. John Ambulance Covid-19: advice for first aiders**: www.sja.org.uk/get-advice/first-aid-advice/covid-19-advice-for-first-aiders/

* **Conducting a SEND risk assessment during the coronavirus outbreak:** www.gov.uk/government/publications/coronavirus-covid-19-send-risk-assessment-guidance/coronavirus-covid-19-send-risk-assessment-guidance

* **HSE. Talking with your workers about preventing coronavirus:** www.hse.gov.uk/news/assets/docs/talking-with-your-workers.pdf

* **Contact for PPE orders if you have difficulties with your own suppliers:**

Leicester City: icrs.service@leicester.gov.uk

Leicester County: enquirylinequality&contracts@leics.gov.uk

Rutland: PPE@rutland.gov.uk

During this activity, what could go wrong resulting in an emergency situation?	1. Child displays symptoms with CV19. 2. Child from teaching group who has been sent home becomes confirmed case. 3. Staff becoming ill and self-isolating.
How could this emergency situation be prevented/controlled?	1. Isolate child until collected. 2. All children in that teaching group to be sent home and told to self-isolate for 14 days. 3. Follow self-isolating guidance, ensure that reporting of illness procedures well understood.
Who should respond to a potential emergency situation and how? Have staff been trained to respond to this emergency situation?	1. Staff to supervise child until collected where 2m rule cannot be implemented PPE to be worn. 2. Make staff aware of guidance in link below, develop guidance on internal monitoring of staff and pupils on self-isolation and student attendance recording. **3.** Follow guidance: www.gov.uk/government/publications/coronavirus-covid-19-implementing-protective-measures-in-education-and-childcare-settings/coronavirus-covid-19-implementing-protective-measures-in-education-and-childcare-settings Consider reallocating staff or capacity of school to remain open. Consult with LA and/or Trust on closure.
Could any non - routine changes affect the safety arrangements in place for this activity? (e.g. weather, people, equipment etc.) What can be done?	Additional pupil numbers in phase 2 and 3 – review procedures and social distancing, refer to any new government guidance.

Risk Assessor (s) Name(s):		Risk Assessor(s) Signature (S):		
Authorised By:		Authoriser Signature:		**Initial**
Date Conducted:		Date of Next Review:		
		Date of Review:		
		Date of Review:		
		Date of Review:		
		Date of Review:		

Potential Severity of Harm		Medium	High	High
	High Death, paralysis, long term serious ill health.			
	Medium An injury requiring further medical assistance or is a RIDDOR incident.	Low	Medium	High
	Low Minor injuries not resulting in any first aid or absence from work.	Low	Low	Medium
		Low The event is unlikely to happen.	**Medium** It is fairly likely to happen.	**High** It is likely to happen.
		Likelihood of Harm Occurring		

Risk Rating Definitions	
Low	This is an acceptable level of risk. No further controls are required as the risk rating cannot be reduced any further. However, it is advised that continual monitoring occurs in order to ensure that no changes/deviation of control measures occur.
Medium	It is advised that further controls are implemented to reduce the risk rating to as low a level as possible. If the risk cannot be reduced to lower than a medium, then on site monitoring should occur to ensure that all stipulated controls are being adhered to.
High	This is an unacceptable risk rating. Urgent interim controls should be implemented to reduce the risk so far as is reasonably practicable. If the risk rating cannot be reduced to lower than a **High**, then a documented safe system of work should be implemented to control the activity. It may be necessary to seek further professional advice. Serious considerations should be given to the validity of carrying out the activity at all. Regular monitoring of the activity should occur.

Annex 4

Primary school (England) – reopening school protocols June 2020

Enabling infrastructure
2. To ensure site safety & management is responsive to latest guidance & facilitates staying open.
Protocol number 1: Classroom Environment Cleaning **Version 1 13.5.20**
Agreed Principles for both schools * Common touch areas will be cleaned throughout the day – clean as you go approach. * Children will wash their hands throughout the day and always on entering school. * Staff will sanitise tables at break, lunchtime, if they go outside, and at the end of the day. * Teachers will wipe digital keyboards and workstations twice a day. * Work surfaces will be kept clear and resources minimised to essential items only. * Practical resources will be cleaned after use (children can contribute to this process). * Rubbish bins will be emptied at lunchtime and at the end of the day.
Specific resourcing * Disposable cleaning wipes /cloths * Additional cleaning station in classroom * Hand sanitiser * Hand wash * Paper towels * Bin liners
School Variations (these may be further varied per classroom to suit age groups) * Cleaning stations will be increased and signposted in classrooms. * Water supply checked daily (especially Yr 6 classes).
Links to government guidance www.gov.uk/government/publications/coronavirus-covid-19-implementing-protective-measures-in-education-and-childcare-settings/coronavirus-covid-19-implementing-protective-measures-in-education-and-childcare-settings www.gov.uk/government/publications/covid-19-decontamination-in-non-healthcare-settings/covid-19-decontamination-in-non-healthcare-settings www.gov.uk/guidance/coronavirus-covid-19-information-for-the-public www.gov.uk/government/news/teach-children-simple-hygiene-to-help-curb-infections
Links to other school documents such as site Risk Assessments or protocols.

Enabling infrastructure
2. To ensure site safety & management is responsive to latest guidance & facilitates staying open.

Protocol number 2: Staffroom and Common areas
Version 1 13.5.20

Agreed Principles for both schools
* 2m social distancing must be observed within the staffroom area at all times. Breaks will be staggered. Do not enter if too full for this.
* All equipment will be wiped with disposable anti bacteria wipes.
* Staff room and other common areas will be cleaned throughout the day – clean as you go approach.
* Staff teams will keep all equipment together to avoid cross-contamination beyond bubbles.
* Water urn/kettle and any other items will be wiped after every use.
* Worktops will be kept clear and for essential items only.
* Fridge and cupboard door handles will be wiped after use.
* Any other equipment used e.g. microwaves will be wiped after use.
* Rubbish bins will be emptied twice daily.

Specific resourcing
* Disposable anti-bacterial cleaning wipes /cloths
* Hand sanitiser
* Hand wash
* Paper towels
* Bin liners

School Variations (these may be further varied per classroom to suit age groups)

Links to government guidance
www.gov.uk/government/publications/coronavirus-covid-19-implementing-protective-measures-in-education-and-childcare-settings/coronavirus-covid-19-implementing-protective-measures-in-education-and-childcare-settings
www.gov.uk/government/publications/covid-19-decontamination-in-non-healthcare-settings/covid-19-decontamination-in-non-healthcare-settings

Links to other school documents such as site Risk Assessments or protocols.

Enabling infrastructure
2. To ensure site safety & management is responsive to latest guidance & facilitates staying open.

Protocol number 3: Using the toilets (children)

Version 2 14.5.20

Agreed Principles for both schools
* Children should be taught how to wash their hands as guidance advises.
* Children should have regular and age appropriate verbal reminders about the importance of handwashing after using the toilet.
* **One child may enter the toilets at a time**.
* Children should use the toilets as normal and wash and dry their hands as the guidance advises.
* Toilets will have clear hand washing guidance above the sinks.
* Toilets will be cleaned at the end of every day.
* Paper towels and hand dryers will be used.
* Paper towel bins will be emptied at lunchtime.
* The cleanliness of children's toilets will be checked at break times and any hygiene supplies should be replenished.
* Any spillages and body fluids should be cleaned in accordance with guidance.

Specific resourcing
* Hand wash
* Paper towels
* Waste bin
* Toilet roll

School Variations (these may be further varied per classroom to suit age groups)

Links to government guidance and other resources to use with children
www.gov.uk/government/publications/covid-19-decontamination-in-non-healthcare-settings/covid-19-decontamination-in-non-healthcare-settings
www.gov.uk/government/news/teach-children-simple-hygiene-to-help-curb-infections#
www.gov.uk/guidance/coronavirus-covid-19-information-for-the-public
https://e-bug.eu/

Links to other school documents such as site Risk Assessments or protocols.

Enabling infrastructure
2. To ensure site safety & management is responsive to latest guidance & facilitates staying open.

Protocol number 3: Using the toilets (staff)

Version 2 14.5.20

Agreed Principles for both schools
* Staff should use the toilets as normal and wash their hands as the guidance suggests.
* Toilets will have clear hand washing guidance above the sinks.
* Toilets will be cleaned at the end of every day as normal.
* Paper towels or hand dryers will be used.
* Paper towel bins will be emptied at lunchtime.
* Staff will replenish any hygiene supplies after use if necessary.

Specific resourcing
* Hand wash
* Paper towels
* Waste bin
* Hand washing signs in all staff toilets

School Variations (these may be further varied per classroom to suit age groups)

Links to government guidance
www.gov.uk/government/publications/coronavirus-covid-19-implementing-protective-measures-in-education-and-childcare-settings/coronavirus-covid-19-implementing-protective-measures-in-education-and-childcare-settings
www.gov.uk/government/publications/covid-19-decontamination-in-non-healthcare-settings/covid-19-decontamination-in-non-healthcare-settings
www.gov.uk/government/news/teach-children-simple-hygiene-to-help-curb-infections

Links to other school documents such as site Risk Assessments or protocols.

Enabling infrastructure
2. To ensure site safety & management is responsive to latest guidance & facilitates staying open.

Protocol number 4: General cleaning

Version 1 13.5.20

Agreed Principles for both schools

* All areas of the school to be cleaned thoroughly at the end of every day.
* All hard surfaces such as tables and worktops cleaned with disinfectant, or detergent then disinfectant.
* All classroom chairs wiped with disinfectant or bleach.
* All carpet areas will be vacuumed.
* All doors door handles to be wiped with disinfectant or bleach. – both internal and external doors.
* All light switches to be wiped with disinfectant or bleach.
* Hard flooring to be mopped with appropriate disinfectant cleaner.
* All bins to be emptied and cleaned with disinfectant or bleach.
* Toilets cleaned using disinfectant or bleach.
* Cleaners will wear aprons and gloves for protection, these should be double bagged and stored for 72 hours before disposing of in normal rubbish.
* Cleaners must wash their hands after removing gloves.

Specific resourcing

* Bleach
* Disinfectant
* Aprons
* Gloves
* Disposable wipes/clothes
* Disposable mop heads

School Variations (these may be further varied per classroom to suit age groups)

Links to government guidance
www.gov.uk/government/publications/coronavirus-covid-19-
implementing-protective-measures-in-education-and-childcare-settings/
coronavirus-covid-19-implementing-protective-measures-in-education-and-childcare-settings
www.gov.uk/government/publications/covid-19-cleaning-of-non-healthcare-settings/
covid-19-cleaning-of-non-healthcare-settings
www.gov.uk/government/news/teach-children-simple-hygiene-to-help-curb-infections

Links to other school documents such as site Risk Assessments or protocols.

Enabling infrastructure
2. To ensure site safety & management is responsive to latest guidance & facilitates staying open.

Protocol number 5: Distancing in Classroom configuration (KS2)

Version 1 13.5.20

Agreed Principles for the junior school

- Children will be sat one pupil to a table at all times.
- All children will have a pack of equipment – pen, pencil, ruler etc. that only they use.
- All children will have access to their own whiteboard pen, whiteboard and rubber.
- Coats will be with them on the back of their chair.
- Children will bring only their lunch box and water bottle to school. These will be stored in designated areas of the classroom.
- Teachers and adults will endeavour to work 2m away from the children when at all possible.
- Shared resources (e.g. felt-tips, paint brushes) will be cleaned after use.
- At no point will paper be passed between children.
- Teacher's hands will be sanitized before and after the distributing of paper/resources to tables.
- Wherever possible, resources will only be given out before children enter the room.
- Children will enter and leave the room at a distance from each other.
- There will be no resources or equipment left on any work surfaces – these will be kept as clear as possible.
- Classrooms will be ventilated with open windows.
- First aid bags are to be placed in all classrooms and minor injuries attended to there (Yr 6 pupils can apply their own plasters and cold compresses with supervision).

Specific resourcing

- Zip lock packs of equipment for each child
- Antibacterial wipes

School Variations (these may be further varied per classroom to suit age groups)

Links to government guidance

www.gov.uk/government/publications/coronavirus-covid-19-
implementing-protective-measures-in-education-and-childcare-settings/
coronavirus-covid-19-implementing-protective-measures-in-education-and-childcare-settings
www.gov.uk/government/news/teach-children-simple-hygiene-to-help-curb-infections
www.england.nhs.uk/south/wp-content/uploads/sites/6/2017/09/catch-bin-kill.pdf

Links to other school documents such as site Risk Assessments or protocols.

Enabling infrastructure
2. To ensure site safety & management is responsive to latest guidance & facilitates staying open.

Protocol number 5: Distancing in Classroom configuration (KS1)

Version 1 13.5.20

Agreed Principles for the infants' school

* Children will sit in table groups for all activities. Children will not be asked to sit on the carpet as part of a larger group.
* Each table will have a limited amount of pencils, crayons, pens & whiteboards to be wiped daily.
* Boxes of toys will be placed on tables for children and rotated on different days.
* Soft toys will be removed or made unavailable for children to play with.
* Coats will be with them on the back of their chair.
* Children will bring only their lunch box and water bottle to school. These will be stored in designated areas of the classroom.
* Teachers and adults will endeavour to socially distance at all times.
* Shared resources (e.g. felt-tips, paint brushes) will be cleaned after use.
* At no point will paper be passed between children.
* Teacher's hands will be sanitized before and after the distributing of paper/resources to tables.
* Resources will only be given out before children enter the room.
* Children will enter and leave the room at a distance from others.
* There will be no unnecessary resources or equipment left on any work surfaces – these will be kept as clear as possible.
* Classrooms will be well ventilated with open windows.
* First aid bags to be placed in all classrooms and minor injuries attended to in their classroom.

Specific resourcing

* Antibacterial wipes/ spray cleaner
* Hand sanitizer

School Variations (these may be further varied per classroom to suit age groups)

Links to government guidance
www.gov.uk/government/publications/coronavirus-covid-19-
implementing-protective-measures-in-education-and-childcare-settings/
coronavirus-covid-19-implementing-protective-measures-in-education-and-childcare-settings
www.gov.uk/government/news/teach-children-simple-hygiene-to-help-curb-infections
www.england.nhs.uk/south/wp-content/uploads/sites/6/2017/09/catch-bin-kill.pdf

Links to other school documents such as site Risk Assessments or protocols.

Enabling infrastructure
2. To ensure site safety & management is responsive to latest guidance & facilitates staying open.
Protocol number 6: Lunchtimes (KS2) **Version 1 13.5.20**
Agreed Principles for the junior school * Each group of children will have a designated time to eat their lunch. * Lunch will be eaten in the classroom. * Children will wash their hands (one at a time) and wipe their tables with soapy water. Staff will also use anti-bacterial spray. This will be a chance for ALL children to go to the toilet. * Children will place all rubbish back into their lunchbox to take back home at the end of the day. * Children will leave the classroom starting with the child nearest the door and walk to the playground ensuring 2m distancing. * Children must only play with children within their bubble. * Games/activities will be encouraged where children can stay 2m apart, without resources. * When the whistle is blown, children will walk into the school when told one at a time, walk with 2m distance between them and will wash their hands on entering the classroom. * Staff on duty will have a first aid bag with them.
Specific resourcing * Hand wash * Sanitiser * Paper towels
School Variations (these may be further varied per classroom to suit age groups)
Links to government guidance www.gov.uk/government/publications/coronavirus-covid-19-implementing-protective-measures-in-education-and-childcare-settings/coronavirus-covid-19-implementing-protective-measures-in-education-and-childcare-settings www.gov.uk/guidance/coronavirus-covid-19-information-for-the-public www.gov.uk/government/news/teach-children-simple-hygiene-to-help-curb-infections
Links to other school documents such as site Risk Assessments or protocols.

Enabling infrastructure
2. To ensure site safety & management is responsive to latest guidance & facilitates staying open.

Protocol number 6: Lunchtimes (KS1)

Version 1 13.5.20

Agreed Principles for the infants' school

* Each group will have a designated dinner lady/LSA.
* Each group of children will have a designated time to eat their lunch.
* Lunch will be eaten in the classroom.
* Children will wash their hands (one at a time) and wipe their tables with soapy water. Staff will also use anti-bacterial spray. This will be a chance for ALL children to go to the toilet.
* Children will place all rubbish back into their lunchbox to take back home at the end of the day.
* Children will play in zoned areas outside with their group.
* Children will have a box of toys for their group.
* Children must only play with children within their bubble.
* When the bell is sounded, children will walk into the school when told one at a time.

A first aider, not attached to any one group, will wear recommended PPE and be available to do first aid.

Specific resourcing

* Hand wash
* Sanitiser
* Paper towels

School Variations (these may be further varied per classroom to suit age groups)

Links to government guidance

www.gov.uk/government/publications/coronavirus-covid-19-implementing-protective-measures-in-education-and-childcare-settings/coronavirus-covid-19-implementing-protective-measures-in-education-and-childcare-settings
www.gov.uk/guidance/coronavirus-covid-19-information-for-the-public
www.gov.uk/government/news/teach-children-simple-hygiene-to-help-curb-infections

Links to other school documents such as site Risk Assessments or protocols.

Enabling infrastructure
2. To ensure site safety & management is responsive to latest guidance & facilitates staying open.

Protocol number 7: Breaktimes

Version 1 13.5.20

Agreed Principles for both schools

- Each group of children will have a designated time to go out on the playground.
- Children will leave the classroom starting with the child nearest the door and walk to the playground ensuring 2m distancing. This will include a chance for ALL children to go to the toilet.
- Games/activities will be encouraged where children can stay 2m apart, without equipment.
- Children must only mix with other children within their bubble.
- When the whistle is blown, children will walk into the school when told one at a time, walk with 2m distance between them and will wash their hands on entering the classroom.
- Staff on duty will have a first aid bag with them.

Specific resourcing

- Hand wash
- Sanitiser
- Paper towels

School Variations (these may be further varied per classroom to suit age groups)

Links to government guidance
www.gov.uk/government/publications/covid-19-decontamination-in-non-healthcare-settings/
covid-19-decontamination-in-non-healthcare-settings
www.gov.uk/government/news/teach-children-simple-hygiene-to-help-curb-infections

Links to other school documents such as site Risk Assessments or protocols.

Enabling infrastructure
2. To ensure site safety & management is responsive to latest guidance & facilitates staying open.

Protocol number 8: Physical Activity

Version 1 13.5.20

Agreed Principles for both schools

* Children will not change into their PE kits for any physical activity.
* All physical activities will be activities that allows children to be 2m apart. (Real PE could be used for ideas.)
* Children will wash their hands when returning to the classroom.
* Class groups to use agreed section of the outside area.

Specific resourcing

* Hand wash
* Sanitiser
* Paper towels

School Variations (these may be further varied per classroom to suit age groups)

Links to government guidance

www.gov.uk/government/publications/coronavirus-covid-19-implementing-protective-measures-in-education-and-childcare-settings/coronavirus-covid-19-implementing-protective-measures-in-education-and-childcare-settings

Links to other school documents such as site Risk Assessments or protocols.

Enabling infrastructure
2. To ensure site safety & management is responsive to latest guidance & facilitates staying open.
Protocol number 9: Dropping off children **Version 1 13.5.20**
Agreed Principles for both schools * Drop off times to be agreed locally but staggered to ensure safer distancing and avoid pinch points. * KS2 children dropped off by parents at school entrance keeping 2M apart, staff to guide children to enter the firedoor of their classroom. * KS1 and EYFS children to be bought into Infant School playground following 2m social distancing, and keeping moving. Children to go independently to the allocated teacher for their bubble as they pass. If a child becomes upset, staff must encourage from a distance. * Signage at each entrance advising parents and children to keep 2M apart. * 2M markings outside each external door. * Children wash/sanitise their hands as they enter the classroom.
Specific resourcing * Signage and two metre markings on Infant playground one way system * Appropriate 2m distance signage at every entrance into school * 2m markings at external doors for up to 15 children * Hand sanitiser * Hand wash * Paper towels
School Variations (these may be further varied per classroom to suit age groups)
Links to government guidance www.gov.uk/government/publications/coronavirus-covid-19- implementing-protective-measures-in-education-and-childcare-settings/ coronavirus-covid-19-implementing-protective-measures-in-education-and-childcare-settings www.gov.uk/government/publications/covid-19-decontamination-in-non-healthcare-settings/ covid-19-decontamination-in-non-healthcare-settings
Links to other school documents such as site Risk Assessments or protocols.

Enabling infrastructure
2. To ensure site safety & management is responsive to latest guidance & facilitates staying open.
Protocol number 10: Picking up at the end of the day. **Version 1 13.5.20**
Agreed Principles for both schools * Pick up times to be agreed locally but staggered to ensure safer distancing and avoid pinch points. * Parents line up 2m apart at agreed pick up point. * Children sent out 1 at a time and leave with their parents before the next child is sent out. * Signage at each pick up point advising parents and children to keep 2M apart. * Signage will be displayed explaining procedures at all pick up points. * 2m distance markings at all pick up points.
Specific resourcing * 2m distance markings at all pick up points. * Appropriate 2m distance signage at every exit. * Signage to explain procedure for picking up children.
School Variations (these may be further varied per classroom to suit age groups)
Links to government guidance www.gov.uk/government/publications/coronavirus-covid-19-implementing-protective-measures-in-education-and-childcare-settings/coronavirus-covid-19-implementing-protective-measures-in-education-and-childcare-settings www.gov.uk/government/publications/covid-19-decontamination-in-non-healthcare-settings/covid-19-decontamination-in-non-healthcare-settings
Links to other school documents such as site Risk Assessments or protocols.

Enabling infrastructure
2. To ensure site safety & management is responsive to latest guidance & facilitates staying open.

Protocol number 11: First aid and illness

Version 2 16.5.20

Agreed Principles for both schools

* Tell parents not to send children to school if they or anyone in their family is showing symptoms of Covid-19.
* If a child becomes ill with a temperature or consistent cough they should be isolated away from the rest of the group.
* The child should be kept in a room behind a closed door if possible under the supervision of a first aider/adult who can keep a 2m distance.
* If the child needs to go to the bathroom while waiting to be collected, the child should use a separate bathroom if possible. The bathroom should be cleaned and disinfected using standard cleaning products before being used by anyone else.
* PPE (disposable gloves, a disposable apron, and a fluid resistant surgical face mask) should be worn by staff caring for the child while they await collection, if they cannot maintain a distance of 2m.
* If there is a risk of splashing to the eyes from coughing, spitting, or vomiting, eye protection should be worn.
* In an emergency, call 999 if the child is seriously ill or injured or their life is at risk.
* Parents should be advised that if the child has a temperature of cough they need to access a Covid -19 test and isolate the child for 7 days with their family self-isolating for 14 days.
* Children will not be allowed back into school before completing self-isolation and until we've seen proof of a test.
* Where the child, young person or staff member tests positive, the rest of their class or group within their 'bubble' will be sent home and advised to self-isolate for 14 days. The other household members of that wider class or group do not need to self-isolate unless the child, young person or staff member they live with in that group subsequently develops symptoms.
* If the Covid-19 test is negative the child may return to school and their family stop isolating.
* If a child becomes ill and needs to be sent home for any other reason, they should be isolated away from the rest of the group.
* First aid should be administered to any child who has an injury in the normal way, however the first aider should wear PPE (see above).
* All hard surfaces should be wiped down with a disposable cloth and sanitised with household disinfectant. Particular attention should be paid to frequently touched areas and surfaces such as bathrooms, grabrails and door handles.
* All PPE equipment worn should be double bagged and stored securely for 72 hours before throwing away in regular rubbish.
* The first aider/adult should wash their hands after disposing of the PPE, with soap and water for 20 seconds.
* Clinical waste bins should be emptied regularly.

Specific resourcing

* Disposable fluid resistant surgical face masks
* Disposable gloves
* Disposable aprons
* Eye protection

Enabling infrastructure
* Soap * Disinfectant * Disposable cloths * Bin bags * First aid kits
School Variations (these may be further varied per classroom to suit age groups)
Links to government guidance www.gov.uk/government/publications/coronavirus-covid-19- implementing-protective-measures-in-education-and-childcare-settings/ coronavirus-covid-19-implementing-protective-measures-in-education-and-childcare-settings www.gov.uk/government/publications/covid-19-decontamination-in-non-healthcare-settings/ covid-19-decontamination-in-non-healthcare-settings
Links to other school documents such as site Risk Assessments or protocols.

Enabling infrastructure
2. To ensure site safety & management is responsive to latest guidance & facilitates staying open.
Protocol number 12: Office areas **Version 1 13.5.20**
Agreed Principles for both schools * Office areas can be manned as normal providing 2m distancing is in place. * Shared phones to be wiped with anti-bacterial wipes after every use. * Workstations areas to be wiped regularly. * Computers and keyboard to be cleaned at the end of each day. * Staff visiting the office to stay 2m apart at all times.
Specific resourcing * Anti-bacterial wipes * Hand sanitiser
School Variations (these may be further varied per classroom to suit age groups)
Links to government guidance www.gov.uk/government/publications/coronavirus-covid-19- implementing-protective-measures-in-education-and-childcare-settings/ coronavirus-covid-19-implementing-protective-measures-in-education-and-childcare-settings www.gov.uk/government/publications/covid-19-decontamination-in-non-healthcare-settings/ covid-19-decontamination-in-non-healthcare-settings www.gov.uk/government/news/teach-children-simple-hygiene-to-help-curb-infections
Links to other school documents such as site Risk Assessments or protocols.

Annex 5

Secondary school (England): specific risk identification and mitigation August 2020

Strategy	Implemenation risk	Likelihood (5 high, 1 low)	Mitigation		
Zoning	Year groups mix		Zoned year group bubbles	**Key**	
			Teachers move not students		
			Hire safe marquees		
			Zoned social areas in large outdoor/indoor spaces		
			Zoned click and collect catering app		
			Zoned bus seating, boarding and departure	High	5
			Zoned learning support service	Fairly High	4
			Mandtory wearing of masks on buses		
	Willful malicious behaviour	3	Strict behaviour protocol	Medium	3
	Inadvertant contravention	5	Spaced staff working bases	Fairly Low	2
			Reconfigured offices and other areas		
			Use of marking, tape and signs	Very Low	1
Social Distancing			Front facing desks		
			Supervision in key areas		
			Remove in main hall		
			PE changing in marquees		
	Required gatherings	2	Staggered departure times		
			No large staff or parent gatherings inc. public events		
			Dining hall closed		

(Continued)

(Cont).

	Arriving with infection	4	Compulsory hand washing points on arrival and departure
			Compusory use of hand sanitisers in rooms and buses
	Air based virus droplets	4	Express preference for student masks
			Catch it, bin it, kill it posters
			No air conditioning
			Doors and windows open
			Use of outdoor spaces where possible
			Strict behaviour protocol
			Wipes and tissues in all rooms
	Surface based transmission	3	Stripped down classrooms
Hygiene			Cleaning registers (signed on completion)
			Roving cleaning team during day
			Rooms disinfected at end of day
			Commonly used surfaces cleaned regularly
			Use of approved cleaning products
			Staff lanyard sanitisers
			Gloves or keyboard protectors for IT use
			No water fountains
			school issued water bottles only
	Exposure to infected persons	5	PPE for exposed/at risk staff e.g. face shields, gloves
			Departure protocol for symptomatic persons
	Food packaging transmission	1	Additional food handling measures
	Exposure to infected persons	3	No visitors, including parents execpt when essential
			Emergency workers only
			Out of hours emergency work where possible
External Interfaces			Sealed off areas for construction work
			Workers follow staff protocol
			Virtual meetings
			Advice to parents on student social mixing in community

(Continued)

(Cont).

Strategy	Implemenation risk	Likelihood (5 high, 1 low)	Mitigation
	Contaminated deliveries	1	Spray with disinfectant
	Exposure to infected persons	5	Instructions to parents
Identify, Isolate and Care			Departure protocol for symptomatic persons
			Staff protocol
			Isolation of all contacts in postive tested cases
			Close bubble for single confirmed cases
			Work with local health protection team with muliple cases
	Failure to make reasonable adjustments for higher risk staff		Staff and student individual risk assessments

Annex 6

Secondary school (England): return to work pandemic risk management strategy August 2020

<rural secondary school uk>
August 2020

Context

Secondary schools are required to re-open to all students in September, while keeping year groups in bubbles to limit transmission of the virus.

Aim

Minimise the risk of COVID-19 to the health of staff, students, their families and the wider community and establish full staff, student and public confidence in the risk management strategy and risk assessment.

Our strategy is organised around six pillars

1   Zoning
2   Social Distancing
3   Hygiene
4   Interface Reduction
5   Identify, Isolate and Care
6   Leadership and Management

Extent of risk

Our county has a relatively low current infection rates 8 cases per 100,000 people and 24 deaths, compared to 5 and 38 deaths (Lincolnshire), 44 and 303 deaths (Northamptonshire), 11 and 528 deaths (Leicestershire) and 51 and 316 deaths in Leicester City as of 9th August. However, the county rate has risen considerably over the summer and was only 0 on the 3rd July. Opening secondary schools *may* affect this situation and increase the possibility of an 'autumn spike' but we simply do not know at this stage. We bear in mind that:

* 70% of our students live outside the county
* Over 50% of staff live outside the county

Evidence also suggests that risk varies widely according to

* demographic factors such as age, gender, and ethnicity
* existing co-morbidities

Where possible, we give due consideration to these factors, but this strategy is about *minimising rather than eliminating the risk entirely*. Employees have a right to a safe workplace, and we will put in place all reasonable measures in line with government guidelines, together with our knowledge of the particular features of our own site to minimise the risk as much possible.

We take a sympathetic line with employees who have particular concerns and approach decisions on a case by case basis, while also giving due regard to the effective operation of the school to ensure that workload is shared fairly, and our educational systems work properly. This approach will be reviewed in line with the changing national and local situation and as much scientific evidence as we can reasonably gather and have confidence in, while recognising that there is rarely a total scientific consensus on such matters and knowledge about the virus is evolving all the time. We will act in good faith, based on our best knowledge at the time.

Legislation

We have given due regard to the following legal responsibilities as employers:

Section 1 **(2) Health and Safety at Work etc Act 1974** which states: 'It shall be the duty of every employer to ensure, so far as is reasonably practicable, the health, safety and welfare at work of all his employees.'

Regulation 3 (1) of the Management of Health and Safety at Work Regulations 1999 which provides that: 'Every employer shall make a suitable and sufficient assessment of the risks to the health and safety of his employees to which they are exposed whilst they are at work; and the risks to the health and safety of persons not in his employment arising out of or in connection with the conduct by him of his undertaking.'

An Equality Impact Assessment or some other means of meeting the requirement of the Public Sector Equality Duty contained in **Section 149 of the Equality Act 2010,** which requires public authorities to have due regard to a number of equality considerations when exercising their functions.

The duty of care is to all staff, and by extension students and visitors. No one should work in an environment where foreseeable risk has not been mitigated or removed as far as is reasonably practicable. Staff (including managers) have a duty of care to themselves, to colleagues, to those they manage or employ and to those they provide services to.

Zoning

The most effective way to maintain year group bubbles is by using a zoning approach. This means that each year group is allocated a zone of movement and all their activities remain in that zone. However, it is not a perfect bubble, because teachers will still move between rooms, classes and year groups, which is why teachers must also adhere to strict social distancing and hygiene rules at all times, not just for their own sake, but for the sake of others around them.

School day

The school day will remain almost as normal except that students will go straight to the first lesson rather than tutor groups in the morning and there will be a slightly staggered end to the day to facilitate the effective boarding of buses. However, the location of learning will be zoned as follows:

Table 1

Year Group (No)	Zone Buildings (rooms)	Social Times		IT Access	Learning Support
		Dry	Wet		
7 (215)	Maths/B+E (7)	Central front field/ brown area of back tarmac	Sports Hall	B and E	Learning Support
8 (210)	Science (8) *	Far left of rear of field	Y8 Marquee	Science IT	Ground floor (new) science prep room

(Continued)

Table 1 (Cont).

Year Group (No)	Zone Buildings (rooms)	Social Times		IT Access	Learning Support
		Dry	Wet		
9 (180)	Millennium (9)	Right side field behind MFL	Y9 Marquee	Alternate days with Y11 Computing/ Business	MFL (French)- use far rear staircase
10 (125)	Main Building (6)	Far right- rear field	Room 2 Room 4	Library IT	Library
11 (125)	Design/E. Arts (11)	Far left side of science block	Design and Arts blocks and canopy courtyard	Graphics HSC Laptop Bank Music Tech Alternate with Y9 Computing/ Business	Music Tech room when required

* Toilets are available in each block
* Remove in the staffroom
* PE changing in marquees Y8 (Girls) and Y9 (Boys) accessed via the field

Table 2 The field will be organised as follows (no ball games permitted).

Year 8					Year 10		
Year 11					MFL/Computing Block	Year 9	
	Science Block	Year 7					
					Nursery		

Arrivals and departures

Parents strongly encouraged to bring their child to school by car, but no car sharing will be permitted outside of family groups.

Cycling and walking will be encouraged where possible.

Bus queues should be socially distant at all times.

* Cars drop off on road only
* Buses dismiss by year group starting with Y7.
* Students embark by year group, starting with Y11.
* Sanitizers used on entry and departure from bus
* Facemasks compulsory on buses and entry to the site
* Named seats and seats grouped by year group from Y7 (front) to Y11 (back)
* Students will proceed immediately to their designated routes to wash their hands (note they must provide their own soap and flannels)

No staff or visitor arrivals or deliveries between 8.15–8.35am (the main car park will close at 8.15am each morning-staff should arrive before that time)

No staff or visitor departures or deliveries between 3.35–4.00pm (staff should not leave before 4pm)

The end of the day will be slightly staggered at 5-minute intervals to assist the departure process and avoid year group mixing. A bell will sound at each of the following times:

3.20	Year 11 leave and board immediately		
3.25	Year 10	"	"
3.30	Year 9	"	"
3.35	Year 8	"	"
3.40	Year 7	"	"

Table 3

Year	Entrance/Exit route	Route to social areas
7	Pupil entrance and single-file corridor to Maths	Maths exit to central front field or sports hall
8	Main entrance and through PE corridor to Science	Coned off corridor from front of science up to left rear of field or y8 marquee
9	Far car park or along roadway to Millennium	Rear exit of Millennium to far right-side field or y9 marquee
10	Side outdoor road to main building library entrance	Side outdoor road and on to a coned off corridor on the field to the right-rear field or rooms 2 and 4
11	Side of expressive arts	Far left side field behind science accessed via side of design or remain in Design/Ex Arts blocks

No shared routes

Access routes and handwashing and social areas will be supervised.

Learning groups

KS3

Taught in sets for a few subjects but many will be taught in consistent groups to minimise unnecessary contacts.

KS4

Students taught in sets, tutor groups and option groups, but with a view to minimising movement where possible.

No locked classrooms so that all staff and students have access without using door handles, creating delays or congestion or sharing keys. Staff should never lock their room.

Lesson changes

Year 7–8 will read in silence in classrooms during lesson changes. When their teacher arrives they will stand behind their chair and when the teacher greets them they will reply collectively with 'good morning or afternoon' Ms or Mr <teacher surname>.

Year 9–11 will often move between rooms within their zone at lesson change and should queue outside in the normal manner until their teacher arrives.

Each corridor/ area will have a designated corridor supervisor for all lesson changes; this will be a member of the teaching staff using that corridor in the preceding lesson. Their role will be to ensure all classes are reading silently or queuing quietly during the period of teacher transit. They will arrive at their new classroom 5 minutes after other staff.

Classroom doors remain open and supervisor patrolling

No valuable or fragile equipment unsupervised

Bells will signal every lesson change

Learning support

To limit and control their exposure, teaching assistants will be allocated to year groups where possible. Learning support rooms are attached to each zone as shown on the table above.

Behaviour

Students cannot use mobiles in the building after 8.45am unless directed otherwise by staff.

Amended behaviour policy-students who wilfully break protocols and rules will not be allowed in school as they are endangering lives.

New classroom routines apply.

Meetings with parents should be virtual where at all possible, or if not in the boardroom.

Remove and detentions will be in the staffroom

Attendance

The attendance policy will be adjusted in line with government guidelines and our identify, isolate and care procedures.

Social times

Students are required to stay in designated zones on the field, or in the event of poor weather, undercover areas which may take the form of marquees. Parents are advised to ensure that their children have warm, waterproof clothing as they will not normally be indoors during social times.

No ball games will be permitted on the field because space will be limited, and contact sports are not allowed by the government guidelines.

Social zones on the field are physically separated to the maximum distance possible. Each area will be physically marked out with cones and supervised.

Extra-curricular activities

These will only be permissible after school when year group bubbles and social distancing can be maintained.

No fixtures or competitions with students from other schools are permitted.

Social distancing

Public health advice is that keeping people 2m apart *substantially* reduces the risk of transmission.

1   Staff must observe this at all times, and offices, classrooms, learning support and social areas will be redesigned to ensure they remain 2m away from each other and students.

2   Staff are prohibited from being *barely* 2m to each other in a confined space (e.g. smaller office) for more than 15 minutes at a time.

3   Year group bubbles will be segregated into zones, but where there is a need for, or possibility of, multi-year gatherings e.g. remove, medical room, after school waiting areas, they will be kept at least 2m apart.

4   Students *within* each year bubble will not observe full social distancing but will be entirely segregated from students in other year bubbles at all times.

While, it is impossible to *guarantee* social distancing rules in all circumstances, we will do everything we can to ensure this rule is adhered to by staff.

Classrooms and learning support areas

* staff/student only zones marked in classrooms by taping with teachers at least 2m away from students at all times
* desks to be forward facing in rows unless fixed permanently to the floor
* teaching assistants not permitted next to students
* learning resources left in piles for students to collect and distribute
* student trays and boxes used to store all exercise books and work
* work completed and sent electronically where possible
* physical work e.g. left in piles/boxes and untouched by staff for 24 hours
* use of arranged outdoor areas for social times and learning where possible
* music tuition will be online

Catering

* no use of courtyard except by catering team, cleaners and premises staff
* app based ordering system Courtyard Collect order by 8.45am
* food carried to food collection points in zones as follows break and lunch deliveries
* bins in each area (recycling where possible)
* students may only use a school water bottle marked with their name

Table 5 Food Collection Points

Year	Zone	Food Collection Point
7	Maths	Bottom of science near lift
8	Science	Science lockers
9	Millennium	Rear of block at bottom of stairs
10	Main	Main lockers

Year	Zone	Food Collection Point
11	Design and Expressive Arts	Canopy courtyard
Staff	All	Staffroom

Gatherings

* gatherings in year group bubbles only
* no large staff gatherings; TEAMS style briefings and training presentations
* no productions or performance evenings
* limited numbers in staff working areas
* no physical whole year group assemblies, though smaller ones may be possible
* distant supervision of year group gatherings

Parking

* staff use main car park but no arrivals between 8.15 and 8.35am
* No visitor spaces
* parents and visitors parking on the designated road

Medical Treatments, Assessments, Accidents and Emergencies

* Enhanced PPE worn by high risk staff when attending or as required
* Medical room reconfigured to ensure distancing and enhanced hygiene measures are possible

Trips and visits

It is envisaged that most trips and visits will be avoided, and overnight trips are prohibited, but in certain circumstances they may be booked in accordance with advice from the relevant centre or destination and with appropriate insurance in the event of cancellation. Enhanced risk assessments will be required.

Fire and emergency evacuation

Fire Assembly points on back tarmac as follows

Year 11	Year 8	Year 7	Year 10	Year 9

Teachers must assemble their class in a line in these areas and register.
Emergency Exit routes

Year 11 design far side behind science
Year 10 library side route
Year 9 rear of millennium
Year 8 front of science
Year 7 front of maths

Teachers must register their class every lesson and ensure they have a written class list
Teachers take written class list with them
Teachers stay with their class and confirm that everyone is present (head count)

Hygiene

Basic hygiene measures significantly reduce risk of transmission. While again, we cannot guarantee that all persons will adhere to these measures on all occasions, we will do everything we can to ensure these measures are followed by staff and students by using the following methods:

Hand washing

* compulsory hand washing for 20 seconds on arrival and departure from site
* compulsory use of wall hand-sanitiser on entry and departure from all classrooms

Students will be required to wash their hands with soap for 20 seconds on arrival via a number of handwashing points and will be required to bring their own soap and flannel (kept in a plastic bag). The following sites are designated:

Year	Handwashing point
7	Side of maths
8	Bike sheds outside main entrance
9	Front of millennium
10	Front of main building
11	Side of Expressive Arts

The use of hand sanitisers on entering and departing classrooms and offices is compulsory. (using the wall dispensers provided)

Staff will be given a small sanitiser to attach their lanyard.

Cleaning protocol

All premises and cleaning staff will be issued with the following protocol:

1 appropriate PPE and strict hygiene precautions must be followed at all times
2 only approved products e.g. 60% alcohol content, bleach/ disinfectant
3 two bins in every classroom and rubbish and bins emptied daily
4 a daytime cleaning team of 3 cleaners will spray/wipe rails, toilets and other commonly touched areas throughout the day
5 cleaning logs to be used at key locations
6 daily disinfection of all rooms and other commonly used surfaces after use
7 tools, vehicles, sports equipment other than balls or shuttlecocks, musical instruments, scientific equipment and machinery including ovens will be cleaned after use and not shared before cleaning. Woodwind and brass instruments will never be shared within 48 hours.
8 tissues, wipes and board cleaning kits in all classrooms replenished regularly
9 meeting desks and furniture must be disinfected after use
10 deep clean of areas which may have been touched by a symptomatic individual or a person suspected of having the virus

All staff are required wipe down whiteboards and surfaces on entering and leaving rooms. Every room will be equipped with a board cleaning kit

A quarantine room will be available for symptomatic students or those suspected of having the virus who are waiting to picked-up by parents. This will be deep cleaned after use and no fabric seating or furniture will stored in that room. A toilet has been designated to *only be* used by a student in this situation and in the event of use it will be deep cleaned immediately.

Facemasks

Older children spread the virus as easily as adults and it is known that facemasks reduce the spread of the virus significantly. Social distancing from the teacher is easier in some classrooms than in others, so we have adopted a mixed-discretionary approach.

The school prefer that students wear facemasks as follows unless exempt from doing so due to a relevant physical disability, mental health issue or because they have an EHCP.

Students must wear facemasks on buses, in corridors and general circulation areas in the building except at social times unless exempt. However, in class, it is left to the discretion of the teacher to decide on whether facemasks are worn except in the case of high-risk staff, partly because the size and shape of our rooms differ ad partly because some staff are at more risk than others.

Staff are not required to wear facemasks when teaching but high and medium risk staff have the option of wearing faceshields. We prefer staff to wear masks in corridors and general circulation areas when students are present.

Catch it, bin it, kill it

Germs spread easily and can live for several hours on tissues and hands.

All staff are therefore required to follow the catch it, bin it, kill it protocol and prominent posters will be displayed in all classrooms and offices.

1   Always carry tissues and use them to catch coughs and sneezes
2   Dispose tissues in a bin as soon as possible
3   Wash or sanitize hands as soon as possible

Stripped down classrooms

Classrooms will be 'stripped down' so that no unprotected items such as textbooks, exercise books, portfolios, folders or resource sheets are left piled on surfaces.

All stored resources must be placed in labelled trays or boxes, preferably with lids.

300 boxes have been ordered; approximately 7–8 per room.

Teachers must ensure their resources are stored in the relevant classroom.

Other resources put in long term storage close in normal classroom areas.

Teacher desks and other shared accessible surfaces must be kept clear of all items except a keyboard and visualiser.

Stripped down classrooms will severely limit the number of exposed surfaces that are difficult or impossible to clean and considerably speed up the efficiency of the cleaning process.

Cleaners and staff should be able to 'wipe and go'.

Food and drink

* food and drinks receptacles must not be shared
* cups and mugs for staff and visitors are banned and will be removed from all cupboards and rooms
* staff must use their own sealed drinks bottle *marked with their name*
* students must use a school water bottle

- students not allowed to bring other cans, or drinks bottles into school, apart from their school water bottle
- no shared metal cutlery or crockery available for staff or students
- single use cardboard cups will be available for visitor hospitality
- water fountains will be shut off and taps shut when not in use
- strict additional measures for the handling and preparation of food are being applied
- no students or staff allowed in food preparation areas apart from catering/premises

Resources

- teacher resources left on desks or in classrooms and not stored in an appropriate labelled box or tray will be removed at the end of the day
- textbooks not shared on same day-scheduled in advance by subject leaders
- arts equipment will be confined to year group bubbles and not shared between year groups. Students will purchase an art pack to take around with them.
- exercise books and textbooks must be stored in a labelled box, preferably with a lid
- textbooks should not be shared *between* year groups on the same day
- textbooks may be shared within year groups on the same day providing they have been wiped down first
- additional stationery will be purchased to avoid sharing where possible
- furniture will not be moved between zones during the week
- staff should keep personal resources with them or in their base

Computers

Keyboards are a potential source of contamination, particularly because teachers are moving from room to room and have to log-on at the start of each lesson. To mitigate against this we are:

- Each member of staff will have a silicone keyboard protector
- Students will use disposable gloves provided

Ventilation

The virus is far less likely to circulate in well ventilated areas. This may lower the temperature in some rooms and suitable clothing may need to be worn.

- premises will open windows and doors in general areas before school
- teachers will ask students to open windows at start of P1

- air conditioning will be turned off at all times
- windows will be kept open at all times where safe to do so
- doors will be kept open or pinned back
- students at social times will be kept outdoors except in very poor or cold weather

Signing-in

- staff will not be required to sign in electronically during the pandemic
- visitors must sign-in electronically ad the screen wiped after use

Interface reduction

The virus cannot enter a site unless invited in, either via a human host or on the surface of an object. We minimise risk by reducing interfaces with the public using the following methods:

- parents and visitor meetings in boardroom only
- no supply staff in school
- spray disinfectant on deliveries where possible
- no objects brought and left in school by students besides work
- use of virtual meetings for governors and external groups
- emergency work to be undertaken out of hours where at all possible
- construction work to take place in sealed areas
- necessary repairs and maintenance workers to follow protocol

Every effort will be made to avoid visitors entering the site but in cases where that is impossible visitors will be advised to

- wear a facemask
- wash hands frequently and sanitise on entry and departure from all rooms
- remain 2m away from all staff and students
- use and dispose of tissues immediately in the event of coughs or sneezes
- if symptoms develop, immediately vacate the building from the nearest outdoor exit, obtain a test as soon as possible and inform the school of the outcome

Identify, isolate and care

Identify and isolate

If, or when, a person is suspected of having the virus, or has been in significant contact with someone who has the virus, the speed of identification and subsequent isolation is critical to minimising the risk of transmission. Senior health advisors are suggesting that up to 40% of infected persons are asymptomatic and infected young people are more likely to be asymptomatic than others. They also estimate that possibly as few as 1 in 4 cases are currently diagnosed. This makes it difficult to identify and isolate cases effectively.

We are also led to understand that up 30% of test results are incorrect, raising the possibility that infected people are undiagnosed and unwittingly spread the virus.

We will full and actively engage with the NHS track and trace system and the local health protection team. The government are providing a number of home testing kits for schools to send home with any symptomatic or suspected person.

Symptoms are defined as a new continuous cough, high temperature, or a loss or change in taste or smell.

Close contact means either direct close contact or proximity contact.

Direct close contact means face to face contact within 2m for any length of time with an infected individual.

Proximity contact means extended close contact within 2m for 15 minutes or more with an infected individual.

All the following apply equally to all staff and students.

Parents must agree to fully abide by the requirements of these measures.

At school we will do everything we can to identify and isolate infected persons as quickly as possible by adopting the following methods:

1   Parents will be required to keep their child off school and make immediate arrangements for a test if they develop symptoms.
2   Parents of children who *test positive* will be required to keep their child off school for a minimum of 14 days from the date when symptoms first appeared, or later until symptoms have disappeared, and provide photo evidence of the positive test as soon as possible.
3   We will inform the local health team immediately if any person tests positive.
4   Parents of children who have had *close contact* with an infected person (tested positive) or are if instructed to do so by NHS track and trace or the local health protection team, will be required to keep their child off school for 14 days and

their child must take a test. If that test is positive, they and their household must self-isolate for at least 14 days or until symptoms disappear after the date the symptoms first appeared. If they test negative, they must remain in self-isolation for the remainder of the 14 days because they may still develop the virus in that period.

5   Parents of children in the same bubble as someone who has tested positive will be instructed to keep their child self-isolated at home for 7 days and only return if no symptoms have appeared.

6   Parents of children with symptoms who *test negative* are required to keep their child off school for 7 days in case of a false negative test and re-test if symptoms persist.

7   If any person on site develops or thinks they might be developing symptoms, they are to leave (staff) or be picked up immediately (students), preferably using outdoor exits and by not re-entering the building or waiting in the isolation room near the student exit.

8   Staff attending a person who has developed symptoms or is suspected of having the virus must wear enhanced PPE and remain a minimum of 2m away if possible.

9   Student services will keep a Covid-register of all students absent from school for a Covid-related reason.

10 All parents will be informed of a positive case, but names will not be shared unless essential to protect others.

11 If we have two or more positive cases within 14 days, or an overall rise in sickness absence where coronavirus is suspected, we will work with the local health protection team and take additional actions as required.

12 Parents and staff who are highly clinically vulnerable, or live with someone who is, are advised to make additional domestic arrangements.

13 Staff are permitted to take any other reasonable additional precautions to protect themselves as they wish, providing they do not prevent them from undertaking their duties as defined in accordance with their risk assessment.

14 Students and staff with protected characteristics that place them at significant additional risk are required to take reasonable additional precautions.

15 Staff or students who deliberately, maliciously or persistently break any of the rules or protocols above will be subject to appropriate disciplinary procedures.

Care

Students

Happier children learn better and we put a high value on student well-being at all times, but in the current pandemic we must give regard to the huge additional strains that have been placed on young people and their families. Directly and indirectly, the pandemic has had an enormous impact on the well-being of our students, although many have also displayed considerable resilience and adapted remarkably well to the circumstances.

In addition to our normal support we are providing:

* bespoke support for the most affected
* dedicated pastoral 'bounce-back' curriculum
* each student with a bounce-back tutor
* additional registers and monitoring systems

We recognise that student experiences of the pandemic will vary hugely from child to child and a single uniform approach would not be appropriate. Our student services team know our children and their families very well and respond in very different ways depending on the circumstances involved. It is this personal level of attention that makes their approach so outstanding.

While care and support is essential for young people, we also recognise that they may have suffered from a lack of structure and boundaries during the lockdown and it is vital that these are restored as quickly as possible. There will be many new protocols and rules to follow in the autumn term and they will be applied strictly in all cases. We will fully explain to students why they have been introduced and why they must be followed at all times.

Caring for young people in school means creating a safe, orderly and respectful environment. We teach children *how* to behave but also know that *every child can behave*, and we will not lower our behaviour expectations. We want children to enjoy being back at school and the best way to do that is by making school a safe and organised place to be.

Staff

Aside from the direct risk of the virus itself, there is likely to be considerable additional pressure on staff as they return to work an adapt to new procedures. Teaching staff are likely to be under considerable extra strain because of the requirement to move from room to room and support staff are also likely to be working under additional strain, particularly in certain front facing roles. Workloads are likely to increase for all staff and if absence levels rise, this will add further pressure on other staff. This is similar to many other workplaces.

It is imperative that staff look after each other in a culture of consultation, mutual respect and support.

When developing and implementing this strategy, and making decisions about it moving forwards, we will give due consideration to

* listening to concerns
* considering workload

* providing support
* communicating sensitively
* monitoring well-being

Staffing and administrative bases

Each member of staff will have a designated permanent work desk base, at least 2m apart from other staff, in one of the following areas. All will have sockets and either IT points or Wi-Fi access and none will be shared.

These areas may be subject to change after review: <The authors have removed staff names and the list of rooms>

The part of the hall not used for remove will be kept available for meetings, cover lessons, assemblies, after school lettings and exams and occasional lessons where required.

The boardroom will be available for meetings with parents and exams.

Individual risk assessments

* all staff and students will be risk assessed and organised into:

    * low risk
    * medium risk
    * high risk

This will be based on self-assessments using a range of criteria based on age, ethnicity, disability, pregnancy, health conditions, those returning to work and proximity to clinically high-risk persons. Requirements and precautions will then be determined as follows

low risk	no additional precautions required
medium risk	limited additional precautions advised
high risk	additional precautions required

The exact nature of the mitigating additional precautions will vary according to the exact circumstances of each individual. These are defined more fully in our individual risk assessment strategy.

All arrangements will be subject to consultation and agreement with medium and high-risk individuals and where necessary appropriate medical advice. An effectiveness review will take place in late September by consultation with affected staff.

A staff risk register and student risk register will be kept and updated as required. Only senior team and one named support staff will have access to the staff register.

Individual risk assessments will be adjusted for students returning to school and staff returning to work, due to any illness likely to significantly compromise their immune system. This will include a record of all support provided.

Supporting the mental health of staff affected by the virus, either directly or indirectly will be incorporated into our staff well-being strategy and our safeguarding and sickness absence policies will be adjusted accordingly.

Remote counselling will be introduced for students and staff.

Leadership and management

A Covid-committee consisting of governors, parents, staff association and union representatives, and representatives of other high-risk groups will be formed to meet virtually on a monthly basis, led by the chair of governors with responsibility for ensuring the risk management and strategy and risk assessment processes are carried out effectively.

Senior Team are responsible leading and managing this strategy on a day to day basis.

The health and safety committee will also meet on a monthly basis.

Author Index

Subject Index

Printed in the United States
by Baker & Taylor Publisher Services